255
aw

Myth

Essays by

Clifford Geertz
James W. Fernandez
Mary Douglas
Frank E. and Fritzie P. Manuel
Judith N. Shklar
Reuben A. Brower
Steven Marcus
Robert M. Adams

Myth, Symbol, and Culture

Edited by CLIFFORD GEERTZ

W · W · NORTON & COMPANY · INC · New York

Copyright © 1971 by the American Academy of
Arts and Sciences

Library of Congress Cataloging in Publication Data
Main entry under title:

Myth, symbol, and culture.

   Originally published as winter 1972 issue of
Daedalus.
   I. Geertz, Clifford, ed. II. Daedalus.
AC5.M93   1974   081   74–4244
ISBN 0–393–04254–5
ISBN 0–393–09409–X (pbk.)

Published simultaneously in Canada
by George J. McLeod Limited, Toronto

Printed in the United States of America

1 2 3 4 5 6 7 8 9 0

CONTENTS

ACKNOWLEDGMENTS

The Ford Foundation is thanked by the Editor for its generous support of this study. Its grant to the American Academy of Arts and Sciences to support interdisciplinary research has been very helpful in making this book possible.

INTRODUCTION

THE HISTORY of the making of a book will sometimes throw light on its contents. This book has a history worth telling. It began with an invitation to scholars, principally from the fields of anthropology and literature, to a conference to discuss what Paul de Man and I chose to call "The Systematic Study of Meaningful Forms." Invitations went out to twelve scholars, in this country and abroad, to meet in Paris for a planning conference. In our letter of invitation, we asked whether the question of the relationship between the social sciences and the humanities is not often approached in the wrong way. We wrote, in part, as follows:

General efforts to connect the work of scholars we take to be occupied with "The Humanities" with those we take to be occupied with "The Social Sciences" tend to adopt a "two cultures" sort of formulation. The "relations" between humanistic and social scientific methods, outlooks, concerns, ambitions, and achievements are described in a rather external fashion, as though two wary sovereign powers were drawing up a treaty of mutual coexistence in order to allow a certain level of carefully regulated commerce between them while guaranteeing their mutual autonomy and right to live their separate lives. Thus one gets discussions, whether or not they are actually called such, of "The Implications (Impact, Convergence, Irrelevance . . .) of Structuralism (Evolutionism, Gestalt Psychology, Generative Grammar, Psychoanalysis . . .) for History (Literary Criticism, Musicology, Law, Philosophy . . .)" and so on. (The Sciences being masculine and the Humanities feminine, the causal arrow is only rarely pointed in the other direction.) Some of these discussions have their uses, if only as statements of a larger faith—or, in some cases, lack of it; but they tend not to contribute much, or at least as much as the grandness of their conception would seem to promise, to the specific development of the fields of study thus "related." They are, a few exceptions aside, part only of parascholarship, public declarations for public occasions which, like Auden's "poetry," make nothing happen.
Yet, in the face of all of this, the conviction continues to grow among leading

figures in the humanities and the social sciences that, as the cliché goes, "they have something to offer one another." The problem is how to effect the offering, reasonably unburnt.

It is our assumption that this will best be done not by general, programmatic considerations of how the humanities, or some corner of them, and the social sciences, or some corner of them, are "related" to one another, or even of what over-all presuppositions they share in common, nor again of their supposedly complementary or contradictory roles in the functioning of modern culture. Rather, it will be done, if it is done at all, when some of the more creative people in specific disciplines discover that they are in fact working, from their contrasting methods, on quite similar problems or ranges of problems.

It is when two (or more) scholars realize that, for all the differences between them, they are attacking highly similar issues, trying to solve closely related puzzles, that communication between them begins to look like a practical policy rather than an academic piety. Specific commonalities of intellectual interest make scholarly interchange possible and useful; and the creation of such interchange demands, and indeed consists in, the discovery and exploitation of such commonalities. It is the coincident perception by historians concerned with the authorship of the Federalist papers and by statisticians concerned with Bayesian interpretations of probability theory that they are confronted with the same kind of problem—how to evaluate "subjective" judgments—which causes them to become genuinely interested in one another. Academic ideologies celebrating the unity of knowledge, decrying the evils of specialization, or dissolving substantive differences into rhetorical agreements do not achieve the same objectives.

Clearly, such commonalities of concern among otherwise discrete disciplines cannot be formulated without prior inquiry. Looking both at the work of our own fields, literary criticism and cultural anthropology, and at that of fields more or less adjacent to them, it seems to us that one such commonality is what might be called—or, when we actually come to look into it, might not—"the systematic study of meaningful forms."

There are a lot of elastic and ill-used words crowded into this little formula— only the article and the preposition seem straightforward—but that it points, in its awkward and preliminary way, to a general area in which "humanists" and "social scientists" (even, in a few cases, some we call natural scientists) are simultaneously engaged in study is beyond much doubt. In the social sciences, structuralist anthropology, socio-linguistics, cognitive psychology, and phenomenological sociology, merely to list a few labels, all represent a sharp turn toward a concern with the analysis of meaningful forms, whether they be South American Indian myths, urban speech styles, children's categorical systems, or the taken-for-granted assumptions of everyday life. In the humanities, where the study of meaningful structures has been a traditional concern, recent developments in the philosophy of language and in the analysis of artistic and literary forms all show a markedly heightened awareness of the need for devising ways of coping more effectively with such structures.

What, dimly perceived, these assorted enterprises seem to have in common is a conviction that meaningful forms, whether they be African passage rites, nineteenth-century novels, revolutionary ideologies, grammatical paradigms, scientific theories, English landscape paintings, or the ways in which moral judgments are phrased, have as good a claim to public existence as horses, stones, and trees, and are therefore as susceptible to objective investigation and systematic analysis as these apparently harder realities.

Everything from modern logic, computer technology, and cybernetics at one extreme to phenomenological criticism, psychohistory, and ordinary language philosophy at the other has conspired to undermine the notion that meaning is so radically "in the head," so deeply subjective, that it is incapable of being firmly grasped, much less analyzed. It may be supremely difficult to deal with such structures of meaning but they are neither a miracle nor a mirage. Indeed, constructing concepts and methods to deal with them and to produce generalizations about them is the primary intellectual task now facing those humanists and social scientists not content merely to exercise habitual skills. The surge of interest in "myth," "fiction," "archetype," "semantics," "systems of relevance," "language games," and so on is but the symptom that this transformation in viewpoint has in fact taken place, and—from the very multiplicity of the terms—that it has taken place in intellectual contexts much more isolated from one another than the commonality of their concerns would warrant.

Whether we have achieved at least a few of the objectives outlined in this letter the reader will judge. A debt is owed Paul de Man for his help in stimulating this study.

CLIFFORD GEERTZ

CLIFFORD GEERTZ

Deep Play: Notes on the Balinese Cockfight

The Raid

EARLY IN April of 1958, my wife and I arrived, malarial and diffident, in a Balinese village we intended, as anthropologists, to study. A small place, about five hundred people, and relatively remote, it was its own world. We were intruders, professional ones, and the villagers dealt with us as Balinese seem always to deal with people not part of their life who yet press themselves upon them: as though we were not there. For them, and to a degree for ourselves, we were nonpersons, specters, invisible men.

We moved into an extended family compound (that had been arranged before through the provincial government) belonging to one of the four major factions in village life. But except for our landlord and the village chief, whose cousin and brother-in-law he was, everyone ignored us in a way only a Balinese can do. As we wandered around, uncertain, wistful, eager to please, people seemed to look right through us with a gaze focused several yards behind us on some more actual stone or tree. Almost nobody greeted us; but nobody scowled or said anything unpleasant to us either, which would have been almost as satisfactory. If we ventured to approach someone (something one is powerfully inhibited from doing in such an atmosphere), he moved, negligently but difinitively, away. If, seated or leaning against a wall, we had him trapped, he said nothing at all, or mumbled what for the Balinese is the ultimate nonword—"yes." The indifference, of course, was studied; the villagers were watching every move we made and they had an enormous amount of quite accurate information about who we were and what we were going to be doing. But they acted as if we simply did not exist, which, in fact, as this behavior was designed to inform us, we did not, or anyway not yet.

This is, as I say, general in Bali. Everywhere else I have been in Indonesia, and more latterly in Morocco, when I have gone into a new village people have poured out from all sides to take a very close look at me, and, often, an all-too-probing feel as well. In Balinese villages, at least those away from the tourist circuit, nothing happens at all. People go on pounding, chatting, making offerings, staring into space, carrying baskets about while one drifts around feeling vaguely disembodied. And the same thing is true

1

on the individual level. When you first meet a Balinese, he seems virtually not to relate to you at all; he is, in the term Gregory Bateson and Margaret Mead made famous, "away."[1] Then—in a day, a week, a month (with some people the magic moment never comes)—he decides, for reasons I have never been quite able to fathom, that you *are* real, and then he becomes a warm, gay, sensitive, sympathetic, though, being Balinese, always precisely controlled person. You have crossed, somehow, some moral or metaphysical shadow line. Though you are not exactly taken as a Balinese (one has to be born to that), you are at least regarded as a human being rather than a cloud or a gust of wind. The whole complexion of your relationship dramatically changes to, in the majority of cases, a gentle, almost affectionate one— a low-keyed, rather playful, rather mannered, rather bemused geniality.

My wife and I were still very much in the gust of wind stage, a most frustrating, and even, as you soon begin to doubt whether you are really real after all, unnerving one, when, ten days or so after our arrival, a large cockfight was held in the public square to raise money for a new school.

Now, a few special occasions aside, cockfights are illegal in Bali under the Republic (as, for not altogether unrelated reasons, they were under the Dutch), largely as a result of the pretensions to puritanism radical nationalism tends to bring with it. The elite, which is not itself so very puritan, worries about the poor, ignorant peasant gambling all his money away, about what foreigners will think, about the waste of time better devoted to building up the country. It sees cockfighting as "primitive," "backward," "unprogressive," and generally unbecoming an ambitious nation. And, as with those other embarrassments—opium smoking, begging, or uncovered breasts—it seeks, rather unsystematically, to put a stop to it.

Of course, like drinking during prohibition or, today, smoking marihuana, cockfights, being a part of "The Balinese Way of Life," nonetheless go on happening, and with extraordinary frequency. And, like prohibition or marihuana, from time to time the police (who, in 1958 at least, were almost all not Balinese but Javanese) feel called upon to make a raid, confiscate the cocks and spurs, fine a few people, and even now and then expose some of them in the tropical sun for a day as object lessons which never, somehow, get learned, even though occasionally, quite occasionally, the object dies.

As a result, the fights are usually held in a secluded corner of a village in semisecrecy, a fact which tends to slow the action a little—not very much, but the Balinese do not care to have it slowed at all. In this case, however, perhaps because they were raising money for a school that the government was unable to give them, perhaps because raids had been few recently, perhaps, as I gathered from subsequent discussion, there was a notion that the necessary bribes had been paid, they thought they could take a chance on the central square and draw a larger and more enthusiastic crowd without attracting the attention of the law.

They were wrong. In the midst of the third match, with hundreds of people, including, still transparent, myself and my wife, fused into a single body around the ring, a superorganism in the literal sense, a truck full of policemen armed with machine guns roared up. Amid great screeching cries of "pulisi! pulisi!" from the crowd, the policemen jumped out, and, springing into the center of the ring, began to swing their guns around like gangsters in a motion picture, though not going so far as actually to fire them. The superorganism came instantly apart as its components scattered in all directions. People raced down the road, disappeared head first over walls, scrambled under platforms, folded themselves behind wicker screens, scuttled up coconut trees. Cocks armed with steel spurs sharp enough to cut off a finger or run a hole through a foot were running wildly around. Everything was dust and panic.

On the established anthropological principle, When in Rome, my wife and I decided, only slightly less instantaneously than everyone else, that the thing to do was run too. We ran down the main village street, northward, away from where we were living, for we were on that side of the ring. About half-way down another fugitive ducked suddenly into a compound—his own, it turned out—and we, seeing nothing ahead of us but rice fields, open country, and a very high volcano, followed him. As the three of us came tumbling into the courtyard, his wife, who had apparently been through this sort of thing before, whipped out a table, a tablecloth, three chairs, and three cups of tea, and we all, without any explicit communication whatsoever, sat down, commenced to sip tea, and sought to compose ourselves.

A few moments later, one of the policemen marched importantly into the yard, looking for the village chief. (The chief had not only been at the fight, he had arranged it. When the truck drove up he ran to the river, stripped off his sarong, and plunged in so he could say, when at length they found him sitting there pouring water over his head, that he had been away bathing when the whole affair had occurred and was ignorant of it. They did not believe him and fined him three hundred rupiah, which the village raised collectively.) Seeing my wife and I, "White Men," there in the yard, the policeman performed a classic double take. When he found his voice again he asked, approximately, what in the devil did we think we were doing there. Our host of five minutes leaped instantly to our defense, producing an impassioned description of who and what we were, so detailed and so accurate that it was my turn, having barely communicated with a living human being save my landlord and the village chief for more than a week, to be astonished. We had a perfect right to be there, he said, looking the Javanese upstart in the eye. We were American professors; the government had cleared us; we were there to study culture; we were going to write a book to tell Americans about Bali. And we had all been there drinking tea and talking about cultural matters all afternoon and did not know anything about any cockfight. Moreover, we had not seen the village chief all day, he must have gone to town. The policeman retreated in rather total disarray. And, after a decent interval, bewildered but relieved to have survived and stayed out of jail, so did we.

The next morning the village was a completely different world for us. Not only were we no longer invisible, we were suddenly the center of all attention, the object of a great outpouring of warmth, interest, and, most especially, amusement. Everyone in the village knew we had fled like everyone else. They asked us about it again and again (I must have told the story, small detail by small detail, fifty times by the end of the day), gently, affectionately, but quite insistently teasing us: "Why didn't you just stand there and tell the police who you were?" "Why didn't you just say you were only watching and not betting?" "Were you really afraid of those little guns?" As always, kinesthetically minded and, even when fleeing for their lives (or, as happened eight years later, surrendering them), the world's most poised people, they gleefully mimicked, also over and over again, our graceless style of running and what they claimed were our panic-stricken facial expressions. But above all, everyone was extremely pleased and even more surprised that we had not simply "pulled out our papers" (they knew about those too) and asserted our Distinguished Visitor status, but had instead demonstrated our solidarity with what were now our covillagers. (What we had actually demonstrated was our cowardice, but there is fellowship in that too.) Even the Brahmana priest, an old, grave, half-way-to-Heaven type who because of its associations with the underworld would never be involved, even distantly, in a cockfight, and was difficult to approach even to other Balinese, had us called into his courtyard to ask us about what had happened, chuckling happily at the sheer extraordinariness of it all.

In Bali, to be teased is to be accepted. It was the turning point so far as our relationship to the community was concerned, and we were quite literally "in." The whole village opened up to us, probably more than it ever would have otherwise (I might actually never have gotten to that priest, and our accidental host became one of my best informants), and certainly very much faster. Getting caught, or almost caught, in a vice raid is perhaps not a very generalizable recipe for achieving that mysterious necessity of anthropological field work, rapport, but for me it worked very well. It led to a sudden and unusually complete acceptance into a society extremely difficult for outsiders to penetrate. It gave me the kind of immediate, inside-view grasp of an aspect of "peasant mentality" that anthropologists not fortunate enough to flee headlong with their subjects from armed authorities normally do not get. And, perhaps most important of all, for the other things might have come in other ways, it put me very quickly on to a combination emotional explosion, status war, and philosophical drama of central significance to the society whose inner nature I desired to understand. By the time I left I had spent about as much time looking into cockfights as into witchcraft, irrigation, caste, or marriage.

Of Cocks and Men

Bali, mainly because it is Bali, is a well-studied place. Its mythology, art, ritual, social organization, patterns of child rearing, forms of law, even styles of trance, have all been microscopically examined for traces of that elusive substance Jane Belo called "The Balinese Temper."[2] But, aside from a few passing remarks, the cockfight has barely been noticed, although as a popular obsession of consuming power it is at least as important a revelation of what being a Balinese "is really like" as these more celebrated phenomena.[3] As much of America surfaces in a ball park, on a golf links, at a race track, or around a poker table, much of Bali surfaces in a cock ring. For it is only apparently cocks that are fighting there. Actually, it is men.

To anyone who has been in Bali any length of time, the deep psychological identification of Balinese men with their cocks is unmistakable. The double entendre here is deliberate. It works in exactly the same way in Balinese as it does in English, even to producing the same tired jokes, strained puns, and uninventive obscenities. Bateson and Mead have even suggested that, in line with the Balinese conception of the body as a set of separately animated parts, cocks are viewed as detachable, self-operating penises, ambulant genitals with a life of their own.[4] And while I do not have the kind of unconscious material either to confirm or disconfirm this intriguing notion, the fact that they are masculine symbols *par excellence* is about as indubitable, and to the Balinese about as evident, as the fact that water runs downhill.

The language of everyday moralism is shot through, on the male side of it, with roosterish imagery. *Sabung*, the word for cock (and one which appears in inscriptions as early as A.D. 922), is used metaphorically to mean "hero," "warrior," "champion," "man of parts," "political candidate," "bachelor," "dandy," "lady-killer," or "tough guy." A pompous man whose behavior presumes above his station is compared to a tailless cock who struts about as though he had a large, spectacular one. A desperate man who makes a last, irrational effort to extricate himself from an impossible situation is likened to a dying cock who makes one final lunge at his tormentor to drag him along to a common destruction. A stingy man, who promises much, gives little, and begrudges that is compared to a cock which, held by the tail, leaps at another without in fact engaging him. A marriageable young man still shy with the opposite sex or someone in a new job anxious to make a good impression is called "a fighting cock caged for the first time."[5] Court trials, wars, political contests, inheritance disputes, and street arguments are all compared to cockfights.[6] Even the very island itself is perceived from its shape as a small, proud cock, poised, neck extended, back taut, tail raised, in eternal challenge to large, feckless, shapeless Java.[7]

But the intimacy of men with their cocks is more than metaphorical. Balinese men, or anyway a large majority of Balinese men, spend an enormous amount of time with their favorites, grooming them, feeding them, discussing them, trying them out against one another, or just gazing at them with a mixture of rapt admiration and dreamy self-absorbtion. Whenever you see a group of Balinese men squatting idly in the council shed or along the road in their hips down, shoulders forward, knees up fashion, half or more of them will have a rooster in his hands, holding it between his thighs, bouncing it gently up and down to strengthen its legs, ruffling its feathers with abstract sensuality, pushing it out against a neighbor's rooster to rouse its spirit, withdrawing it toward his loins to calm it again. Now and then, to get a feel for another bird, a man will fiddle this way with someone else's cock for a while, but usually by moving around to squat in place behind it, rather than just having it passed across to him as though it were merely an animal.

In the houseyard, the high-walled enclosures where the people live, fighting cocks are kept in wicker cages, moved frequently about so as to maintain the optimum balance of sun and shade. They are fed a special diet, which varies somewhat according to individual theories but which is mostly maize, sifted for impurities with far more care than it is when mere humans are going to eat it and offered to the animal kernel by kernel. Red pepper is stuffed down their beaks and up their anuses to give them spirit. They are bathed in the same ceremonial preparation of tepid water, medicinal herbs, flowers, and onions in which infants are bathed, and for a prize cock just about as often. Their combs are cropped, their plumage dressed, their spurs trimmed, their legs massaged, and they are inspected for flaws with the squinted concentration of a diamond merchant. A man who has a passion for cocks, an enthusiast in the literal sense of the term, can spend most of his life with them, and even those, the overwhelming majority, whose passion though intense has not entirely run away with them, can and do spend what seems not only to an outsider, but also to themselves, an inordinate amount of time with them. "I am cock crazy," my landlord, a quite ordinary *afficionado* by Balinese standards, used to moan as he went to move another cage, give another bath, or conduct another feeding. "We're all cock crazy."

The madness has some less visible dimensions, however, because although it is true that cocks are symbolic expressions or magnifications of their owner's self, the narcissistic male ego writ out in Aesopian terms, they are also expressions—and rather more immediate ones—of what the Balinese regard as the direct inversion, aesthetically, morally, and metaphysically, of human status: animality.

The Balinese revulsion against any behavior regarded as animal-like can hardly be overstressed. Babies are not allowed to crawl for that reason. Incest, though hardly approved, is a much less horrifying crime than bestiality. (The appropriate punishment for the second is death by drowning, for the first being forced to live like an animal.)[8] Most demons are represented—in sculpture, dance, ritual, myth—in some real or fantastic animal form. The main puberty rite consists in filing the child's teeth so they will not look like animal fangs. Not only defecation but eating is regarded as a disgusting, almost obscene activity, to be conducted hurriedly and privately, because of its association with animality. Even falling down or any form of clumsiness is considered to be bad for these reasons. Aside from cocks and a few domestic animals—oxen, ducks—of no emotional significance, the Balinese are aversive to animals and treat their large number of dogs not merely callously but with a phobic cruelty. In identifying with his cock, the Balinese man is identifying not just with his ideal self, or even his penis, but also, and at the same time, with what he most fears, hates, and ambivalence being what it is, is fascinated by—The Powers of Darkness.

The connection of cocks and cockfighting with such Powers, with the animalistic demons that threaten constantly to invade the small, cleared off space in which the Balinese have so carefully built their lives and devour its inhabitants, is quite explicit. A cockfight, any cockfight, is in the first instance a blood sacrifice offered, with the appropriate chants and oblations, to the demons in order to pacify their ravenous, cannibal hunger. No temple festival should be conducted until one is made. (If it is omitted someone will inevitably fall into a trance and command with the voice of an angered spirit that the oversight be immediately corrected.) Collective responses to natural evils—illness, crop failure, volcanic eruptions—almost always involve them. And that famous holiday in Bali, The Day of Silence (Njepi), when everyone sits silent and immobile all day long in order to avoid contact with a sudden influx of demons chased momentarily out of hell, is preceded the previous day by large-scale cockfights (in this case legal) in almost every village on the island.

In the cockfight, man and beast, good and evil, ego and id, the creative power of aroused masculinity and the destructive power of loosened animality fuse in a bloody drama of hatred, cruelty, violence, and death. It is little wonder that when, as is the invariable rule, the owner of the winning cock takes the carcass of the loser—often torn limb from limb by its enraged owner—home to eat, he does so with a mixture of social embarrassment, moral satisfaction, aesthetic disgust, and cannibal joy. Or that a man who has lost an important fight is sometimes driven to wreck his family shrines and curse the gods, an act of metaphysical (and social) suicide. Or that in seeking earthly analogues for heaven and hell the Balinese compare the former to the mood of a man whose cock has just won, the latter to that of a man whose cock has just lost.

The Fight

Cockfights (*tetadjen; sabungan*) are held in a ring about fifty feet square. Usually they begin toward late afternoon and run three or four hours until sunset. About nine or ten separate matches (*sehet*) comprise a program. Each match is precisely like the others in general pattern: there is no main match, no connection between individual matches, no variation in their format, and each is arranged on a completely ad hoc basis. After a fight has ended and the emotional debris is cleaned away—the bets paid, the curses cursed, the carcasses possessed—seven, eight, perhaps even a dozen men slip negligently into the ring with a cock and seek to find there a logical opponent for it. This process, which rarely takes less than ten minutes, and often a good deal longer, is conducted in a very subdued, oblique, even dissembling manner. Those not immediately involved give it at best but disguised, sidelong attention; those who, embarrassedly, are, attempt to pretend somehow that the whole thing is not really happening.

A match made, the other hopefuls retire with the same deliberate indifference, and the selected cocks have their spurs (*tadji*) affixed—razor sharp, pointed steel swords, four or five inches long. This is a delicate job which only a small proportion of men, a half-dozen or so in most villages, know how to do properly. The man who attaches the spurs also provides them, and if the rooster he assists wins its owner awards him the spur-leg of the victim. The spurs are affixed by winding a long length of string around the foot of the spur and the leg of the cock. For reasons I shall come to presently, it is done somewhat differently from case to case, and is an obsessively deliberate affair. The lore about spurs is extensive—they are sharpened only at eclipses and the dark of the moon, should be kept out of the sight of women, and so forth. And they are handled, both in use and out, with the same curious combination of fussiness and sensuality the Balinese direct toward ritual objects generally.

The spurs affixed, the two cocks are placed by their handlers (who may or may not be their owners) facing one another in the center of the ring.[9] A coconut pierced with a small hole is placed in a pail of water, in which it takes about twenty-one seconds to sink, a period known as a *tjeng* and marked at beginning and end by the beating of a slit gong. During these twenty-one seconds the handlers (*pengangkeb*) are not permitted to touch their roosters. If, as sometimes happens, the animals have not fought during this time, they are picked up, fluffed, pulled, prodded, and otherwise insulted, and put back in the center of the ring and the process begins again. Sometimes they refuse to fight at all, or one keeps running away, in which case they are imprisoned together under a wicker cage, which usually gets them engaged.

Most of the time, in any case, the cocks fly almost immediately at one another in a wing-beating, head-thrusting, leg-kicking explosion of animal fury so pure, so absolute, and in its own way so beautiful, as to be almost abstract, a Platonic concept of hate. Within moments one or the other drives home a solid blow with his spur. The handler whose cock has delivered the blow immediately picks it up so that it will not get a return blow, for if he does not the match is likely to end in a mutually mortal tie as the two birds wildly hack each other to pieces. This is particularly true if, as often happens, the spur sticks in its victim's body, for then the aggressor is at the mercy of his wounded foe.

With the birds again in the hands of their handlers, the coconut is now sunk three times after which the cock which has landed the blow must be set down to show that he is firm, a fact he demonstrates by wandering idly around the rink for a coconut sink. The coconut is then sunk twice more and the fight must recommence.

During this interval, slightly over two minutes, the handler of the wounded cock has been working frantically over it, like a trainer patching a mauled boxer between rounds, to get it in shape for a last, desperate try for victory. He blows in its mouth, putting the whole chicken head in his own mouth and sucking and blowing, fluffs it, stuffs its wounds with various sorts of medicines, and generally tries anything he can think of to arouse the last ounce of spirit which may be hidden somewhere within it. By the time he is forced to put it back down he is usually drenched in chicken blood, but, as in prize fighting, a good handler is worth his weight in gold. Some of them can virtually make the dead walk, at least long enough for the second and final round.

In the climactic battle (if there is one; sometimes the wounded cock simply expires in the handler's hands or immediately as it is placed down again), the cock who landed the first blow usually proceeds to finish off his weakened opponent. But this is far from an inevitable outcome, for if a cock can walk he can fight, and if he can fight, he can kill, and what counts is which cock expires first. If the wounded one can get a stab in and stagger on until the other drops, he is the official winner, even if he himself topples over an instant later.

Surrounding all this melodrama—which the crowd packed tight around the ring follows in near silence, moving their bodies in kinesthetic sympathy with the movement of the animals, cheering their champions on with wordless hand motions, shiftings of the shoulders, turnings of the head, falling back *en masse* as the cock with the murderous spurs careens toward one side of the ring (it is said that spectators sometimes lose eyes and fingers from being too attentive), surging forward again as they glance off toward another—is a vast body of extraordinarily elaborate and precisely detailed rules.

These rules, together with the developed lore of cocks and cockfighting which accompanies them, are written down in palm leaf manuscripts (*lontar; rontal*) passed on from generation to generation as part of the general legal and cultural tradition of the villages. At a fight, the umpire (*saja komong; djuru kembar*)—the man who manages the coconut—is in charge of their application and his authority is absolute. I have never seen an umpire's judgment questioned on any subject, even by the more despondent losers, nor have I ever heard, even in private, a charge of unfairness directed against one, or, for that matter, complaints about umpires in general. Only exceptionally well-trusted, solid, and, given the complexity of the code, knowledgeable citizens perform this job, and in fact men will bring their cocks only to fights presided over by such men. It is also the umpire to whom accusations of cheating, which, though rare in the extreme, occasionally arise, are referred; and it is he who in the not infrequent cases where the cocks expire virtually together decides which (if either, for, though the Balinese do not care for such an outcome, there can be ties) went first. Likened to a judge, a king, a priest, and a policeman, he is all of these, and under his assured direction the animal passion of the fight proceeds within the civic certainty of the law. In the dozens of cockfights I saw in Bali, I never once saw an altercation about rules. Indeed, I never saw an open altercation, other than those between cocks, at all.

This crosswise doubleness of an event which, taken as a fact of nature, is rage untrammeled and, taken as a fact of culture, is form perfected, defines the cockfight as a sociological entity. A cockfight is what, searching for a name for something not vertebrate enough to be called a group and not structureless enough to be called a crowd, Erving Goffman has called a "focused gathering"—a set of persons engrossed in a common flow of activity and relating to one another in terms of that flow.[10] Such gatherings meet and disperse; the participants in them fluctuate; the activity that focuses them is discreet—a particulate process that reoccurs rather than a continuous one that endures. They take their form from the situation that evokes them, the floor on which they are placed, as Goffman puts it; but it is a form, and an articulate one, nonetheless. For the situation, the floor is itself created, in jury deliberations, surgical operations, block meetings, sit-ins, cockfights, by the cultural preoccupations—here, as we shall see, the celebration of status rivalry—which not only specify the focus but, assembling actors and arranging scenery, bring it actually into being.

In classical times (that is to say, prior to the Dutch invasion of 1908), when there were no bureaucrats around to improve popular morality, the staging of a cockfight was an explicitly societal matter. Bringing a cock to an important fight was, for an adult male, a compulsory duty of citizenship; taxation of fights, which were usually held on market day, was a major source of public revenue; patronage of the art was a stated responsibility of princes; and the cock ring, or *wantilan*, stood in the center of the village near those other monuments of Balinese civility—the council house, the origin temple, the marketplace, the signal tower, and the banyan tree. Today, a few special occasions aside, the newer rectitude makes so open a statement of the connection between the excitements of collective life and those of blood sport impossible, but, less directly expressed, the connection itself remains intimate and intact. To expose it, however, it is necessary to turn to the aspect of cockfighting around which all the others pivot, and through which they exercise their force, an aspect I have thus far studiously ignored. I mean, of course, the gambling.

Odds and Even Money

The Balinese never do anything in a simple way that they can contrive to do in a complicated one, and to this generalization cockfight wagering is no exception.

In the first place, there are two sorts of bets, or *toh*.[11] There is the single axial bet in the center between the principals (*toh ketengah*), and there is the cloud of peripheral ones around the ring between members of the audience (*toh kesasi*). The first is typically large; the second typically small. The first is collective, involving coalitions of bettors clustering around the owner; the second is individual, man to man. The first is a matter of deliberate, very quiet, almost furtive arrangement by the coalition members and the umpire huddled like conspirators in the center of the ring; the second is a matter of impulsive shouting, public offers, and public acceptances by the excited throng around its edges. And most curiously, and as we shall see most revealingly, *where the first is always, without exception, even money, the second, equally without exception, is never such.* What is a fair coin in the center is a biased one on the side.

The center bet is the official one, hedged in again with a webwork of rules, and is made between the two cock owners, with the umpire as overseer and public witness.[12] This bet, which, as I say, is always relatively and sometimes very large, is never raised simply by the owner in whose name it is made, but by him together with four or five, sometimes seven or eight, allies—kin, village mates, neighbors, close friends. He may, if he is not especially well-to-do, not even be the major contributor, though, if only to show that he is not involved in any chicanery, he must be a significant one.

Of the fifty-seven matches for which I have exact and reliable data on the center bet, the range is from fifteen ringgits to five hundred, with a mean at eighty-five and with the distribution being rather noticeably trimodal: small fights (15 ringgits either side of 35) accounting for about 45 per cent of the total number; medium ones (20 ringgits either side of 70) for about 25 per cent; and large (75 ringgits either side of 175) for about 20 per cent, with a few very small and very large ones out at the extremes. In a society where the normal daily wage of a manual laborer—a brickmaker, an ordinary farmworker, a market porter—was about three ringgits a day, and considering the fact that fights were held on the average about every two-and-a-half days in the immediate area I studied, this is clearly serious gambling, even if the bets are pooled rather than individual efforts.

The side bets are, however, something else altogether. Rather than the solemn, legalistic pactmaking of the center, wagering takes place rather in the fashion in which the stock exchange used to work when it was out on the curb. There is a fixed and known odds paradigm which runs in a continuous series from ten-to-nine at the short end to two-to-one at the long: 10-9, 9-8, 8-7, 7-6, 6-5, 5-4, 4-3, 3-2, 2-1. The man who wishes to back the *underdog cock* (leaving aside how favorites, *kebut*, and underdogs, *ngai*, are established for the moment) shouts the short-side number indicating the odds he wants *to be given*. That is, if he shouts *gasal*, "five," he wants the underdog at five-to-four (or, for him, four-to-five); if he shouts "four," he wants it at four-to-three (again, he putting up the "three"), if "nine," at nine-to-eight, and so on. A man backing the favorite, and thus considering giving odds if he can get them short enough, indicates the fact by crying out the color-type of that cock—"brown," "speckled," or whatever.[13]

As odds-takers (backers of the underdog) and odds-givers (backers of the favorite) sweep the crowd with their shouts, they begin to focus in on one another as potential betting pairs, often from far across the ring. The taker tries to shout the giver into longer odds, the giver to shout the taker into shorter ones.[14] The taker, who is the wooer in this situation, will signal how large a bet he wishes to make at the odds he is shouting by holding a number of fingers up in front of his face and vigorously waving them. If the giver, the wooed, replies in kind, the bet is made; if he does not, they unlock gazes and the search goes on.

The side betting, which takes place after the center bet has been made and its size announced, consists then in a rising crescendo of shouts as backers of the underdog offer their propositions to anyone who will accept them, while those who are backing the favorite but do not like the price being offered, shout equally frenetically the color of the cock to show they too are desperate to bet but want shorter odds.

Almost always odds-calling, which tends to be very consensual in that at any one time almost all callers are calling the same thing, starts off toward the long end of the range—five-to-four or four-to-three—and then moves, also consensually, toward the short end with greater or lesser speed and to a greater or lesser degree. Men crying "five" and finding themselves answered only with cries of "brown" start crying "six," either drawing the other callers fairly quickly with them or retiring from the scene as their too-generous offers are snapped up. If the change is made and partners are still scarce, the procedure is repeated in a move to "seven," and so on, only rarely, and in the very largest fights, reaching the ultimate "nine" or "ten" levels. Occasionally, if the cocks are clearly mismatched, there may be no upward movement at all, or even a movement down the scale to four-to-three, three-to-two, very, very rarely two-to-one, a shift which is accompanied by a declining number of bets as a shift upward is accompanied by an increasing number. But the general pattern is for the betting to move a shorter or longer distance up the scale toward the, for sidebets, nonexistent pole of even money, with the overwhelming majority of bets falling in the four-to-three to eight-to-seven range.[15]

As the moment for the release of the cocks by the handlers approaches, the screaming, at least in a match where the center bet is large, reaches almost frenzied proportions as the remaining unfulfilled bettors try desperately to find a last minute partner at a price they can live with. (Where the center bet is small, the opposite tends to occur: betting dies off, trailing into silence, as odds lengthen and people lose interest.) In a large-bet, well-made match—the kind of match the Balinese regard as "real cockfighting"— the mob scene quality, the sense that sheer chaos is about to break loose, with all those waving, shouting, pushing, clambering men is quite strong, an effect which is only heightened by the intense stillness that falls with instant suddenness, rather as if someone had turned off the current, when the slit gong sounds, the cocks are put down, and the battle begins.

When it ends, anywhere from fifteen seconds to five minutes later, *all bets are immediately paid*. There are absolutely no IOU's, at least to a betting opponent. One may, of course, borrow from a friend before offering or accepting a wager, but to offer or accept it you must have the money already in hand and, if you lose, you must pay it on the spot, before the next match begins. This is an iron rule, and as I have never heard of a disputed umpire's decision (though doubtless there must sometimes be some), I have also never heard of a welshed bet, perhaps because in a worked-up cockfight crowd the consequences might be, as they are reported to be sometimes for cheaters, drastic and immediate.

It is, in any case, this formal assymetry between balanced center bets and unbalanced side ones that poses the critical analytical problem for a theory which sees cockfight wagering as the link connecting the fight to the wider world of Balinese culture. It also suggests the way to go about solving it and demonstrating the link.

The first point that needs to be made in this connection is that the higher the center bet, the more likely the match will in actual fact be an even one. Simple considerations of rationality suggest that. If you are betting fifteen ringgits on a cock, you might be willing to go along with even money even if you feel your animal somewhat the less promising. But if you are betting five hundred you are very, very likely to be loathe to do so. Thus, in large-bet fights, which of course involve the better animals, tremendous care is taken to see that the cocks are about as evenly matched as to size, general condition, pugnacity, and so on as is humanly possible. The different ways of adjusting the spurs of the animals are often employed to secure this. If one cock seems stronger, an agreement will be made to position his spur at a slightly less advantageous angle—a kind of handicapping, at which spur affixers are, so it is said, extremely skilled. More care will be taken, too, to employ skillful handlers and to match them exactly as to abilities.

In short, in a large-bet fight the pressure to make the match a genuinely fifty-fifty proposition is enormous, and is consciously felt as such. For medium fights the pressure is somewhat less, and for small ones less yet, though there is always an effort to make things at least approximately equal, for even at fifteen ringgits (five days work) no one wants to make an even money bet in a clearly unfavorable situation. And, again, what statistics I have tend to bear this out. In my fifty-seven matches, the favorite won thirty-three times over-all, the underdog twenty-four, a 1.4 to 1 ratio. But if one splits the figures at sixty ringgits center bets, the ratios turn out to be 1.1 to 1 (twelve favorites, eleven underdogs) for those above this line, and 1.6 to 1 (twenty-one and thirteen) for those below it. Or, if you take the extremes, for very large fights, those with center bets over a hundred ringgits the ratio is 1 to 1 (seven and seven); for very small fights, those under forty ringgits, it is 1.9 to 1 (nineteen and ten).[16]

Now, from this proposition—that the higher the center bet the more exactly a fifty-fifty proposition the cockfight is—two things more or less immediately follow: (1) the higher the center bet, the greater is the pull on the side betting toward the short-odds end of the wagering spectrum and vice versa; (2) the higher the center bet, the greater the volume of side betting and vice versa.

The logic is similar in both cases. The closer the fight is in fact to even money, the less attractive the long end of the odds will appear and, therefore, the shorter it must be if there are to be takers. That this is the case is apparent from mere inspection, from the Balinese's own analysis of the matter, and from what more systematic observations I was able to collect. Given the difficulty of making precise and complete recordings of side betting, this argument is hard to cast in numerical form, but in all my cases the odds-giver, odds-taker consensual point, a quite pronounced mini-max saddle where the bulk (at a guess, two-thirds to three-quarters in most cases) of the bets are actually made, was three or four points further along the scale toward the shorter end for the large-center-bet fights than for the small ones, with medium ones generally in between. In detail, the fit is not, of course, exact, but the general pattern is quite consistent: the power of the center bet to pull the side bets toward its own even-money pattern is directly proportional to its size, because its size is directly proportional to the degree to which the cocks are in fact evenly matched. As for the volume question, total wagering is greater in large-center-bet fights because such fights are considered more "interesting," not only in the sense that they are less predictable, but, more crucially, that more is at stake in them—in terms of money, in terms of the quality of the cocks, and consequently, as we shall see, in terms of social prestige.[17]

The paradox of fair coin in the middle, biased coin on the outside is thus a merely apparent one. The two betting systems, though formally incongruent, are not really contradictory to one another, but part of a single larger system in which the center bet is, so to speak, the "center of gravity," drawing, the larger it is the more so, the outside bets toward the short-odds end of the scale. The center bet thus "makes the game," or perhaps better, defines it, signals what, following a notion of Jeremy Bentham's, I am going to call its "depth."

The Balinese attempt to create an interesting, if you will, "deep," match by making the center bet as large as possible so that the cocks matched will be as equal and as fine as possible, and the outcome, thus, as unpredictable as possible. They do not always succeed. Nearly half the matches are relatively trivial, relatively uninteresting—in my borrowed terminology, "shallow"—affairs. But that fact no more argues against my interpretation than the fact that most painters, poets, and playwrights are mediocre argues against the view that artistic effort is directed toward profundity and, with a certain frequency, approximates it. The image of artistic technique is indeed exact: the center bet is a means, a device, for creating "interesting," "deep" matches, *not* the reason, or at least not the main reason, *why* they are interesting, the source of their fascination, the substance of their depth. The question why such matches are interesting—indeed, for the Balinese, exquisitely absorbing—takes us out of the realm of formal concerns into more broadly sociological and social-psychological ones, and to a less purely economic idea of what "depth" in gaming amounts to.[18]

Playing with Fire

Bentham's concept of "deep play" is found in his *The Theory of Legislation*.[19] By it he means play in which the stakes are so high that it is, from his utilitarian standpoint, irrational for men to engage in it at all. If a man whose fortune is a thousand pounds (or ringgits) wages five hundred of it on an even bet, the marginal utility of the pound he stands to win is clearly less than the marginal disutility of the one he stands to lose. In genuine deep play, this is the case for both parties. They are both in over their heads. Having come together in search of pleasure they have entered into a relationship which will bring the participants, considered collectively, net pain rather than net pleasure. Bentham's conclusion was, therefore, that deep play was immoral from first principles and, a typical step for him, should be prevented legally.

But more interesting than the ethical problem, at least for our concerns here, is that despite the logical force of Bentham's analysis men do engage in such play, both passionately and often, and even in the face of law's revenge. For Bentham and those who think as he does (nowdays mainly lawyers, economists, and a few psychiatrists), the explanation is, as I have said, that such men are irrational—addicts, fetishists, children, fools, savages, who need only to be protected against themselves. But for the Balinese, though naturally they do not formulate it in so many words, the explanation lies in the fact that in such play money is less a measure of utility, had or expected, than it is a symbol of moral import, perceived or imposed.

It is, in fact, in shallow games, ones in which smaller amounts of money are involved, that increments and decrements of cash are more nearly synonyms for utility and disutility, in the ordinary, unexpanded sense—for pleasure and pain, happiness and unhappiness. In deep ones, where the amounts of money are great, much more is at stake than material gain: namely, esteem, honor, dignity, respect—in a word, though in Bali a profoundly freighted word, status.[20] It is at stake symbolically, for (a few cases of ruined addict gamblers aside) no one's status is actually altered by the outcome of a cockfight; it is only, and that momentarily, affirmed or insulted. But for the Balinese, for whom nothing is more pleasurable than an affront obliquely delivered or more painful than one obliquely received—particularly when mutual acquaintances, undeceived by surfaces, are watching—such appraisive drama is deep indeed.

This, I must stress immediately, is *not* to say that the money does not matter, or that the Balinese is no more concerned about losing five hundred ringgits than fifteen. Such a conclusion would be absurd. It is because money *does*, in this hardly unmaterialistic society, matter and matter very much that the more of it one risks the more of a lot of other things, such as one's pride, one's poise, one's dispassion, one's masculinity, one also risks, again only momentarily but again very publicly as well. In deep cockfights an owner and his collaborators, and, as we shall see, to a lesser but still quite real extent also their backers on the outside, put their money where their status is.

It is in large part *because* the marginal disutility of loss is so great at the higher levels of betting that to engage in such betting is to lay one's public self, allusively and metaphorically, through the medium of one's cock, on the line. And though to a Benthamite this might seem merely to increase the irrationality of the enterprise that much further, to the Balinese what it mainly increases is the meaningfulness of it all. And as (to follow Weber rather than Bentham) the imposition of meaning on life is the major end and primary condition of human existence, that access of significance more than compensates for the economic costs involved.[21] Actually, given the even-money quality of the larger matches, important changes in material fortune among those who regularly participate in them seem virtually nonexistent, because matters more or less even out over the long run. It is, actually, in the smaller, shallow fights, where one finds the handful of more pure, addict-type gamblers involved—those who *are* in it mainly for the money—that "real" changes in social position, largely downward, are affected. Men of this sort, plungers, are highly dispraised by "true cockfighters" as fools who do not understand what the sport is all about, vulgarians who simply miss the point of it all. They are, these addicts, regarded as fair game for the genuine enthusiasts, those who do understand, to take a little money away from, something that is easy enough to do by luring them, through the force of their greed, into irrational bets on mismatched cocks. Most of them do indeed manage to ruin themselves in a remarkably short time, but there always seems to be one or two of them around, pawning their land and selling their clothes in order to bet, at any particular time.[22]

This graduated correlation of "status gambling" with deeper fights and, inversely, "money gambling" with shallower ones is in fact quite general. Bettors themselves form a sociomoral hierarchy in these terms. As noted earlier, at most cockfights there are, around the very edges of the cockfight area, a large number of mindless, sheer-chance type gambling games (roulette, dice throw, coin-spin, pea-under-the-shell) operated by concessionaires. Only women, children, adolescents, and various other sorts of people who do not (or not yet) fight cocks—the extremely poor, the socially despised, the personally idiosyncratic—play at these games, at, of course, penny ante levels. Cockfighting men would be ashamed to go anywhere near them. Slightly above these people in standing are those who, though they do not themselves fight cocks, bet on the smaller matches around the edges. Next, there are those who fight cocks in small, or occasionally medium matches, but have not the status to join in the large ones, though they may bet from time to time on the side in those. And finally, there are those, the really substantial members of the community, the solid citizenry around whom local life revolves, who fight in the larger fights and bet on them around the side. The focusing element in these focused gatherings, these men generally dominate and define the sport as they dominate and define the society. When a Balinese male talks, in that almost venerative way, about "the true cockfighter," the *bebatoh* ("bettor") or *djuru kurung* ("cage keeper"), it is this sort of person, not those who bring the mentality of the pea-and-shell game into the quite different, inappropriate context of the cockfight, the driven gambler (*potét*, a word which has the secondary meaning of thief or reprobate), and the wistful hanger-on, that they mean. For such a man, what is really going on in a match is something rather closer to an *affaire d'honneur* (though, with the Balinese talent for practical fantasy, the blood that is spilled is only figuratively human) than to the stupid, mechanical crank of a slot machine.

What makes Balinese cockfighting deep is thus not money in itself, but what, the more of it that is involved the more so, money causes to happen: the migration of the Balinese status hierarchy into the body of the cockfight. Psychologically an Aesopian representation of the ideal/demonic, rather narcissistic, male self, sociologically it is an equally Aesopian representation of the complex fields of tension set up by the controlled, muted, ceremonial, but for all that deeply felt, interaction of those selves in the context of everyday life. The cocks may be surrogates for their owners' personalities, animal mirrors of psychic form, but the cockfight is—or more exactly, deliberately is made to be—a simulation of the social matrix, the involved system of crosscutting, overlapping, highly corporate groups— villages, kingroups, irrigation societies, temple congregations, "castes"—in which its devotees live.[23] And as prestige, the necessity to affirm it, defend it, celebrate it, justify it, and just plain bask in it (but not, given the strongly ascriptive character of Balinese stratification, to seek it), is perhaps the central driving force in the society, so also—ambulant penises, blood sacrifices, and monetary exchanges aside—is it of the cockfight. This apparent amusement and seeming sport is, to take another phrase from Erving Goffman, "a status bloodbath."[24]

The easiest way to make this clear, and at least to some degree to demonstrate it, is to invoke the village whose cockfighting activities I observed the closest—the one in which the raid occurred and from which my statistical data are taken.

As all Balinese villages, this one—Tihingan, in the Klungkung region of southeast Bali—is intricately organized, a labyrinth of alliances and oppositions. But, unlike many, two sorts of corporate groups, which are also status groups, particularly stand out, and we may concentrate on them, in a part-for-whole way, without undue distortion.

First, the village is dominated by four large, patrilineal, partly endogamous descent groups which are constantly vying with one another and form the major factions in the village. Sometimes they group two and two, or rather the two larger ones versus the two smaller ones plus all the unaffiliated people; sometimes they operate independently. There are also subfactions within them, subfactions within the subfactions, and so on to rather fine levels of distinction. And second, there is the village itself, almost entirely endogamous, which is opposed to all the other villages round about in its cockfight circuit (which, as explained, is the market region), but which also forms alliances with certain of these neighbors against certain others in various supra-village political and social contexts. The exact situation is thus, as everywhere in Bali, quite distinctive; but the general pattern of a tiered hierarchy of status rivalries between highly corporate but various based groupings (and, thus, between the members of them) is entirely general.

Consider, then, as support of the general thesis that the cockfight, and especially the deep cockfight, is fundamentally a dramatization of status concerns, the following facts, which to avoid extended ethnographic description I will simply pronounce to be facts—though the concrete evidence-examples, statements, and numbers that could be brought to bear in support of them is both extensive and unmistakable:

1. A man virtually never bets against a cock owned by a member of his own kingroup. Usually he will feel obliged to bet for it, the more so the closer the kin tie and the deeper the fight. If he is

certain in his mind that it will not win, he may just not bet at all, particularly if it is only a second cousin's bird or if the fight is a shallow one. But as a rule he will feel he must support it and, in deep games, nearly always does. Thus the great majority of the people calling "five" or "speckled" so demonstratively are expressing their allegiance to their kinsman, not their evaluation of his bird, their understanding of probability theory, or even their hopes of unearned income.

2. This principle is extended logically. If your kingroup is not involved you will support an allied kingroup against an unallied one in the same way, and so on through the very involved networks of alliances which, as I say, make up this, as any other, Balinese village.

3. So, too, for the village as a whole. If an outsider cock is fighting any cock from your village you will tend to support the local one. If, what is a rarer circumstance but occurs every now and then, a cock from outside your cockfight circuit is fighting one inside it you will also tend to support the "home bird."

4. Cocks which come from any distance are almost always favorites, for the theory is the man would not have dared to bring it if it was not a good cock, the more so the further he has come. His followers are, of course, obliged to support him, and when the more grand-scale legal cockfights are held (on holidays, and so on) the people of the village take what they regard to be the best cocks in the village, regardless of ownership, and go off to support them, although they will almost certainly have to give odds on them and to make large bets to show that they are not a cheapskate village. Actually, such "away games," though infrequent, tend to mend the ruptures between village members that the constantly occurring "home games," where village factions are opposed rather than united, exacerbate.

5. Almost all matches are sociologically relevant. You seldom get two outsider cocks fighting, or two cocks with no particular group backing, or with group backing which is mutually unrelated in any clear way. When you do get them, the game is very shallow, betting very slow, and the whole thing very dull, with no one save the immediate principals and an addict gambler or two at all interested.

6. By the same token, you rarely get two cocks from the same group, even more rarely from the same subfaction, and virtually never from the same sub-subfaction (which would be in most cases one extended family) fighting. Similarly, in outside village fights two members of the village will rarely fight against one another, even though, as bitter rivals, they would do so with enthusiasm on their home grounds.

7. On the individual level, people involved in an institutionalized

hostility relationship, called *puik,* in which they do not speak or otherwise have anything to do with each other (the causes of this formal breaking of relations are many: wife-capture, inheritance arguments, political differences) will bet very heavily, sometimes almost maniacally, against one another in what is a frank and direct attack on the very masculinity, the ultimate ground of his status, of the opponent.

8. The center bet coalition is, in all but the shallowest games, *always* made up by structural allies—no "outside money" is involved. What is "outside" depends upon the context, of course, but given it, no outside money is mixed in with the main bet; if the principals cannot raise it, it is not made. The center bet, again especially in deeper games, is thus the most direct and open expression of social opposition, which is one of the reasons why both it and match making are surrounded by such an air of unease, furtiveness, embarrassment, and so on.

9. The rule about borrowing money—that you may borrow *for* a bet but not *in* one—stems (and the Balinese are quite conscious of this) from similar considerations: you are never at the *economic* mercy of your enemy that way. Gambling debts, which can get quite large on a rather short-term basis, are always to friends, never to enemies, structurally speaking.

10. When two cocks are structurally irrelevant or neutral so far as *you* are concerned (though, as mentioned, they almost never are to each other) you do not even ask a relative or a friend whom he is betting on, because if you know how he is betting and he knows you know, and you go the other way, it will lead to strain. This rule is explicit and rigid; fairly elaborate, even rather artificial precautions are taken to avoid breaking it. At the very least you must pretend not to notice what he is doing, and he what you are doing.

11. There is a special word for betting against the grain, which is also the word for "pardon me" (*mpura*). It is considered a bad thing to do, though if the center bet is small it is sometimes all right as long as you do not do it too often. But the larger the bet and the more frequently you do it, the more the "pardon me" tack will lead to social disruption.

12. In fact, the institutionalized hostility relation, *puik,* is often formally initiated (though its causes always lie elsewhere) by such a "pardon me" bet in a deep fight, putting the symbolic fat in the fire. Similarly, the end of such a relationship and resumption of normal social intercourse is often signalized (but, again, not actually brought about) by one or the other of the enemies supporting the other's bird.

13. In sticky, cross-loyalty situations, of which in this extraordinarily complex social system there are of course many, where a man is

caught between two more or less equally balanced loyalties, he tends to wander off for a cup of coffee or something to avoid having to bet, a form of behavior reminiscent of that of American voters in similar situations.[25]

14. The people involved in the center bet are, especially in deep fights, virtually always leading members of their group—kinship, village, or whatever. Further, those who bet on the side (including these people) are, as I have already remarked, the more established members of the village—the solid citizens. Cockfighting is for those who are involved in the everyday politics of prestige as well, not for youth, women, subordinates, and so forth.

15. So far as money is concerned, the explicitly expressed attitude toward it is that it is a secondary matter. It is not, as I have said, of no importance; Balinese are no happier to lose several weeks' income than anyone else. But they mainly look on the monetary aspects of the cockfight as self-balancing, a matter of just moving money around, circulating it among a fairly well-defined group of serious cockfighters. The really important wins and losses are seen mostly in other terms, and the general attitude toward wagering is not any hope of cleaning up, of making a killing (addict gamblers again excepted), but that of the horseplayer's prayer: "Oh, God, please let me break even." In prestige terms, however, you do not want to break even, but, in a momentary, punctuate sort of way, win utterly. The talk (which goes on all the time) is about fights against such-and-such a cock of So-and-So which your cock demolished, not on how much you won, a fact people, even for large bets, rarely remember for any length of time, though they will remember the day they did in Pan Loh's finest cock for years.

16. You must bet on cocks of your own group aside from mere loyalty considerations, for if you do not people generally will say, "What! Is he too proud for the likes of us? Does he have to go to Java or Den Pasar [the capital town] to bet, he is such an important man?" Thus there is a general pressure to bet not only to show that you are important locally, but that you are not so important that you look down on everyone else as unfit even to be rivals. Similarly, home team people must bet against outside cocks or the outsiders will accuse it—a serious charge—of just collecting entry fees and not really being interested in cockfighting, as well as again being arrogant and insulting.

17. Finally, the Balinese peasants themselves are quite aware of all this and can and, at least to an ethnographer, do state most of it in approximately the same terms as I have. Fighting cocks, almost every Balinese I have ever discussed the subject with has said, is like playing with fire only not getting burned. You activate village

and kingroup rivalries and hostilities, but in "play" form, coming dangerously and entrancingly close to the expression of open and direct interpersonal and intergroup aggression (something which, again, almost never happens in the normal course of ordinary life), but not quite, because, after all, it is "only a cockfight."

More observations of this sort could be advanced, but perhaps the general point is, if not made, at least well-delineated, and the whole argument thus far can be usefully summarized in a formal paradigm:

THE MORE A MATCH IS . . .

1. Between near status equals (and/or personal enemies)
2. Between high status individuals

THE DEEPER THE MATCH.

THE DEEPER THE MATCH . . .

1. The closer the identification of cock and man (or: more properly, the deeper the match the more the man will advance his best, most closely-identified-with cock).
2. The finer the cocks involved and the more exactly they will be matched.
3. The greater the emotion that will be involved and the more the general absorbtion in the match.
4. The higher the individual bets center and outside, the shorter the outside bet odds will tend to be, and the more betting there will be over-all.
5. The less an "economic" and the more a "status" view of gaming will be involved, and the "solider" the citizens who will be gaming.[26]

Inverse arguments hold for the shallower the fight, culminating, in a reversed-signs sense, in the coin-spinning and dice-throwing amusements. For deep fights there are no absolute upper limits, though there are of course practical ones, and there are a great many legend-like tales of great Duel-in-the-Sun combats between lords and princes in classical times (for cockfighting has always been as much an elite concern as a popular one), far deeper than anything anyone, even aristocrats, could produce today anywhere in Bali.

Indeed, one of the great culture heroes of Bali is a prince, called after his passion for the sport, "The Cockfighter," who happened to be away at a very deep cockfight with a neighboring prince when the whole of his family—father, brothers, wives, sisters—were assassinated by commoner usurpers. Thus spared, he returned to dispatch the upstarts, regain the throne, reconstitute the Balinese high tradition, and build its most powerful, glorious, and prosperous state. Along with everything else that the Balinese see in fighting cocks—themselves, their social order, abstract hatred, masculinity, demonic power—they also see the archetype of status virtue, the arrogant, resolute, honor-mad player with real fire, the ksatria prince.[27]

Feathers, Blood, Crowds, and Money

"Poetry makes nothing happen," Auden says in his elegy of Yeats, "it survives in the valley of its saying . . . a way of happening, a mouth." The cockfight too, in this colloquial sense, makes nothing happen. Men go on allegorically humiliating one another and being allegorically humiliated by one another, day after day, glorying quietly in the experience if they have triumphed, crushed only slightly more openly by it if they have not. *But no one's status really changes.* You cannot ascend the status ladder by winning cockfights; you cannot, as an individual, really ascend it at all. Nor can you descend it that way.[28] All you can do is enjoy and savor, or suffer and withstand, the concocted sensation of drastic and momentary movement along an aesthetic semblance of that ladder, a kind of behind-the-mirror status jump which has the look of mobility without its actuality.

As any art form—for that, finally, is what we are dealing with—the cockfight renders ordinary, everyday experience comprehensible by presenting it in terms of acts and objects which have had their practical consequences removed and been reduced (or, if you prefer, raised) to the level of sheer appearances, where their meaning can be more powerfully articulated and more exactly perceived. The cockfight is "really real" only to the cocks—it does not kill anyone, castrate anyone, reduce anyone to animal status, alter the hierarchical relations among people, nor refashion the hierarchy; it does not even redistribute income in any significant way. What it does is what, for other peoples with other temperaments and other conventions, *Lear* and *Crime and Punishment* do; it catches up these themes—death, masculinity, rage, pride, loss, beneficence, chance—and, ordering them into an encompassing structure, presents them in such a way as to throw into relief a particular view of their essential nature. It puts a construction on them, makes them, to those historically positioned to appreciate the construction, meaningful—visible, tangible, graspable—"real," in an ideational sense. An image, fiction, a model, a metaphor, the cockfight is a means of expression; its function is neither to assuage social passions nor to heighten them (though, in its play-with-fire way, it does a bit of both), but, in a medium of feathers, blood, crowds, and money, to display them.

The question of how it is that we perceive qualities in things—paintings, books, melodies, plays—that we do not feel we can assert literally to be there has come, in recent years, into the very center of aesthetic theory.[29] Neither the sentiments of the artist, which remain his, nor those of the audience, which remain theirs, can account for the agitation of one painting or the serenity of another. We attribute grandeur, wit, despair, exuberance to strings of sounds; lightness, energy, violence, fluidity to blocks of stone. Novels are said to have strength, buildings eloquence, plays momentum, ballets repose. In this realm of eccentric predicates, to say that the cock-fight, in its perfected cases at least, is "disquietful" does not seem at all unnatural, merely, as I have just denied it practical consequence, somewhat puzzling.

The disquietfulness arises, "somehow," out of a conjunction of three attributes of the fight: its immediate dramatic shape; its metaphoric content; and its social context. A cultural figure against a social ground, the fight is at once a convulsive surge of animal hatred, a mock war of symbolical selves, and a formal simulation of status tensions, and its aesthetic power derives from its capacity to force together these diverse realities. The reason it is disquietful is not that it has material effects (it has some, but they are minor); the reason that it is disquietful is that, joining pride to selfhood, selfhood to cocks, and cocks to destruction, it brings to imaginative realization a dimension of Balinese experience normally well-obscured from view. The transfer of a sense of gravity into what is in itself a rather blank and unvarious spectacle, a commotion of beating wings and throbbing legs, is effected by interpreting it as expressive of something unsettling in the way its authors and audience live, or, even more ominously, what they are.

As a dramatic shape, the fight displays a characteristic that does not seem so remarkable until one realizes that it does not have to be there: a radically atomistical structure.[30] Each match is a world unto itself, a particulate burst of form. There is the match making, there is the betting, there is the fight, there is the result—utter triumph and utter defeat—and there is the hurried, embarrassed passing of money. The loser is not consoled. People drift away from him, look through him, leave him to assimilate his momentary descent into nonbeing, reset his face, and return, scarless and intact, to the fray. Nor are winners congratulated, or events rehashed; once a match is ended the crowd's attention turns totally to the next, with no looking back. A shadow of the experience no doubt remains with the principals, perhaps even with some of the witnesses, of a deep fight, as it remains with us when we leave the theater after seeing a powerful play well-performed; but it quite soon fades to become at most a schematic memory—a diffuse glow or an abstract shudder—and usually not even that. Any expressive form lives only in its own present—the one it itself creates. But, here, that present is severed into a string of flashes, some more bright than others, but all of them disconnected, aesthetic quanta. Whatever the cockfight says, it says in spurts.

But, as I have argued lengthily elsewhere, the Balinese live in spurts.[31] Their life, as they arrange it and perceive it, is less a flow, a directional movement out of the past, through the present, toward the future than an on-off pulsation of meaning and vacuity, an arhythmic alternation of short periods when "something" (that is, something significant) is happening and equally short ones where "nothing" (that is, nothing much) is—between what they themselves call "full" and "empty" times, or, in another idiom, "junctures" and "holes." In focusing activity down to a burning-glass dot, the cockfight is merely being Balinese in the same way in which everything from the monadic encounters of everyday life, through the clanging pointillism of *gamelan* music, to the visiting-day-of-the-gods temple celebrations are. It is not an imitation of the punctuateness of Balinese social life, nor a depiction of it, nor even an expression of it; it is an example of it, carefully prepared.[32]

If one dimension of the cockfight's structure, its lack of temporal directionality, makes it seem a typical segment of the general social life, however, the other, its flat-out, head-to-head (or spur-to-spur) agressiveness, makes it seem a contradiction, a reversal, even a subversion of it. In the normal course of things, the Balinese are shy to the point of obsessiveness of open conflict. Oblique, cautious, subdued, controlled, masters of indirection and dissimulation—what they call *alus*, "polished," "smooth,"—they rarely face what they can turn away from, rarely resist what they can evade. But here they portray themselves as wild and murderous, manic explosions of instinctual cruelty. A powerful rendering of life as the Balinese most deeply do not want it (to adapt a phrase Frye has used of Gloucester's blinding) is set in the context of a sample of it as they do in fact have it.[33] And, because the context suggests that the rendering, if less than a straightforward description is nonetheless more than an idle fancy, it is here that the disquietfulness—the disquietfulness of the *fight*, not (or, anyway, not necessarily) its patrons, who seem in fact rather thoroughly to enjoy it—emerges. The slaughter in the cock ring is not a depiction of how things literally are among men, but, what is almost worse, of how, from a particular angle, they imaginatively are.[34]

The angle, of course, is stratificatory. What, as we have already seen, the cockfight talks most forcibly about is status relationships, and what it says about them is that they are matters of life and death. That prestige is a profoundly serious business is apparent everywhere one looks in Bali—in the village, the family, the economy, the state. A peculiar fusion of Polynesian title ranks and Hindu castes, the hierarchy of pride is the moral backbone of the society. But only in the cockfight are the sentiments upon which that hierarchy rests revealed in their natural colors. Enveloped elsewhere in a haze of etiquette, a thick cloud of euphemism and ceremony, gesture and allusion, they are here expressed in only the thinnest disguise of an animal mask, a mask which in fact demonstrates them far more effectively than it conceals them. Jealousy is as much a part of Bali as poise, envy as grace, brutality as charm; but without the cockfight the

Balinese would have a much less certain understanding of them, which is, presumably, why they value it so highly.

Any expressive form works (when it works) by disarranging semantic contexts in such a way that properties conventionally ascribed to certain things are unconventionally ascribed to others, which are then seen actually to possess them. To call the wind a cripple, as Stevens does, to fix tone and manipulate timbre, as Schoenberg does, or, closer to our case, to picture an art critic as a dissolute bear, as Hogarth does, is to cross conceptual wires; the established conjunctions between objects and their qualities are altered and phenomena—fall weather, melodic shape, or cultural journalism —are clothed in signifiers which normally point to other referents.[35] Similarly, to connect—and connect, and connect— the collision of roosters with the devisiveness of status is to invite a transfer of perceptions from the former to the latter, a transfer which is at once a description and a judgment. (Logically, the transfer could, of course, as well go the other way; but, like most of the rest of us, the Balinese are a great deal more interested in understanding men than they are in understanding cocks.)

What sets the cockfight apart from the ordinary course of life, lifts it from the realm of everyday practical affairs, and surrounds it with an aura of enlarged importance is not, as functionalist sociology would have it, that it reinforces status discriminations (such reinforcement is hardly necessary in a society where every act proclaims them), but that it provides a metasocial commentary upon the whole matter of assorting human beings into fixed hierarchical ranks and then organizing the major part of collective existence around that assortment. Its function, if you want to call it that, is interpretive: it is a Balinese reading of Balinese experience; a story they tell themselves about themselves.

Saying Something of Something

To put the matter this way is to engage in a bit of metaphorical refocusing of one's own, for it shifts the analysis of cultural forms from an endeavor in general parallel to dissecting an organism, diagnosing a symptom, deciphering a code, or ordering a system—the dominant analogies in contemporary anthropology—to one in general parallel with penetrating a literary text. If one takes the cockfight, or any other collectively sustained symbolic structure, as a means of "saying something of something" (to invoke a famous Aristotelian tag), then one is faced with a problem not in social mechanics but social semantics.[36] For the anthropologist, whose concern is with formulating sociological principles, not with promoting or appreciating cockfights, the question is, what does one learn about such principles from examining culture as an assemblage of texts?

Such an extension of the notion of a text beyond written material, and even beyond verbal, is, though metaphorical, not, of course, all that novel.

The *interpretatio naturae* tradition of the middle ages, which, culminating in Spinoza, attempted to read nature as Scripture, the Nietszchean effort to treat value systems as glosses on the will to power (or the Marxian one to treat them as glosses on property relations), and the Freudian replacement of the enigmatic text of the manifest dream with the plain one of the latent, all offer precedents, if not equally recommendable ones.[37] But the idea remains theoretically undeveloped; and the more profound corollary, so far as anthropology is concerned, that cultural forms can be treated as texts, as imaginative works built out of social materials, has yet to be systematically exploited.[38]

In the case at hand, to treat the cockfight as a text is to bring out a feature of it (in my opinion, the central feature of it) that treating it as a rite or a pastime, the two most obvious alternatives, would tend to obscure: its use of emotion for cognitive ends. What the cockfight says it says in a vocabulary of sentiment—the thrill of risk, the despair of loss, the pleasure of triumph. Yet what it says is not merely that risk is exciting, loss depressing, or triumph gratifying, banal tautologies of affect, but that it is of these emotions, thus exampled, that society is built and individuals put together. Attending cockfights and participating in them is, for the Balinese, a kind of sentimental education. What he learns there is what his culture's ethos and his private sensibility (or, anyway, certain aspects of them) look like when spelled out externally in a collective text; that the two are near enough alike to be articulated in the symbolics of a single such text; and— the disquieting part—that the text in which this revelation is accomplished consists of a chicken hacking another mindlessly to bits.

Every people, the proverb has it, loves its own form of violence. The cockfight is the Balinese reflection on theirs: on its look, its uses, its force, its fascination. Drawing on almost every level of Balinese experience, it brings together themes—animal savagery, male narcissism, opponent gambling, status rivalry, mass excitement, blood sacrifice—whose main connection is their involvement with rage and the fear of rage, and, binding them into a set of rules which at once contains them and allows them play, builds a symbolic structure in which, over and over again, the reality of their inner affiliation can be intelligibly felt. If, to quote Northrop Frye again, we go to see *Macbeth* to learn what a man feels like after he has gained a kingdom and lost his soul, Balinese go to cockfights to find out what a man, usually composed, aloof, almost obsessively self-absorbed, a kind of moral autocosm, feels like when, attacked, tormented, challenged, insulted, and driven in result to the extremes of fury, he has totally triumphed or been brought totally low. The whole passage, as it takes us back to Aristotle (though to the *Poetics* rather than the *Hermeneutics*), is worth quotation:

But the poet [as opposed to the historian], Aristotle says, never makes any real statements at all, certainly no particular or specific ones. The poet's job is not to

tell you what happened, but what happens: not what did take place, but the kind
of thing that always does take place. He gives you the typical, recurring, or what
Aristotle calls universal event. You wouldn't go to *Macbeth* to learn about the
history of Scotland—you go to it to learn what a man feels like after he's gained
a kingdom and lost his soul. When you meet such a character as Micawber in
Dickens, you don't feel that there must have been a man Dickens knew who was
exactly like this: you feel that there's a bit of Micawber in almost everybody you
know, including yourself. Our impressions of human life are picked up one by one,
and remain for most of us loose and disorganized. But we constantly find things
in literature that suddenly co-ordinate and bring into focus a great many such
impressions, and this is part of what Aristotle means by the typical or universal
human event.[39]

It is this kind of bringing of assorted experiences of everyday life to
focus that the cockfight, set aside from that life as "only a game" and
reconnected to it as "more than a game," accomplishes, and so creates
what, better than typical or universal, could be called a paradigmatic
human event—that is, one that tells us less what happens than the kind
of thing that would happen if, as is not the case, life were art and could
be as freely shaped by styles of feeling as *Macbeth* and *David Copperfield*
are.

Enacted and reenacted, so far without end, the cockfight enables the
Balinese, as, read and reread, *Macbeth* enables us, to see a dimension of
his own subjectivity. As he watches fight after fight, with the active watching of an owner and a bettor (for cockfighting has no more interest as a
pure spectator sport than croquet or dog racing do), he grows familiar
with it and what it has to say to him, much as the attentive listener to
string quartets or the absorbed viewer of still lifes grows slowly more
familiar with them in a way which opens his subjectivity to himself.[40]

Yet, because—in another of those paradoxes, along with painted feelings and unconsequenced acts, which haunt aesthetics—that subjectivity
does not properly exist until it is thus organized, art forms generate and
regenerate the very subjectivity they pretend only to display. Quartets,
still lifes, and cockfights are not merely reflections of a preexisting sensibility analogically represented; they are positive agents in the creation and
maintenance of such a sensibility. If we see ourselves as a pack of Micaw-
bers it is from reading too much Dickens (if we see ourselves as un-
illusioned realists, it is from reading too little); and similarly for Balinese,
cocks, and cockfights. It is in such a way, coloring experience with the light
they cast it in, rather than through whatever material effects they may
have, that the arts play their role, as arts, in social life.[41]

In the cockfight, then, the Balinese forms and discovers his temperament and his society's temper at the same time. Or, more exactly, he
forms and discovers a particular face of them. Not only are there a great
many other cultural texts providing commentaries on status hierarchy and
self-regard in Bali, but there are a great many other critical sectors of

Balinese life besides the stratificatory and the agonistic that receive such commentary. The ceremony consecrating a Brahmana priest, a matter of breath control, postural immobility, and vacant concentration upon the depths of being, displays a radically different, but to the Balinese equally real, property of social hierarchy—its reach toward the numinous transcendent. Set not in the matrix of the kinetic emotionality of animals, but in that of the static passionlessness of divine mentality, it expresses tranquility not disquiet. The mass festivals at the village temples, which mobilize the whole local population in elaborate hostings of visiting gods— songs, dances, compliments, gifts—assert the spiritual unity of village mates against their status inequality and project a mood of amity and trust.[42] The cockfight is not the master key to Balinese life, any more than bullfighting is to Spanish. What it says about that life is not unqualified nor even unchallenged by what other equally eloquent cultural statements say about it. But there is nothing more surprising in this than in the fact that Racine and Molière were contemporaries, or that the same people who arrange chrysanthemums cast swords.[43]

The culture of a people is an ensemble of texts, themselves ensembles, which the anthropologist strains to read over the shoulders of those to whom they properly belong. There are enormous difficulties in such an enterprise, methodological pitfalls to make a Freudian quake, and some moral perplexities as well. Nor is it the only way that symbolic forms can be sociologically handled. Functionalism lives, and so does psychologism. But to regard such forms as "saying something of something," and saying it to somebody, is at least to open up the possibility of an analysis which attends to their substance rather than to reductive formulas professing to account for them.

As in more familiar exercises in close reading, one can start anywhere in a culture's repertoire of forms and end up anywhere else. One can stay, as I have here, within a single, more or less bounded form and circle steadily within it. One can move between forms in search of broader unities or informing contrasts. One can even compare forms from different cultures to define their character in reciprocal relief. But whatever the level at which one operates, and however intricately, the guiding principle is the same: societies, like lives, contain their own interpretations. One has only to learn how to gain access to them.

REFERENCES

1. Gregory Bateson and Margaret Mead, *Balinese Character: A Photographic Analysis* (New York: New York Academy of Sciences, 1942), p. 68.

2. Jane Belo, "The Balinese Temper," in Jane Belo, ed., *Traditional Balinese Culture* (New York: Columbia University Press, 1970; originally published in 1935), pp. 85-110.

3. The best discussion of cockfighting is again Bateson and Mead's (*Balinese Character*, pp. 24-25, 140), but it, too, is general and abbreviated.

4. *Ibid.*, pp. 25-26. The cockfight is unusual within Balinese culture in being a single-sex public activity from which the other sex is totally and expressly excluded. Sexual differentiation is culturally extremely played down in Bali and most activities, formal and informal, involve the participation of men and women on equal ground, commonly as linked couples. From religion, to politics, to economics, to kinship, to dress, Bali is a rather "uni-sex" society, a fact both its customs and its symbolism clearly express. Even in contexts where women do not in fact play much of a role—music, painting, certain agricultural activities—their absence, which is only relative in any case, is more a mere matter of fact than socially enforced. To this general pattern, the cockfight, entirely of, by, and for men (women—at least *Balinese* women —do not even watch), is the most striking exception.

5. Christiaan Hooykaas, *The Lay of the Jaya Prana* (London, 1958), p. 39. The lay has a stanza (no. 17) with the reluctant bridegroom use. Jaya Prana, the subject of a Balinese Uriah myth, responds to the lord who has offered him the loveliest of six hundred servant girls: "Godly King, my Lord and Master/I beg you, give me leave to go/such things are not yet in my mind;/like a fighting cock encaged/indeed I am on my mettle/I am alone/as yet the flame has not been fanned."

6. For these, see V. E. Korn, *Het Adatrecht van Bali*, 2d ed. ('S-Gravenhage: G. Naeff, 1932), index under *toh*.

7. There is indeed a legend to the effect that the separation of Java and Bali is due to the action of a powerful Javanese religious figure who wished to protect himself against a Balinese culture hero (the ancestor of two Ksatria castes) who was a passionate cockfighting gambler. See Christiaan Hooykaas, *Agama Tirtha* (Amsterdam: Noord-Hollandsche, 1964), p. 184.

8. An incestuous couple is forced to wear pig yokes over their necks and crawl to a pig trough and eat with their mouths there. On this, see Jane Belo, "Customs Pertaining to Twins in Bali," in Belo, ed., *Traditional Balinese Culture*, p. 49; on the abhorence of animality generally, Bateson and Mead, *Balinese Character*, p. 22.

9. Except for unimportant, small-bet fights (on the question of fight "importance," see below) spur affixing is usually done by someone other than the owner. Whether the owner handles his own cock or not more or less depends on how skilled he is at it, a consideration whose importance is again relative to the importance of the fight. When spur affixers and cock handlers are someone other than the owner, they are almost always a quite close relative—a brother or cousin—or a very intimate friend of his. They are thus almost extensions of his personality, as the fact that all three will refer to the cock as "mine," say "I" fought So-and-So, and so on, demonstrates. Also, owner-handler-affixer triads tend to be fairly fixed, though individuals may participate in several and often exchange roles within a given one.

10. Erving Goffman, *Encounters: Two Studies in the Sociology of Interaction* (Indianapolis: Bobbs-Merrill, 1961), pp. 9-10.

11. This word, which literally means an indelible stain or mark, as in a birthmark or a vein in a stone, is used as well for a deposit in a court case, for a pawn, for security offered in a loan, for a stand-in for someone else in a legal or ceremonial context, for an earnest advanced in a business deal, for a sign placed in a field to indicate its ownership is in dispute, and for the status of an unfaithful wife from whose lover her husband must gain satisfaction or surrender her to him. See Korn, *Het Adatrecht*

van Bali; Theodoor Pigeaud, *Javaans-Nederlands Handwoordenboek* (Groningen: Wolters, 1938); H. H. Juynboll, *Oudjavaansche-Nederlandsche Woordenlijst* (Leiden: Brill, 1923).

12. The center bet must be advanced in cash by both parties prior to the actual fight. The umpire holds the stakes until the decision is rendered and then awards them to the winner, avoiding, among other things, the intense embarrassment both winner and loser would feel if the latter had to pay off personally following his defeat. About 10 per cent of the winner's receipts are subtracted for the umpire's share and that of the fight sponsors.

13. Actually, the typing of cocks, which is extremely elaborate (I have collected more than twenty classes, certainly not a complete list), is not based on color alone, but on a series of independent, interacting, dimensions, which include, beside color, size, bone thickness, plumage, and temperament. (But *not* pedigree. The Balinese do not breed cocks to any significant extent, nor, so far as I have been able to discover, have they ever done so. The *asil*, or jungle cock, which is the basic fighting strain everywhere the sport is found, is native to southern Asia, and one can buy a good example in the chicken section of almost any Balinese market for anywhere from four or five ringgits up to fifty or more.) The color element is merely the one normally used as the type name, except when the two cocks of different types—as on principle they must be—have the same color, in which case a secondary indication from one of the other dimensions ("large speckled" v. "small speckled," etc.) is added. The types are coordinated with various cosmological ideas which help shape the making of matches, so that, for example, you fight a small, headstrong, speckled brown-on-white cock with flat-lying feathers and thin legs from the east side of the ring on a certain day of the complex Balinese calendar, and a large, cautious, all-black cock with tufted feathers and stubby legs from the north side on another day, and so on. All this is again recorded in palm-leaf manuscripts and endlessly discussed by the Balinese (who do not all have identical systems), and full-scale componential-cum-symbolic analysis of cock classifications would be extremely valuable both as an adjunct to the description of the cockfight and in itself. But my data on the subject, though extensive and varied, do not seem to be complete and systematic enough to attempt such an analysis here. For Balinese cosmological ideas more generally see Belo, ed., *Traditional Balinese Culture,* and J. L. Swellengrebel, ed., *Bali: Studies in Life, Thought, and Ritual* (The Hague: W. van Hoeve, 1960); for calendrical ones, Clifford Geertz, *Person, Time, and Conduct in Bali: An Essay in Cultural Analysis* (New Haven: Southeast Asia Studies, Yale University, 1966), pp. 45-53.

14. For purposes of ethnographic completeness, it should be noted that it is possible for the man backing the favorite—the odds-giver—to make a bet in which he wins if his cock wins or there is a tie, a slight shortening of the odds (I do not have enough cases to be exact, but ties seem to occur about once every fifteen or twenty matches). He indicates his wish to do this by shouting *sapih* ("tie") rather than the cock-type, but such bets are in fact infrequent.

15. The precise dynamics of the movement of the betting is one of the most intriguing, most complicated, and, given the hectic conditions under which it occurs, most difficult to study, aspects of the fight. Motion picture recording plus multiple observers would probably be necessary to deal with it effectively. Even impressionistically—the only approach open to a lone ethnographer caught in the middle of all this—it is clear that certain men lead both in determining the favorite (that is, making the opening cock-type calls which always initiate the process) and in

directing the movement of the odds, these "opinion leaders" being the more accomplished cockfighters-cum-solid-citizens to be discussed below. If these men begin to change their calls, others follow; if they begin to make bets, so do others and
—though there is always a large number of frustrated bettors crying for shorter or
longer odds to the end—the movement more or less ceases. But a detailed understanding of the whole process awaits what, alas, it is not very likely ever to get: a
decision theorist armed with precise observations of individual behavior.

16. Assuming only binomial variability, the departure from a fifty-fifty expectation in
the sixty ringgits and below case is 1.38 standard deviations, or (in a one direction
test) an eight in one hundred possibility by chance alone; for the below forty
ringgits case it is 1.65 standard deviations, or about five in one hundred. The fact
that these departures though real are not extreme merely indicates, again, that even
in the smaller fights the tendency to match cocks at least reasonably evenly persists.
It is a matter of relative relaxation of the pressures toward equalization, not their
elimination. The tendency for high-bet contests to be coin-flip propositions is, of
course, even more striking, and suggests the Balinese know quite well what they
are about.

17. The reduction in wagering in smaller fights (which, of course, feeds on itself; one
of the reasons people find small fights uninteresting is that there is less wagering in
them, and contrariwise for large ones) takes place in three mutually reinforcing
ways. First, there is a simple withdrawal of interest as people wander off to have
a cup of coffee or chat with a friend. Second, the Balinese do not mathematically
reduce odds, but bet directly in terms of stated odds as such. Thus, for a nine-to-
eight bet, one man wagers nine ringgits, the other eight; for five-to-four, one wagers
five, the other four. For any given currency unit, like the ringgit, therefore, 6.3
times as much money is involved in a ten-to-nine bet as in a two-to-one bet, for
example, and, as noted, in small fights betting settles toward the longer end.
Finally, the bets which are made tend to be one- rather than two-, three-, or in
some of the very largest fights, four- or five-finger ones. (The fingers indicate
the *multiples* of the stated bet odds at issue, not absolute figures. Two fingers in a
six-to-five situation means a man wants to wager ten ringgits on the underdog
against twelve, three in an eight-to-seven situation, twenty-one against twenty-four,
and so on.)

18. Besides wagering there are other economic aspects of the cockfight, especially its
very close connection with the local market system which, though secondary both
to its motivation and to its function, are not without importance. Cockfights are
open events to which anyone who wishes may come, sometimes from quite distant
areas, but well over 90 per cent, probably over 95, are very local affairs, and
the locality concerned is defined not by the village, nor even by the administrative
district, but by the rural market system. Bali has a three-day market week with the
familiar "solar-system" type rotation. Though the markets themselves have never
been very highly developed, small morning affairs in a village square, it is the
micro-region such rotation rather generally marks out—ten or twenty square miles,
seven or eight neighboring villages (which in contemporary Bali is usually going
to mean anywhere from five to ten or eleven thousand people) from which the
core of any cockfight audience, indeed virtually all of it, will come. Most of the
fights are in fact organized and sponsored by small combines of petty rural merchants
under the general premise, very strongly held by them and indeed by all Balinese,
that cockfights are good for trade because "they get money out of the house, they
make it circulate." Stalls selling various sorts of things as well as assorted sheer-
chance gambling games (see below) are set up around the edge of the area so that

this even takes on the quality of a small fair. This connection of cockfighting with markets and market sellers is very old, as, among other things, their conjunction in inscriptions (Roelof Goris, *Prasasti Bali*, 2 vols. [Bandung: N. V. Masa Baru, 1954]) indicates. Trade has followed the cock for centuries in rural Bali and the sport has been one of the main agencies of the island's monetization.

19. The phrase is found in the Hildreth translation, International Library of Psychology, 1931, note to p. 106; see L. L. Fuller, *The Morality of Law* (New Haven: Yale University Press, 1964), pp. 6ff.

20. Of course, even in Bentham, utility is not normally confined as a concept to monetary losses and gains, and my argument here might be more carefully put in terms of a denial that for the Balinese, as for any people, utility (pleasure, happiness . . .) is merely identifiable with wealth. But such terminological problems are in any case secondary to the essential point: the cockfight is not roulette.

21. Max Weber, *The Sociology of Religion* (Boston: Beacon Press, 1963). There is nothing specifically Balinese, of course, about deepening significance with money, as Whyte's description of corner boys in a working-class district of Boston demonstrates: "Gambling plays an important role in the lives of Cornerville people. Whatever game the corner boys play, they nearly always bet on the outcome. When there is nothing at stake, the game is not considered a real contest. This does not mean that the financial element is all-important. I have frequently heard men say that the honor of winning was much more important than the money at stake. The corner boys consider playing for money the real test of skill and, unless a man performs well when money is at stake, he is not considered a good competitor." W. F. Whyte, *Street Corner Society*, 2d ed. (Chicago: University of Chicago Press, 1955), p. 140.

22. The extremes to which this madness is conceived on occasion to go—and the fact that it is considered madness—is demonstrated by the Balinese folktale *I Tuhung Kuning*. A gambler becomes so deranged by his passion that, leaving on a trip, he orders his pregnant wife to take care of the prospective newborn if it is a boy but to feed it as meat to his fighting cocks if it is a girl. The mother gives birth to a girl, but rather than giving the child to the cocks she gives them a large rat and conceals the girl with her own mother. When the husband returns the cocks, crowing a jingle, inform him of the deception and, furious, he sets out to kill the child. A goddess descends from heaven and takes the girl up to the skies with her. The cocks die from the food given them, the owner's sanity is restored, the goddess brings the girl back to the father who reunites him with his wife. The story is given as "Geel Komkommertje" in Jacoba Hooykaas-van Leeuwen Boomkamp, *Sprookjes en Verhalen van Bali* ('S-Gravenhage: Van Hoeve, 1956), pp. 19-25.

23. For a fuller description of Balinese rural social structure, see Clifford Geertz, "Form and Variation in Balinese Village Structure," *American Anthropologist*, 61 (1959), 94-108; "Tihingan, A Balinese Village," in R. M. Koentjaraningrat, *Villages in Indonesia* (Ithaca: Cornell University Press, 1967), pp. 210-243; and, though it is a bit off the norm as Balinese villages go, V. E. Korn, *De Dorpsrepubliek tnganan Pagringsingan* (Santpoort [Netherlands]: C. A. Mees, 1933).

24. Goffman, *Encounters*, p. 78.

25. B. R. Berelson, P. F. Lazersfeld, and W. N. McPhee, *Voting: A Study of Opinion Formation in a Presidential Campaign* (Chicago: University of Chicago Press, 1954).

26. As this is a formal paradigm, it is intended to display the logical, not the causal, structure of cockfighting. Just which of these considerations leads to which, in what order, and by what mechanisms, is another matter—one I have attempted to shed some light on in the general discussion.

27. In another of Hooykaas-van Leeuwen Boomkamp's folk tales ("De Gast," *Sprookies en Verhalen van Bali,* pp. 172-180), a low caste *Sudra,* a generous, pious, and carefree man who is also an accomplished cock fighter, loses, despite his accomplishment, fight after fight until he is not only out of money but down to his last cock. He does not despair, however—"I bet," he says, "upon the Unseen World."

His wife, a good and hard-working woman, knowing how much he enjoys cockfighting, gives him her last "rainy day" money to go and bet. But, filled with misgivings due to his run of ill luck, he leaves his own cock at home and bets merely on the side. He soon loses all but a coin or two and repairs to a food stand for a snack, where he meets a decrepit, odorous, and generally unappetizing old beggar leaning on a staff. The old man asks for food, and the hero spends his last coins to buy him some. The old man then asks to pass the night with the hero, which the hero gladly invites him to do. As there is no food in the house, however, the hero tells his wife to kill the last cock for dinner. When the old man discovers this fact, he tells the hero he has three cocks in his own mountain hut and says the hero may have one of them for fighting. He also asks for the hero's son to accompany him as a servant, and, after the son agrees, this is done.

The old man turns out to be Siva and, thus, to live in a great palace in the sky, though the hero does not know this. In time, the hero decides to visit his son and collect the promised cock. Lifted up into Siva's presence, he is given the choice of three cocks. The first crows: "I have beaten fifteen opponents." The second crows, "I have beaten twenty-five opponents." The third crows, "I have beaten the King." "That one, the third, is my choice," says the hero, and returns with it to earth.

When he arrives at the cockfight, he is asked for an entry fee and replies, "I have no money; I will pay after my cock has won." As he is known never to win, he is let in because the king, who is there fighting, dislikes him and hopes to enslave him when he loses and cannot pay off. In order to insure that this happens, the king matches his finest cock against the hero's. When the cocks are placed down, the hero's flees, and the crowd, led by the arrogant king, hoots in laughter. The hero's cock then flies at the king himself, killing him with a spur stab in the throat. The hero flees. His house is encircled by the king's men. The cock changes into a Garuda, the great mythic bird of Indic legend, and carries the hero and his wife to safety in the heavens.

When the people see this, they make the hero king and his wife queen and they return as such to earth. Later their son, released by Siva, also returns and the hero-king announces his intention to enter a hermitage. ("I will fight no more cockfights. I have bet on the Unseen and won.") He enters the hermitage and his son becomes king.

28. Addict gamblers are really less declassed (for their status is, as everyone else's, inherited) than merely impoverished and personally disgraced. The most prominent addict gambler in my cockfight circuit was actually a very high caste *satria* who sold off most of his considerable lands to support his habit. Though everyone privately regarded him as a fool and worse (some, more charitable, regarded him as sick), he was publicly treated with the elaborate deference and politeness due his rank. On the independence of personal reputation and public status in Bali, see Geertz, *Person, Time, and Conduct,* pp. 28-35.

29. For four, somewhat variant, treatments, see Susanne Langer, *Feeling and Form*

(New York: Scribners, 1953); Richard Wollheim, *Art and Its Objects* (New York: Harper and Row, 1968); Nelson Goodman, *Languages of Art* (Indianapolis: Bobbs-Merrill, 1968); Maurice Merleau-Ponty, "The Eye and the Mind," in his, *The Primacy of Perception* (Evanston: Northwestern University Press, 1964), pp. 159-190.

30. British cockfights (the sport was banned there in 1840) indeed seem to have lacked it, and to have generated, therefore, a quite different family of shapes. Most British fights were "mains," in which a preagreed number of cocks were aligned into two teams and fought serially. Score was kept and wagering took place both on the individual matches and on the main as a whole. There were also "battle Royales," both in England and on the Continent, in which a large number of cocks were let loose at once with the one left standing at the end the victor. And in Wales, the so-called "Welsh main" followed an elimination pattern, along the lines of a present-day tennis tournament, winners proceeding to the next round. As a genre, the cockfight has perhaps less compositional flexibility than, say, Latin comedy, but it is not entirely without any. On cockfighting more generally, see Arch Ruport, *The Art of Cockfighting* (New York: Devin-Adair, 1949); G. R. Scott, *History of Cockfighting* (1957); and Lawrence Fitz-Barnard, *Fighting Sports* (London: Odhams Press, 1921).

31. *Person, Time, and Conduct*, esp. pp. 42ff. I am, however, not the first person to have argued it: see G. Bateson, "Bali, the Value System of a Steady State," and "An Old Temple and a New Myth," in Belo, ed., *Traditional Balinese Culture*, pp. 384-402 and 111-136.

32. For the necessity of distinguishing among "description," "representation," "exemplification," and "expression" (and the irrelevance of "imitation" to all of them) as modes of symbolic reference, see Goodman, *Languages of Art*, pp. 6-10, 45-91, 225-241.

33. Northrop Frye, *The Educated Imagination* (Bloomington: University of Indiana Press, 1964), p. 99.

34. There are two other Balinese values and disvalues which, connected with punctuate temporality on the one hand and unbridled aggressiveness on the other, reinforce the sense that the cockfight is at once continuous with ordinary social life and a direct negation of it: what the Balinese call *ramé*, and what they call *paling*. *Ramé* means crowded, noisy, and active, and is a highly sought after social state: crowded markets, mass festivals, busy streets are all *ramé*, as, of course, is, in the extreme, a cockfight. *Ramé* is what happens in the "full" times (its opposite, *sepi*, "quiet," is what happens in the "empty" ones). *Paling* is social vertigo, the dizzy, disoriented, lost, turned around feeling one gets when one's place in the coordinates of social space is not clear, and it is a tremendously disfavored, immensely anxiety-producing state. Balinese regard the exact maintenance of spatial orientation ("not to know where north is" is to be crazy), balance, decorum, status relationships, and so forth, as fundamental to ordered life (*krama*) and *paling*, the sort of whirling confusion of position the scrambling cocks exemplify as its profoundest enemy and contradiction. On *ramé*, see Bateson and Mead, *Balinese Character*, pp. 3, 64; on *paling*, *ibid.*, p. 11, and Belo, ed., *Traditional Balinese Culture*, pp. 90ff.

35. The Stevens reference is to his "The Motive for Metaphor," ("You like it under the trees in autumn,/Because everything is half dead./The wind moves like a cripple among the leaves/And repeats words without meaning"); the Schoenberg reference is to the third of his *Five Orchestral Pieces* (Opus 16), and is borrowed

from H. H. Drager, "The Concept of 'Tonal Body,'" in Susanne Langer, ed., *Reflections on Art* (New York: Oxford University Press, 1961), p. 174. On Hogarth, and on this whole problem—there called "multiple matrix matching"—see E. H. Gombrich, "The Use of Art for the Study of Symbols," in James Hogg, ed., *Psychology and the Visual Arts* (Baltimore: Penguin Brooks, 1969), pp. 149-170. The more usual term for this sort of semantic alchemy is "metaphorical transfer," and good technical discussions of it can be found in M. Black, *Models and Metaphors* (Ithaca: Cornell University Press, 1962), pp. 25ff; Goodman, *Language as Art*, pp. 44ff; and W. Percy, "Metaphor as Mistake," *Sewanee Review*, 66 (1958), 78-99.

36. The tag is from the second book of the *Organon, On Interpretation*. For a discussion of it, and for the whole argument for freeing "the notion of text . . . from the notion of scripture or writing," and constructing, thus, a general hermeneutics, see Paul Ricoeur, *Freud and Philosophy* (New Haven: Yale University Press, 1970), pp. 20ff.

37. *Ibid.*

38. Lévi-Strauss's "structuralism" might seem an exception. But it is only an apparent one, for, rather than taking myths, totem rites, marriage rules, or whatever as texts to interpret, Lévi-Strauss takes them as ciphers to solve, which is very much not the same thing. He does not seek to understand symbolic forms in terms of how they function in concrete situations to organize perceptions (meanings, emotions, concepts, attitudes); he seeks to understand them entirely in terms of their internal structure, *indépendent de tout sujet, de tout objet, et de toute contexte*. For my own view of this approach—that is suggestive and indefensible—see Clifford Geertz, "The Cerebral Savage: On the Work of Lévi-Strauss," *Encounter*, 48 (1967), 25-32.

39. Frye, *The Educated Imagination*, pp. 63-64.

40. The use of the, to Europeans, "natural" visual idiom for perception—"see," "watches," and so forth—is more than usually misleading here, for the fact that, as mentioned earlier, Balinese follow the progress of the fight as much (perhaps, as fighting cocks are actually rather hard to see except as blurs of motion, more) with their bodies as with their eyes, moving their limbs, heads, and trunks in gestural mimicry of the cocks' maneuvers, means that much of the individual's experience of the fight is kinesthetic rather than visual. If ever there was an example of Kenneth Burke's definition of a symbolic act as "the dancing of an attitude" (*The Philosophy of Literary Form*, rev. ed. [New York: Vintage Books, 1957], p. 9) the cockfight is it. On the enormous role of kinesthetic perception in Balinese life, Bateson and Mean, *Balinese Character*, pp. 84-88; on the active nature of aesthetic perception in general, Goodman, *Language of Art*, pp. 241-244.

41. All this coupling of the occidental great with the oriental lowly will doubtless disturb certain sorts of aestheticians as the earlier efforts of anthropologists to speak of Christianity and totemism in the same breath disturbed certain sorts of theologians. But as ontological questions are (or should be) bracketed in the sociology of religion, judgmental ones are (or should be) bracketed in the sociology of art. In any case, the attempt to deprovincialize the concept of art is but part of the general anthropological conspiracy to deprovincialize all important social concepts—marriage, religion, law, rationality—and though this is a threat to aesthetic theories which regard certain works of art as beyond the reach of sociological analysis, it is no threat to the conviction, for which Robert Graves claims to have been reprimanded at his Cambridge tripos, that some poems are better than others.

42. For the consecration ceremony, see V. E. Korn, "The Consecration of the Priest," in Swellengrebel, ed., *Bali,* pp. 131-154; for (somewhat exaggerated) village communion, Roelof Goris, "The Religious Character of the Balinese Village," *ibid.,* pp. 79-100.

43. That what the cockfight has to say about Bali is not altogether without perception and the disquiet it expresses about the general pattern of Balinese life is not wholly without reason is attested by the fact that in two weeks of December 1965, during the upheavals following the unsuccessful coup in Djakarta, between forty and eighty thousand Balinese (in a population of about two million) were killed, largely by one another—the worst outburst in the country. (John Hughes, *Indonesian Upheaval* [New York: McKay, 1967], pp. 173-183. Hughes's figures are, of course, rather casual estimates, but they are not the most extreme.) This is not to say, of course, that the killings were caused by the cockfight, could have been predicted on the basis of it, or were some sort of enlarged version of it with real people in the place of the cocks—all of which is nonsense. It is merely to say that if one looks at Bali not just through the medium of its dances, its shadowplays, its sculpture, and its girls, but—as the Balinese themselves do—also through the medium of its cockfight, the fact that the massacre occurred seems, if no less appalling, less like a contradiction to the laws of nature. As more than one real Gloucester has discovered, sometimes people actually get life precisely as they most deeply do not want it.

JAMES W. FERNANDEZ

Persuasions and Performances: Of the Beast in Every Body . . . And the Metaphors of Everyman

> He who only cricket knows,
> knows not cricket.
> —C. L. R. James, *Beyond a Boundary*

> Anybody who learns to become a crow can see
> it . . . it is possible to become a lion or
> a bear but that is rather dangerous . . . it
> takes too much energy to become one.
> —Don Juan in Castaneda, *The Teachings of Don Juan*

A Cattle Complex

I AM situated as I write this between cows and rodents. At night the rodents rustle and gnaw in the attic while the cows and calves periodically shift their weight, stomp, and sigh heavily in the stable below. During the day the cattle are driven out and up to the pastures and the rats descend to their nests in the stable. The house is left to us and occasionally to a donkey who brays at being left in the stable during the day.

These animals have become very much a part of our world, although I cannot pretend they mean as much to me as to the Asturian mountain countrymen with whom we are living. We have been in these green mountains a bare two months and little yet can be said with confidence. Asturias is another part of Spain, green and lush, covered most often with celtic mists and clouds off the Cantabrian sea. It has scarcely a month of sunny weather a year. These mists evaporate on the high passes and divides—*los puertos*—that open out upon the Castillian plateau, brown and sere already with its summer burnt look under the Sahara sun.

The cattle in the summer are driven up to those *puertos* and hence they and those that go and live with them up in the *caserias* have more of the benefit of the sun. Men turn brown up in the *puertos* but the immaculate tan cow of Asturias, the *casina*, grazing back and forth between *sol* and *sombra*, retains her placid and reflective character. There is nothing in

39

these cows of the *vaca brava*—the brave black bulls of Salamanca or Andalucia. In fact one sees very few bulls at all. Heifers are carefully tended and brought to maturity for milk and progeny but *novillos* are butchered early for veal. Artificial insemination has been accepted everywhere.

Cows and calves have an enormous weight in village life. They are a constant topic of conversation. When one is shown the family pictures, photos of cows and calves are as likely to tumble out amidst the shuffle. And a family given a picture taken five years earlier of the father and baby posing before a cow team pulling a hay cart, spent most of an excited half hour remembering those cows with nostalagia. I don't know all there is to walking cows from the stable through the streets and up to the pastures. But there is a satisfaction in it for men and women that makes them highly resistant to government efforts to consolidate their scattered meadows—their stubborn *minifundia*. For if they were consolidated one would no longer walk one's cows about one's wide world. In part, of course, one is parading one's fortune. A good milk cow is worth several month's wages and a herd of fifteen is a sizable nest egg—to mix our metaphors.

The love of calves equals the *cariño* for young children. Both loves are very great and volubly expressed, and in the closest association. The urban middle class deplores the villagers' attitude toward education. "They raise them like calves that they should be strong and fecund, capable of climbing to the *puertos* in the summer and with enough fat to survive the winter." As for boys beyond five they are more likely to be treated as *quajes, rapaces*—fractious, superfluous elements in the society who serve principally to get into trouble, break things, soil clothes, interrupt their sisters who are working hard at various tasks. Girls grow up usefully to produce in their time more of the milk of human kindness and the babies upon which it can be lavished. This cattle complex has something to do with the quite central place of women in this society, and perhaps even with the Cult of the Virgin.

Asturian mountain character, formed by mists and the encirclement of the sierra and the following-after of cows, is unhurried, contemplative. It is austere even dour when compared with the ebullience of the Andaluz or the briskness of the Castilian. But if one is tempted to say that it is cowed by this round of life and the celtic twilight in which it develops, then one forgets that this is the only part of Spain never fully under Roman control, never conquered by the Moors—a rebellious outpost of Carlism in the last century and, in this century—in the militant collectivity of its miners—a turbulent challenge to many succeeding regimes including the present one.

One remembers that there are other animals men study to situate themselves. There are the bears in the forests whose demise in hand-to-hand conflict with the many folk heroes is celebrated in tale after tale. Of the donkey there is not much to be said. Other parts of Spain seem to be in greater communion with its qualities as was Jimenez with Platero. Donkeys carry no names here—only wood, hay, manure, and blows. But of course, there are the rats whose furtive life is contrary to right nature. They come up at night and go down in the day and they are never to be seen. Women say to children "If you don't eat your food or keep yourself clean we will put you into the attic tonight and the rats will eat you," as they eat anything that is carelessly left around and not well formed, well disciplined, or well seen. And when one is very hungry one says "the rats are running around in the drawer," in chagrin that the stomach should have gotten so empty and oneself so careless as to be taken over by that furtive animal nature. It is not well formed or well seen to admit to hunger or to accept food, like rats, in any house other than one's own.

A cow in short is everything a rat is not and men are wise to draw the appropriate lessons that each nature has to teach. Men can be and are, through the diverse powers of culture, many things. Their choices are manifold. If they can look around and find some lesson in cows and calves, bears and rats, their choices are made easier.

The Study of Metaphor

This is as far as I can presently take the reader into the preoccupation with animals in the Asturian mountains—a paleolithic preoccupation, after all, throughout Franco-Cantabrian country. It seems apparent to me that the intimate contact these villagers have with these animals has an impact upon them. In a sense, those we domesticate have domesticated us and those we have not domesticated are still useful in measuring the achievement or excesses of our domestication. If life becomes too much a following about of cows, men may be excused for turning a bit bearish.

What all this points to, it seems to me, is the importance of the analysis of metaphors in anthropological inquiry. In fact, the analysis of metaphor seems to me to be the very nature of that inquiry. One always feels a bit sheepish of course about bringing the metaphor concept into the social sciences and perhaps this is because one always feels there is something soft and wooly about it. Yet one recognizes that the finest anthropological field studies[1] have been highly sensitive to figures of speech of all kinds and surely to metaphor. As one of our epigraphs reminds us, the anthropological literature on religion and folklore is full of those shape shiftings and possessions which constitute in most dramatic form the assumption of a metaphoric identity. And even behaviorists recognize that metaphor is one of the few devices we have for leaping beyond the essential privacy of the experiential process.[2]

Indeed, metaphors jump out at us from every side in human behavior. As S. E. Asch has said, if we but reflect on it we find like Moliere's character "we have been speaking metaphor all our lives!"[3] In November of 1970 the American press gave front page coverage to the director of the

Federal Bureau of Investigation. He called the former Attorney General a jellyfish. The Attorney General had criticized the director for imposing upon the bureau a preoccupation with the director's own image and for giving the bureau an ideological character.

Perhaps this was mere petulance. If so, the somber work of Herman Kahn may be more telling. In a book entitled *On Escalation: Metaphors and Scenarios* (1965), Kahn takes two metaphors as models of international relations; that of the strike, on the one hand, in which both parties though antagonistic recognize mutual need, and that of the teenage game of chicken, on the other, in which both parties are concerned to establish their manly (or at least nonchicken) identity. In part Kahn takes these metaphors as analytic models to aid his understanding, but at the same time these metaphors can be adopted by actors. They can lead to performance and create a scenario. I will argue here that the metaphoric assertions men make about themselves or about others influence their behavior. Such assertions make manageable objects of the self or of others and facilitate performance. In respect to behavior such assertions—you are a chicken, I am not a chicken, you are a hawk or a dove or a rat or a donkey—provide images in relation to which the organization of behavior can take place. We can call them organizing or performative metaphors. I am going to define the uses of several kinds of metaphor, persuasive or colocative metaphor in the first place, and performative or organizing metaphor in the second. I am then going to ask how these metaphors operate in respect to culture conceived of as a "quality space."

Resistance to the study of metaphor arises for several reasons. One reason is that structural analysis in linguistics has made so important an impact on anthropological analysis. The burden of this influence rests upon the study of the discriminations and contrasts by means of which intellectual structures (paradigms and taxonomies) are built up. But a good reason for studying metaphoric assertion is that it is a way of avoiding building up precise intellectual structures. It is so congenial a thought style to many of the third world peoples anthropologists have studied because it has the profundity of a concrete immediacy. Many of these people incline to rhetorical devices of representation—iconic and enactive rather than symbolic forms of representation.[4] They incline toward assessment by analogy. Our subtle analyses of the discriminations they make within various domains of their experience is matched by their subtlety in linking these domains in unexpected and creative ways.

If we have much to learn from painstaking dissections of our informants' kinship terminology, diseases, or firewood lexicon, we can also learn from their powers of extension and synthesis. More is involved in the games people play than the rules and boundaries by which they play them. Our epigraphs from the Trinidadian, James, and the Yaqui, Juan, remind us of that. We have only to consider the popularity of proverbs and riddles in many parts of the world—a genre which rests in large measure upon leaping to metaphoric similarities between two distinct domains of experience.

Another reason for resistance to the study of metaphor arises from the fact that metaphor has so much to do with feelings. Such obscure matters have quite naturally provoked the distrust of social scientists. J. Piaget in his essay on structuralism[5] strongly supports C. Lévi-Strauss's "penetrating critique of explanations in terms of affectivity," and lauds his axiom[6] that that which is refractory to explanation cannot ipso facto serve as explanation.

One may well wish to create explanations by preventing what is refractory from intruding, but to deny its existence and importance is another matter. Emotions in human affairs may easily, and regrettably, outweigh the influence of logical structures. And those who want to write their ethnologies where they conceive the action to be, in the midst of affectivity and the conditioning of the emotions, are entitled to our attention. It is too easy to say that they are soft. In any case a false dichotomy can too easily prevail. Might not there be a structure to sentiment?

In respect to affectivity Robert P. Armstrong[7] has recently given us a revelatory anthropological essay which seeks to dwell in the very center of what he calls "the affecting presence." He uses metaphor as a central term of analysis. His discussion of metaphor is essentially contemplative, as one would expect in an essay written from the aesthetic point of view. That is to say, Armstrong assumes the enduring status of the objects and events he studies as expressions of existing (universal or cultural) feeling states. But the student of behavior wants to know what metaphors do, where they come from, and how they emerge. How do they work in human affairs? To use Armstrong's own vocabulary: in the "affecting transaction" what emotions are transferred and how is this done? Perhaps metaphors are not alone arresting repositories of feelings. Perhaps they can be strategies taken in respect to feelings.

Metaphoric Strategies

Though I cannot do justice to all these questions I should like to approach them by defining metaphor simply as "a strategic predication upon an inchoate pronoun (an I, a you, a we, a they) which makes a movement and leads to performance." More can be said about metaphor than that, but it should carry us a little distance. There is nothing new in regarding a metaphor as a strategy. The notion is present throughout the work of Kenneth Burke[8] and is expressed in his well-known definition of a proverb as a "strategy for dealing with a situation."[9] Since a proverb, as we have said, rests upon a metaphoric sense of similarity between two domains of experience, Burke's definition applies equally to metaphor. A proverb in its way is, like the metaphors I will discuss, a predication upon an inchoate situation. It says that something much more concrete and graspable—a rolling stone, a bird in the hand—is equivalent to the essential elements in another situation we have difficulty in grasping.

The strategic element in metaphor glares at us from this contretemps we have reviewed between the Attorney General and the director of the FBI. Obviously the director intended a put-down. It became the Attorney General's lot to put up or shut up. Already the reader will see that the language we both speak shows us a continuum: a continuum of ups and downs. As it happened, the Attorney General responded in balanced prose about the ideological conformity imposed upon the FBI and the director's preoccupation with his self-image. It is difficult to remember what he said, though the director's salty metaphor still sticks.

The Attorney General had various options. He could put up by staying in the same metaphoric domain. He might have responded, in turn, that the director was a walrus, or more sharply a shark, or a Portuguese man-of-war, or an octopus—"a thousand tentacled octopus releasing the ink of ideological obfuscation over the land." Or the Attorney General might have shifted to another domain, the familiar gastrointestinal one. Here the opportunities are rich. Perhaps the director thought of himself as a man of heart or real guts. The Attorney General could put him down by referring to him as an old flatus. That would have deflated him!

Of course people do not simply jump into a strategic posture willy-nilly. They do occupy positions, by force of their social condition and the fate of physiology, both in their own estimation and the estimation of others. Everyone knows where the director stands and has stood foursquare for fifty years. If we had not followed his pronouncements over that time as he has admirably constructed his agency brick by brick we might gather it from his concentrated boxer's gaze—his bulldog jaw. As for the Attorney General, who built nothing but occupied an existing edifice of office with compassion and intelligence, we see something of his position in his long bloodhound's face, his aristocratic nose, his troubled eyes. These are pre-possessing men and to some extent are prepositioned—prepostured as are we all. We see that the bulldog who knows throughout his fiber the mass and power of his opponent must be impatient with the bloodhound who does not really know his opponent except as traces in the air to be followed with uncertainty amidst a multitude of other stimuli. The bloodhound lives in a much more complicated world than the bulldog, but the bulldog has reason to believe that his is the more real.

We will assume that metaphoric strategies involve the placing of self and other pronouns on continua. The salient continuum here chosen by the director to confirm his position is the hard-soft one which is omnipresent in American life, as far as men are concerned. The first strategy of anyone who puts forth a metaphor in predication about a pronoun is to pick a domain of equivalence whose members have some apt shock value when applied to a pronoun and give perspective by incongruity. Almost any domain will do if people know enough about it and the strategist is ingenious.

The strategy is to make it appear that the incumbent occupies a desirable or undesirable place in the continuum of whatever domain has been chosen. As Aristotle says, "To adorn, borrow metaphor from things superior, to disparage, borrow from things inferior." And while metaphors may be put forth in an honest attempt to assess the position the pronoun actually occupies as a consequence of its physical and social condition, we are generally inspired to metaphor for purposes of adornment or disparagement. If a pronoun inspires predication we generally want to move it about on the continuum. We want to put down or put up.

The second strategy belongs to the subject upon whom a metaphor has been predicated. If he does not accept the way he has been moved, he may choose to reorient the continuum. Reorientation is obtained first by finding members of the domain relatively less desirable and more opprobrious than the metaphor with which you are saddled: for jellyfish return octopus. Better a jellyfish than an octopus if one must dwell in the sea. For the one floats blithely upon its surface and the other is sinister and sunk in its tangled depths. We see here, incidentally, a complexity in metaphor which we should not deny though we will for the main part ignore it. A number of continua may be involved in any metaphoric predication. In the above example we have hard and soft, light and dark, above and below, grasping and relaxing. The continua may be so melded as to be indistinguishable, or they may be in an interesting state of tension.

Reorientation is obtained secondly by suggesting an alternative metaphor better placed on the continuum or continua. If a hawk calls you a dove, you suggest rather owl. Reorientation is obtained thirdly not by finding even more undesirable members of the domain or by offering an alternative metaphor but by giving a positive interpretation to what is ostensibly undesirable. If you are made out to be a bleeding heart on the corporeal continuum you return numbskull. For there is, after all, nothing intrinsically good about the end of any continuum. No culture is so unambiguous about its choices that a clever man cannot turn a continuum to his advantage. In a culture that lauds whiteness there is yet an attraction and an energy to blackness. In a competitive culture the last shall yet be first.

The final strategy in this enterprise of metaphoric placement is to change the venue. One simply chooses to pass beyond a boundary and as a consequence, it is another ball game. If one is disadvantaged in the domain of sea creatures, one shifts to the domain of corporeality and a desirable postition in the gastrointestinal continuum.

The Quality of Cultural Space

In the intellectual sense the movement accomplished by these metaphors is from the inchoate in the pronomial subject to the concrete in the predicate. These are basic if not kernel predications in social life which enable us to escape the privacy of experience. For what is more inchoate and in need of a concrete predication than a pronoun! Personal experience and social life cries out to us, to me, to you, to predicate some identity upon "others" and "selves." We need to become objects to ourselves, and others need to become objects to us as well. At the earliest moment our infants receive metaphoric attributions: they become sweet peas, tigers, little bears, kittens, little fish. How often those earliest objects are animals. And how inclined we are to comb the world for cunning animals to surround our children with. Is it that without them we feel helpless to give definition to the infantile inchoate? For millennia of course we have been in the most intimate contact with animals who have provided us with just such reference points in our quest for identity. But intellectual concretization is not the movement we are really interested in.

Let us say of George that he is a lobster. Men, faced with the inchoate pronoun, always have hard alternatives. Most reasonably we can appeal for clarification to the customary domains to which the subject belongs and offer a predication by superordination or subordination within that domain. Of George we say: he is a teller, he is a banker, he is a businessman, he is a Harvard alumnus, he is a father, he is an adult, he is a homo sapien, he is anthropoid, he is a vertebrate, and so on. Of course men belong to a number of domains and hence in qualifying the inchoate pronoun we must choose one domain or another: the domain of business activity, of educational activity, of domestic activity, of phylogenetic classification. We can combine domains but that always makes for problems—if not for us, surely for George. He is an ivy league anthropoid, or a businesslike father.

But to say of George that he is a lobster is to learn something very different about him. For it is to follow a different kind of logic in defining George than the logic of superordination or subordination within customary domains. George is not really an anthropoid. He really has, logically, more backbone than that. But in a deeper sense perhaps he does not. Perhaps he is a scuttling, snappish, popeyed, soft-centered, rigidly defensive creature. It is true that the mind by abstractions can integrate all its experiences. Thus, at a very high level of abstraction both George and lobster are members of the same domain. They are both metazoa. But for all practical purposes we see how metaphor accomplishes an unaccustomed linking of domains.

The shift in feeling tone—of adornment and disparagement—is also most always present and may be the dominant impulse to metaphor. Every metaphor has its mood which has motivated its employment and is perhaps a major part of the satisfaction of having employed it. Metaphor is, like synesthesia, the translation of experience from one domain into another by virtue of a common factor which can be generalized between the experiences in the two domains. These generalizable factors can be of a variety, but there are two main kinds: structural and textual.[10] In the case of structural metaphor the translation between realms is based on some isomorphism of structure or similarity of relationship of parts. By textual metaphor we mean an assimilation made on the basis of similarity in feeling tone. Thus in synesthesia when we speak of music being hot we are moving from one domain of experience, that of sound, to another, that of temperature. The Law of Parallel Alignment prevails. That is, in the domain of sound the rapid beat of jazz music has a parallel intensity on the scale of fast to slow to that on the temperature scale of hot to cold. Somehow that which is hot feels like that which is rapid of rhythm.

The metaphors in which we are interested make a movement. They take their subjects and move them along a dimension or a set of dimensions. They are not satisfied with parallel alignment, if indeed that were possible, given the inchoate nature of the pronomial subject. The Attorney General is really not as soft as a jellyfish, but the strategist hopes that saying it will move him and make it so in the eyes of others. On the continuum of purposiveness in the domain of sea creatures, the Attorney General is, perhaps, *really* a porpoise. The strategy is to make him out a jellyfish.

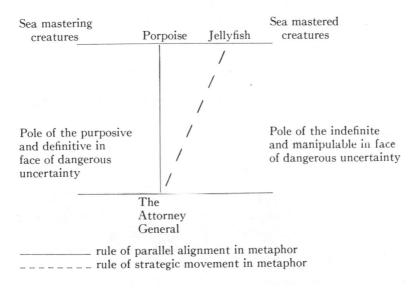

Behind this discussion, as the reader will have perceived, lies a topographic model of society and culture. I am inordinately attracted to it, but it may be useful. Culture from this view is a quality space of "n" dimensions or continua, and society is a movement about of pronouns within this space. Of course, pronouns move about by many means of locomotion, but the metaphoric assertion of identity by the linking of domains is one important way.

Since it is so difficult to think of a space as defined by "n" dimensions, we may have a Euclidean space by taking, for illustrative purposes, Charles E. Osgood's semantic space.[11] This space is defined by the three dimensions of goodness, potency, and activity. The meaning that Osgood's method explores and plots in semantic space is connotation—the feelings held about various concepts. Similarly, the topographic model proposed here would suggest that in cultural life pronouns come to possess appropriate or inappropriate feelings of potency, activity, and goodness attached to them. Language has devices of representation at its disposal, mainly metaphor, by which pronouns can be moved about—into better or worse position—in quality space. Social life from the perspective of this model is the set of those transactions by which pronouns, the foci of identity, change their feeling tone—the sense of potency, activity, and goodness attached to them.

Lest our discussion evolve into an "idee fixe" we had best remind ourselves that metaphors can serve a variety of functions: informative, expressive, declarative, directive, and so forth. I do not pretend that what I want to say about metaphor here encompasses all these uses. The point is that there is an important social use of metaphor involving the occupancy of various continua which in sum constitute a cultural quality space. Persuasive metaphors situate us and others with whom we interact in that space.

Some Fang Metaphors of Debate and Supplication

If we have spent some time here among cattle and rodents and with the implications of an acrimonious exchange that arose between two government officials, it is only because what that husbandry and that politics teaches us is an everyday lesson and a commonplace of the idiom of interaction in many cultures known to anthropologists. I learned a good deal about the skillful use of metaphor some years ago sitting day in and day out in the "palabra house" of the Fang people of western equatorial Africa. The Fang are a neo-Bantu culture practicing slash and burn agriculture in the equatorial forest. They rewarded me for paying such unrelenting attention to things that had no obvious personal implications with the sobriquet "the dispeptic one" (*nkwan minsili*)—that is, he who is sick by reason of the many questions he has on his stomach. In some quarters I was at first known as *nsinga*, the cat, probably because I was obliged to insinuate myself a bit too much. In any case having laid out our definitions and our model, I would like to discuss some metaphors characteristic of the Fang and say something about the continua upon which these metaphors operate.

The Fang institution of the palabra or council house (*aba*) is the most salient in the lives of men. Activity in the *aba* is almost constant, whether it be the manufacture of various crafts, folkloric performances of an evening, or the daily discussions, debates, and moots involving marriage, divorce, brideprice, fraternal rights and debts, territorial claims, and inheritance. The Fang are a very open, unstructured, and egalitarian society and men are not appointed nor do they gain permanent positions as judges *(nkik mesang)* in village moots and litigation. But men are selected to hear and make judgments in the conflicts of others by virtue of a reputation they have achieved. And though selections are made on an ad hoc basis according to the affair at hand, the same set of men tend to appear as judges in repeated instances.

In general these men are called upon because they have a reputation, *ewôga,* that is a kind of authority granted to them because they are listened to (*wôk*, to listen, understand) and can make themselves understood. To say that they have this authority because they are eloquent, or persuasive, or intelligent, or wise is to deal in abstract descriptions which, though used by the Fang themselves, do not capture the metaphoric predications upon these people on the basis of which their reputation is established. One does not start out in any convincing way saying of a man he is wise, or eloquent. One starts by saying that he breaks palabra (*a buk adzô*) or he slices them (*a kik adzô*). For if you are so clumsy, however powerful, as to break apart a palabra you leave jagged ends which are hard to fit back together again. You do not resolve it; you simply put it off to another day when it shall surge forth again in perhaps more festered condition. But if you cut or slice it, the two parts may be easily put back together again.

In an egalitarian society where there is no effective hierarchy to enforce judgments, the slicing of a palabra demands careful ambiguity of statement. Aphorisms and proverbial statements, various kinds of metaphor in short, are very suitable for such purposes for they provide ways of commenting upon the essentials of experience in one domain by extending these essentials to analogous experiences in another domain. The essential wisdom of the comment may be preserved in the extension while a painful and indeed unenforceable precision is obscured.

But the point I wish to make is that the metaphoric description of juridic techniques—he is a slicer or he is a breaker of palabras—refers the listener to the domain of what we may call forest work. In Western culture we can easily understand the difference between breaking and cutting. But the distinction is much more loaded with meaning in Fang culture, where everyman, if he was to provide successfully for himself and his family, had to work the forest skillfully. He had to be a craftsman carefully cutting and not breaking raffia palm wands, lianes and other fibers, and all the various woods of the forest. Out of the equatorial forest Fang men make their shelters, their essential tools, their comforts, and their admirable carvings. For a people heavily involved in forest exploitation and forest crafts, the linking of this realm to techniques of argument and judgment is particularly convincing. Men cannot well survive nor be esteemed if they break rather than carefully cut in either arena.

Nkikmesang a kui elik—"The judge has arrived at the *elik*," the site of the former village deep in the forest. The implication is that the judge has found the old clearing in the forest where the resentments which have given rise to the present conflict lie. By casting light on these resentments he has clarified them, if not cleared them up. He has made his way skillfully through the forest (the affair). He has also—this is implied in returning to the *elik*—encouraged in the parties in conflict the sentiment of their common origins. One basic use of the variety of metaphor we have under view here is to encourage social sentiments—the primordial sentiments of a community and a common belonging or, on the other hand, of a lack of community and an exclusion. The apt judge is he whose verbal powers are able to encourage in the disputants a sentiment of common belonging.

Let me mention a final metaphor in this domain—there are so many— which are predicated upon participants. Not only is the palabra an obstruction which must be carefully sliced, it is also, as we have seen, a forest that one must wend one's way through. The clumsy disputant or judge chops down the forest, but that only leads to a conflagration. The able judge leads the parties in his judgment carefully through the forest to the discovery of the *elik*. And the able litigant as well should be capable of wending his way through the forest. In the process of argument a litigant (*nteamadzô*) may be complimented or may compliment himself on being an *nyamoro nsôm adzô*, "a mature man and a hunter in the affair." He is proceeding carefully and skillfully through the "forest." He breaks no twigs. By his verbal powers he reaches the "game" and makes it his own. Should he wish to disparage his opponent, he may refer to him as *nyamoro ôzem*—"a man mature as the bearded monkey" (*cercopithecus talapoin*). With his beard he may appear as a full man but he is a chatterer not a debater. He does not dominate the "forest" by making his way skillfully through it, but simply plays around within it failing, as we would say, to know the forest for the trees. Moreover, rather than the hunter he is the hunted—in short, the dominated in the palabra situation. Here is another continuum, hunter-hunted or more abstractly dominating-dominated.

There are then a variety of continua upon which these palabra metaphors operate: slicing-breaking (chopping), skillful hunting-clumsy hunting (pathfinding), hunting-being hunted. By examination of this variety of continua we may come to the conclusion that we are dealing with one factor only, competence-incompetence. But such an abstraction does not capture a rich domain of Fang experience—the domain of forest and woods working—to which the events of the palabra house are referred by metaphoric extension. Because of the complexity of the palabra situation, it seems, it is difficult to see what makes a good litigant or judge. Metaphor extends that inchoate experience to more concrete domains of Fang experience where comparisons in performance are more easily recognized.

Everyone knows the difference between a good and a bad hunter. The evidence comes home in his bag. In the adversarial situation of the palabra house the strategy is to situate oneself advantageously and one's opponent undesirably in respect to the continua which characterize the relevant domains of metaphoric reference. The sum of the relevant domains and the set of respective continua constitute the quality space of Fang litigation. In that quality space, reputation is not first a matter of wisdom or eloquence. It is a matter of cutting or slicing, pathfinding, hunting. By such metaphoric predications do the Fang come to know their judges.

The adversary nature of life in the palabra house may perhaps give a special quality to the use of metaphor that we find there. Let us submit this proposition—that metaphors operate in respect to quality space—in another situation. Let us examine the metaphors put forth in supplications to divine powers (*evangiles*) in a Fang syncretist cult called Bwiti.[12] This cult has been active among the Fang since the First World War. Originally it was a reworking of various western equatorial ancestor cults, but recently it has been incorporating many Christian elements. One might say, of course, that the members of Bwiti do exist in an adversary relationship with the condition of the African in the colonial world. And they are using metaphor to situate themselves more desirably in respect to that condition.

The packing of meaning is typical of Bwiti sermons, but it happens that the particular branch of this cult from which the *evangiles* are taken (*Asumege Ening*—New Life) puts exceptional value on recondite speech and regards it as a sign of power in the cult leader. This packing of imagery and the illusive and often determinedly arcane manner in which sermons are put forth has led me elsewhere to discuss them as "unbelievably subtle words." As subtle as they may be, we may note a resonance with those metaphors of the palabra house which extend to the domain of forest work. The following text is taken from the *Evangile Fete Kumba,* the September 1959 Bwiti festival held before planting and preparation of the earth. It was given by the cult leader at Kougouleu chapel (Kango District, Gabon Republic), Ekang Engono, called *Akikos Zambi Avanga.*

Eboka tells us that the afterbirth of the spirit is the blood. Women must close the backdoor of the cookhouse before the setting of the sun. The member of Bwiti is buried in a white robe with ashes on his face for it is by means of fire that the Fang can chop down the trees to heaven. The spirit flees the body because of the noise of the body but when the body sleeps the spirit wanders fitfully. The Fang have come to divine that vibrating string on which music is made between heaven and earth—between God above and God below. That string is played sweetly. God below is the bath of the soul, the seat of the soul. For a child in being born falls to earth and must be cleaned of dirt that he may arise to the wind which is God above. Man can be tied as a package with that string— as his afterbirth is tied and buried in the earth—as the umbilical cord is tied and buried in the earth—as leftover food is tied in a leaf package to be eaten

later. We are all of us leaf packages of leftover food—the food of God above—
we should not rot in that package for our brothers to eat us in witchcraft—we
should open up that package so that God above may eat us—we should untie
that string that leads us from God below to God above.[13]

Let us begin with the Bwiti name of the leader of the cult—*Akikos Zambi
Avanga*. He is the "parrot's egg—god who creates." We also note the general name for the cult members—*Banzie* (angels, or those who fly). Both
of these are metaphors of height, of loftiness, of heavenly connotation.
The African gray parrot nests in the tallest trees of the equatorial forest
and frequently in the *Adzap* (*minusops djave*), the sacred tree of the
Banzie. The parrot has the power to speak. His red tail feathers have always been important in Fang ritual and folklore and are highly significant
in Bwiti ritual which is organized around something they call the red
"path of life and death" *(zen abiale ye awu)*. The parrot is surely a liminal
creature and difficult to categorize. But what I would emphasize is his
occupancy of the high realms of the forest, his capacity to communicate,
his characteristically purposeful, rapid, and unambiguous flight.

Now these metaphors are both very apt—that is, they make a proper
movement—in respect to the situation of the Fang. For the Fang have in
recent decades found themselves badly situated. As they would put it, they
are too much of the ground—of things of dirt and earth and thickets.
Figuratively, they find themselves meandering through dense undergrowth.
Images of the ground and undergrowth abound in Bwiti *evangiles*. Clay
and swamps and fens appear and men lost in the leaves of the underbrush
who wander unable to see each other, let alone their tutelary supernat-
urals. There are powers of the below of course. These were the powers
cultivated by the old religion—the ancestor cult and the witchcraft societies
—powers of the dead, powers of the forest, secret powers of the living.
Many of the Fang have come to adopt the generic term *Zame Asi*, God of
the below, for these powers and their rituals. In Bwiti, Fang recognize
the inescapable attraction of the evangelical God of the above, and in
Bwiti they seek to establish by syncretism a communication between these
two gods—a communication that is represented in this *evangile* by the
vibrating cord of the one string harp, *béng*, seen as binding God below
and God above together.

The metaphors of Bwiti *evangiles*—this should not surprise us—move
the membership toward higher things—toward realms of the above. They
do this by treating the members as *Banzie*—spirits of the wind. They do
this by giving the leader his name—"the egg of the parrot"—the essence
of the potential of superior knowledge. For the leader, like the parrot
with his arresting cry and unambiguous flight, calls out to men below strug-
gling and wandering in the suffocating thickets of the forest and gives
them direction upwards.

Because this *evangile* does in fact give us a continuum of gods below and above joined by a vibrating cord, it supports my point that metaphors operate upon continua—in this case belowness and aboveness—moving people and things aptly about on the continua. I think this understanding is essential if we are to see how the *evangile* works, though admittedly the matter is not so simple. Rare is the communication between men and surely rare is the *evangile* that moves us only in one direction on one continuum. In the *evangile* given, something is surely said for belowness. Men are born to it. It gives them stability. They can stand on it though it dirties their feet and obscures their vision and, in the end, they stand on belowness, really, the better to launch themselves to aboveness. The Bwitiest does not abandon *Zame Asi* in moving upwards. It is a rich source of creative tension in this cult to try to keep *Zame* below in mind as they search for the above. It is the tension between *Zame* above and *Zame* below that keep the cord vibrating.

To reduce any of these *evangiles* to movement on a continuum or a set of continua violates a deep richness they possess, a richness contained in some of their most apt metaphors. Consider the metaphor of man as a leaf package of leftover food tied by a string that should be connecting the below and the above. How aptly that image captures the notion of forest-bound man closed in by leaves. How aptly it captures the feeling of bodily decay, so widespread a feeling in the colonial period. How aptly it summarizes the anxiety Fang felt about the increase in witchcraft and the consumption of brother by brother. "Men are as food to each other." At the same time there is a positive element in the image, for these leaf packets of leftover food are a great delight and solace to hunters and gatherers in the deep forest at noontime.

Who can deny that there are many subtle things to be said about the work of metaphor and symbol? Strategies may so often end in poetry, perhaps the ultimate strategy, where instead of being moved anywhere we are accommodated in many subtle ways to our condition in all its contrarieties and complexities.

At the same time we should avoid making a mystery of these subtleties—making a seance out of science—if we can find a relatively reduced number of dimensions upon which we can follow essentials of movement in metaphoric predication. Despite all the things that can and must be said about the package metaphor, its object in the end is to convince the *Banzie* to disentangle themselves and become properly attached to the above.

The Performance of Metaphors

The metaphors which have interested us to this point have been mainly rhetorical. They have been put forth for reason of persuading feelings in certain directions. Still there are always the implications for action in them. The metaphoric predication can be self-fulfilling. The king can be told so often that he is a lion that he comes to believe it. He roars at his subjects and stealthily stalks those he thinks are enemies to his interest. He finally springs upon them in fell and summary justice. In the privacy of our experience we are usually not sure who we really are. A metaphor thrust upon us often enough as a model can become compelling.

Such persistence in the application of metaphors does not often occur, so that persuasion does not usually pass over into performance. But at a deeper level of fantasy men may hold to predications which cause them irresistably to organize their world, insofar as they can, so as to facilitate or make inevitable certain scenarios. It has been frequently remarked that the current American entanglement in Southeast Asia, complete with air cavalry, ranger battalions, and native scouts, is a scenario based upon a deep definition of our national pronouns as frontierman or Indian fighter extending enlightenment and civilization over against the "hostiles" on the dark side of the frontier. Whether fantasies are lived out or not, they may still be defined as scenarios arising from metaphoric predication on pronouns.

In Bwiti we have a particular opportunity to witness metaphors arise in fantasy and be put into action. For the cult is especially atune to fantasies and even promotes them through dependence upon the alkaloid narcotic *tabernanthe eboka*. The members of Bwiti feel that they obtain knowledge useful to ritual elaborations from their dreams and visions.

In a syncretist religious movement undergoing, before our eyes, its rapid evolution, we can readily discover what it is tempting to call the kernel metaphoric statements: the deep lying metaphoric subject (pronouns) and metaphoric predicate out of which by a series of transformations we see arise the complex surface structure of cult ritual. In my study of some six of these movements in Africa I have attempted to give an account of the organizing metaphors that appear time and again in ritual performance. These metaphors include the militant metaphor of Christian soldiering in the Apostle's Revelation Society in Ghana, the pastoral metaphor of the bull who crashes in the kraal in the Church of God in Christ in Natal, South Africa, the atmospheric metaphor of the circumambient Holy Wind (or Ghost) in Zulu Zionism, the linguistic metaphor of the voices of God in Christianisme Celeste in Dahomey, and the sylvan metaphor of the lost hunters and the parrot's egg in the Bwiti cult.[14] These metaphors and their performative implications may be listed.

Metaphoric assertion	*Performative consequence*
We are Christian soldiers.	Our church activities must show our militance in fighting against the forces of the devil.
I (the pastor) am the bull who	In my sermons I must show my powers and

maintains order in the cattle kraal. You the members are the cattle I protect and invest with my substance.

I must lay on hands in the healing circles with such force that my power will shoot into the membership and they will be disciplined and directed. We must open ourselves up to the power of the pastor.

We are vessels of the Holy Wind.

Our actions must build up the presence of the wind around us and open us up so that we may incorporate it. We must fly.

We are the voices of God.

We must study the Bible so that we can learn God's language. We must concentrate our attention on sermons and seek speaking in tongues.

We are lost hunters in the forest searching for its secrets. I (the leader of this cult) am the parrot's egg holding a secret for which the membership must search.

Our liturgy and our leader must guide us through the forest and lead us to the secrets that the forest holds—principally communication with the wandering shades of the dead.

It should not be presumed that these are the only metaphors that appear in each of these cults though, I believe, they are the ones which set the dominant feeling tone of the cults and most do something for the members in a strategic sense.

Let us take just one metaphor from the Bwiti cult. It is a metaphor subsidiary to the one we have given above but it is in the same domain. It is the metaphor of the rituals of entrance into the cult house—*minkin*. The members say at this time *bi ne esamba* (we are a trading team). Historically the main association of this metaphor is with that adventurous team of young men that collected rubber and ivory at the turn of the century and took it to the coast to exchange for trade goods. These groups were characterized by high solidarity, the euphoria of hunting and gathering, and the satisfaction of a rewarding trading relation with the colonial world. It was a group with a sense of purpose which led to significant fulfillment. The aptness of this metaphor is readily understood when the goallessness, the lack of solidarity in village and kinship, and the high degree of ambivalence about the larger colonial world is grasped. For these conditions make for feelings to which the metaphor is a compensatory representation.

If metaphors are a compensatory representation in themselves, they are even more so when they are acted upon, when they are images in the sense of plans of behavior.[15] In the case of the *esamba* metaphor, we see that it is an organizing force in the performance of the rituals of entrance and exit. These rituals, of course, are an accretion of many elements. But when we see narrow paths being cut through the underbrush on the margins of the village so that the membership at the midnight exit from the chapel can wend their way through the forest and then return, we have reason to assume a metaphor is being put into action as a plan of ritual behavior. And when we see the rituals of entrance begin at the margins of the forest and dance as a tightly packed mass across the village plaza into the chapel, we have reason to assume we are seeing the realization of a metaphoric assertion. It is an old question as to how rituals arise. We may avoid the fruitless debate on the primacy of myth or ritual by stating simply: rituals are the acting out of metaphoric predication upon inchoate pronouns which are in need of movement.

People undertake religious experiences because they desire to change the way they feel about themselves and the world in which they live. They come into their particular cult with some constellation of feelings—isolation, disengagement, powerlessness, enervation, debasement, contamination —from which they need to move away. Metaphors put forth in these movements accomplish that. By persuasion and performance they operate upon the member allowing him eventually to exit from the ritual incorporated, empowered, activated, euphoric. They allow him eventually to exit better situated in quality space. Of course these are just psychological abstractions. My point here is that we come to understand these operations only if we study metaphoric predications upon pronouns as they appear in persuasion and performance. The strategy of emotional movement in religion lies in them.

Conclusion: What It Means to be Moved

The materials we have examined bear first on the way that appropriate impressions of persons are formed, but further they cast light upon the important question of the images of the ideal personality and how these images are generated. Boulding called our attention to the importance of this problem and to our persisting ignorance of how these images arise, compete, change, and decline. "Like the gods and goddesses of ancient mythology one almost gets the impression of ideal types battling above the clouds for the minds and allegiances of men. It is the fall of the ideal image that leads to the collapse of empires and the decay of cultures. Yet how little we know about the forces which support or destroy these powerful beings."[16]

I may not have accounted for the collapse of empires, but what I have said may relate to processes of decay in acculturation. It has been my view that the images of social beings are generated by metaphoric predications upon pronouns which are themselves the primary—if not primordial—ideal types. These metaphoric extensions generate qualities in pronouns. They invest pronouns with emotional meaningfulness if the domains into which extension takes place are important arenas of activity for the culture involved. If the forest, for example, becomes a less preoccupying arena of life for the Fang—as, in fact, because of their increasing activity along the arteries of commerce, it is—then it becomes harder and harder for the Fang to form meaningful images of the peoples involved in the palabra house except by employing vitiated abstractions (wise, eloquent, forceful) or old metaphors dead or dying because they extend into moribund aspects of their lives. The vitiation of metaphor through drastic change in the domains of activity of a people is an aspect of acculturation that has not been fully enough explored. This vitiation makes it difficult for a people to have satisfactory feelings about their pronouns.

I have not been content, however, with examining the ways in which by use of metaphor we learn to have feelings about the qualities of people. I have suggested that there is a strategy involved in the adversarial condition of social life and that strategy involves placement of self or other on the various continua of the important domains of experience of a culture. The set of these continua define the quality space of that culture—the quality space within which the pronouns of that culture operate, or are operated upon.

It is my argument, therefore, that the systematic study of those most meaningful forms in human intercommunication—metaphors—involves among many other approaches the study of the movement they make in semantic space. A sensitive ethnography must obtain the metaphors that men predicate upon themselves so as to locate the movements they desire to make in the culture they occupy.

But we should not overestimate the applicability of this model. Though it indicates the method by which we must discover a structure of sentiment, it remains essentially topographic. To be a structural model[17] it should specify the transformations to which the parts of the model are susceptible. Systematic description must show how the state of the space, that is the nature of the culture, imposes or inspires certain characteristic kinds of shifts in pronouns—toward, for example, greater potency or activity or goodness.[18]

In any event it is my view that these complicated and, so often, opaque structural matters must begin with a topographic model of quality space and with some idea of the movement that kernel metaphoric predications make in that space. And though this model may be problematic there is precedent in believing that our minds organize our perceptualized experiences by reference to their relative distances from each other on some prelinguistic quality space which arises out of the very nature of life in a world defined by gravitational forces.[19] Metaphoric predication would be the dynamic element in such a space. There may even be reason for believing, if we can learn from frogs in this regard, that what our ears, eyes, mouths are really telling our brains—or what the brain finally understands from what it is told—about the bloom and buzz of experience is the essential qualitative pattern of potency, activity, and goodness (edibility) of the things which catch our attention.[20]

It will be enough if anthropologists pay attention in the field to the ways in which men are aided in conveying inchoate psychological experiences by appealing to a range of more easily observable and concrete events in other domains of their lives. There must surely be some universals involved. It is likely that the domain of corporeal experience is used everywhere to clarify the heart and the head of many inchoate matters or the warmth or coolness of any personality. And it is likely, since the succession of bodily sensations is also a sequence of social experiences which arise to accommodate and control them as men mature, that the extension of social experience into the domain of corporeality and vice versa is also a universal.

While I first felt sheepish about taking up the problem of metaphor in the social sciences, I now feel more bullish. At the least we should have been tossed on the horns of the following dilemma which I believe fundamental to the understanding of culture. However men may analyze their experiences within any domain, they inevitably know and understand them best by referring them to other domains for elucidation. It is in that metaphoric cross-referencing of domains, perhaps, that culture is integrated, providing us with the sensation of wholeness. And perhaps the best index of cultural integration or disintegration, or of genuineness or spuriousness in culture for that matter, is the degree to which men can feel the aptness of each other's metaphors.

La Casona
El Pino
Alto Aller
Asturias

My thinking on the problem of "representations" and upon metaphor specifically has been aided by discussions with Robert Kleck, John Lanzetta, and Edward Yonan. I am grateful to the Ford Foundation for their support and to the Social Science Research Council and American Council of Learned Societies for support of the African field work. The National Science Foundation is supporting the Asturian field work.

REFERENCES

1. Bronislaw Malinowski, *Coral Gardens and Their Magic*, 2 vols. (London: Allen and Unwin, 1935); E. E. Evans-Pritchard, *Witchcraft, Oracles and Magic Among the Azanda* (Oxford: Clarendon Press, 1937), and *Nuer Religion* (Oxford: Clarendon Press, 1956).

2. B. F. Skinner, "The Operational Analysis of Psychological Terms," *Cumulative Record* (Boston, 1945), pp. 272-286.

3. S. E. Asch, "On the Use of Metaphors in the Descriptions of Persons," in Heinz Werner, ed., *On Expressive Language* (Worcester, Mass.: Clark University Press, 1955), p. 30.

4. Jerome Bruner, "The Course of Cognitive Growth," *American Psychologist*, 19 (1963), 1-27.

5. J. Piaget, *Structuralism* (New York: Basic Books, 1970).

6. C. Lévi-Strauss, *The Savage Mind* (Chicago: University of Chicago Press, 1962), p. 69.

7. Robert P. Armstrong, *The Affecting Presence: An Essay in Humanistic Anthropology* (Urbana: University of Illinois Press, 1971).

8. Kenneth Burke, *Permanence and Change*, 2d rev. ed. (Los Altos: Hermes Publications, 1954), and *The Philosophy of Literary Form*, rev. ed. (New York: Vintage Books, 1957).

9. Burke, *Philosophy of Literary Form*, p. 256.

10. D. Berggren, "The Use and Abuse of Metaphor," *The Review of Metaphysics*, 16 (1962-1963), 238-258.

11. Charles E. Osgood and others, *The Measurement of Meaning* (Urbana: University of Illinois Press, 1957).

12. James W. Fernandez, "Symbolic Consensus in a Fang Reformative Cult," *American Anthropologist*, 67 (1965), 902-929.

13. The Fang from which this is a running translation is the following, a little over half of the full text: Ebôka a zô na: ku nsisim a ne meki. Nyi na nkawla mewala mesaman ye etun ôngoase mininga ye ayong nyingwan mebege a yian dzip nda mbi atarega. Môt a dzebe ye mfum étô ening mon Fang é dzô alé. Nsisim wa mara ékôkôm akale a ne engôngôm. Edô a ne oyô. Mwan Fang a nga sô a zu a sok beng nye na; Zame esi Zame ôyô. Nya na beng é ne nkôl, nya na e ne fe etuge nzum, nya na Nzame esi enye éne etok nsisim, Nzame oyo a ne mfonga. Minkol mite emyo Nyingwan Mebege a nga eka mwan . . . bininga bi kak ekôp. Bia bise bi ne nyim Zame. Edô nyim a nga sô sô etôm. Bôbedzang be dzi nyim . . . ô ta dzi nyim, nyim Nzame. Aki Kos Zambi Avanga enye a nga kôbô. Me mana dzô. Bi nga van tsi beng nyim Zame.

14. References to each of these cults and their organizing metaphors may be found in the following: Fernandez, "Revitalized Words from the Parrot's Egg and the Bull Who Crashes in the Kraal: African Cult Sermons," *Proceedings of the American Ethnological Society for 1966: Essays on the Verbal and Visual Arts* (1967), pp. 45-63; *Microcosmogeny and Modernization*, Occasional Papers, Centre for Developing Area Studies, McGill University (1969), pp. 1-34; "Rededication and Prophetism in Ghana," *Cahiers d'Etudes Africaines*, no. 38, VII (1970), 228-305.

15. George A. Miller, E. Galenter, and K. H. Pribram, *Plans and the Structure of Behavior* (New York: Holt, 1960).

16. K. Boulding, *The Image: Knowledge in Life and Society* (Ann Arbor: University of Michigan Press, 1956), pp. 144-145.

17. Piaget, *Structuralism*.

18. Some of these things can be worked out with the model as it stands, where all we need to investigate are predications across domains of the form; P is A [I (a man) am a hawk]. Of greater interest are complex associations within and across domains of the form, still derived from these basic predications; P1 : P2 :: A : B [I (a man) am to you (a woman) as hawk is to dove]. For in these formulae we begin to get a sense of order in culture—a sense of congruences in sets of associations within and across domains. And beyond that and still of greater interest are the characteristic

transformations that metaphoric associations undergo in various bodies of expressive culture, such as ritual. These are purportedly summed up for us in the sybelline Lévi-Strauss formula over which so much blood has been shed.

$$f_x(a) \; : \; f_y(b) \; :: \; f_x(b) \; : \; f_{a-1}(y)$$

This may be read in terms of our argument here as: The emotional movement or function (x) accomplished by some metaphor (a) is to the movement (y) accomplished by some metaphor (b) as the appropriation by metaphor (b) of its complementary movement (x) is to the transformation of a previous metaphor (a) into a significantly new movement $(a\text{-}1)$ of a new metaphor (y) itself transformed from a previous movement. The only thing this can mean in terms of our discussion here is that movement can be transformed into metaphor and metaphor into movement within a given quality space.

An article on "The Performance of Ritual Metaphors," which attempts to give an account of metaphoric transformations in ritual, will appear in a collection of articles on *The Social Use of Metaphor,* edited by David Sapir for Cornell University Press.

19. W. V. O. Quine, *Word and Object* (Cambridge, Mass.: MIT Press, 1963), pp. 83ff. *Proceedings of the Institute of Radio Electronics,* 47 (November 1959), 1940-1959.

MARY DOUGLAS

Deciphering a Meal

IF LANGUAGE is a code, where is the precoded message? The question is phrased to expect the answer: nowhere. In these words a linguist is questioning a popular analogy.[1] But try it this way: if food is a code, where is the precoded message? Here, on the anthropologist's home ground, we are able to improve the posing of the question. A code affords a general set of possibilities for sending particular messages. If food is treated as a code, the messages it encodes will be found in the pattern of social relations being expressed. The message is about different degrees of hierarchy, inclusion and exclusion, boundaries and transactions across the boundaries. Like sex, the taking of food has a social component, as well as a biological one.[2] Food categories therefore encode social events. To say this is to echo Roland Barthes[3] on the sartorial encoding of social events. His book, *Système de la mode*, is primarily about methodology, about code-breaking and code-making taken as a subject in itself. The next step for the development of this conceptual tool is to take up a particular series of social events and see how they are coded. This will involve a close understanding of a microscale social system. I shall therefore start the exercise by analyzing the main food categories used at a particular point in time in a particular social system, our home. The humble and trivial case will open the discussion of more exalted examples.

Sometimes at home, hoping to simplify the cooking, I ask, "Would you like to have just soup for supper tonight? I mean a good thick soup—instead of supper. It's late and you must be hungry. It won't take a minute to serve." Then an argument starts: "Let's have soup now, and supper when you are ready." "No no, to serve two meals would be more work. But if you like, why not start with the soup and fill up with pudding?" "Good heavens! What sort of a meal is that? A beginning and an end and no middle." "Oh, all right then, have the soup as it's there, and I'll do a Welsh rarebit as well." When they have eaten soup, Welsh rarebit, pudding, and cheese: "What a lot of plates. Why do you make such elaborate suppers?" They proceed to argue that by taking thought I could satisfy the full requirements of a meal with a single, copious dish. Several rounds of this conversation have given me a practical interest in the categories and

61

meanings of food. I needed to know what defines the category of a meal in our home.

The first source for enlightenment will obviously be Claude Lévi-Strauss's *The Raw and the Cooked* and the other volumes of his *Mythologiques*[4] which discuss food categories and table manners. But this is only a beginning. He fails us in two major respects. First, he takes leave of the small-scale social relations which generate the codification and are sustained by it. Here and there his feet touch solid ground, but mostly he is orbiting in rarefied space where he expects to find universal food meanings common to all mankind. He is looking for a precoded, panhuman message in the language of food, and thus exposing himself to the criticism implicit in the quoted linguist's question. Second, he relies entirely on the resources of binary analysis. Therefore he affords no technique for assessing the relative value of the binary pairs that emerge in a local set of expressions. Worse than clumsy, his technical apparatus produces meanings which cannot be validated. Yea, or nay, he and Roman Jakobson may be right on the meanings in a sonnet of Baudelaire's.[5] But even if the poet himself had been able to judge between theirs and Riffaterre's alternative interpretation of the same work[6] and to say that one was closer to his thought than the other, he would be more likely to agree that all these meanings are there. This is fair for literary criticism, but when we are talking of grammar, coding, and the "science of the concrete,"[7] it is not enough.

For analyzing the food categories used in a particular family the analysis must start with why those particular categories and not others are employed. We will discover the social boundaries which the food meanings encode by an approach which values the binary pairs according to their position in a series. Between breakfast and the last nightcap, the food of the day comes in an ordered pattern. Between Monday and Sunday, the food of the week is patterned again. Then there is the sequence of holidays and fast days through the year, to say nothing of life cycle feasts, birthdays, and weddings. In other words, the binary or other contrasts must be seen in their syntagmatic relations. The chain which links them together gives each element some of its meaning. Lévi-Strauss discusses the syntagmatic relation in his earlier book, *The Savage Mind*, but uses it only for the static analysis of classification systems (particularly of proper names). It is capable of a much more dynamic application to food categories, as Michael Halliday has shown. On the two axes of syntagm and paradigm, chain and choice, sequence and set, call it what you will, he has shown how food elements can be ranged until they are all accounted for either in grammatical terms, or down to the last lexical item.

Eating, like talking, is patterned activity, and the daily menu may be made to yield an analogy with linguistic form. Being an analogy, it is limited in relevance; its purpose is to throw light on, and suggest problems of, the categories of grammar by relating these to an activity which is familiar and for much of which a terminology is ready to hand.

The presentation of a framework of categories for the description of eating might proceed as follows:

Units: Daily menu
Meal
Course
Helping
Mouthful

Unit: Daily Menu

Elements of primary structure	$\overrightarrow{E, M, L, S}$ ("early," "main," "light," "snack")
Primary structures	EML EMLS (conflated as EML(S))
Exponents of these elements (primary classes of unit "meal")	E: 1 (breakfast) M: 2 (dinner) L: 3 ⎫ (no names available; see secondary S: 4 ⎭ classes)
Secondary structures	EL_aS_aM EL_aM EML_bS_b EMS_aL_c
Exponents of secondary elements (systems of secondary classes of unit "meal")	L_a: 3.1 (lunch) L_b: 3.2 (high tea) L_c: 3.3 (supper) S_a: 4.1 (afternoon tea) S_b: 4.2 (nightcap)
System of sub-classes of unit "meal"	E: 1.1 (English breakfast) 1.2 (continental breakfast)

Passing to the rank of the "meal," we will follow through the class "dinner:"

Unit: Meal, Class: dinner

Elements of primary structure	$\longrightarrow$ F, S, M, W, Z ("first," "second," "main," "sweet," "savoury")
Primary structures	MW MWZ MZW FMW FMWZ FMZW FSMW FSMWZ FSMZW (conflated as (F(S)MW(Z))
Exponents of these elements (primary classes of unit "course")	F: 1(antipasta) S: 2 (fish) M: 3 (entrée) W: 4 (dessert) Z: 5 (cheese*)
Secondary structures	(various, involving secondary elements $F_{a..d}$, $M_{a,b}$, $W_{a..c}$)
Exponents of secondary elements (systems of secondary classes of unit "course")	F_a: 1.1 (soup) F_b: 1.2 (hors d'oeuvres) F_c: 1.3 (fruit) F_d: 1.4 (fruit juice) M_a: 3.1 (meat dish) M_b: 3.2 (poultry dish) W_a: 4.1 (fruit*) W_b: 4.2 (pudding) W_c: 4.3 (ice cream*)

Systems of sub-classes of unit "course"	F_a:	1.11 (clear soup*)
		1.12 (thick soup*)
	S:	2.01 (grilled fish*)
		2.02 (fried fish*)
		2.03 (poached fish*)
	W_b:	4.21 (streamed pudding*)
		4.22 (milk pudding*)
Exponential systems operating in meal structure	F_c:	grapefruit/melon
	F_d:	grapefruit juice/pineapple juice/ tomato juice
	M_a:	beef/mutton/pork
	M_b:	chicken/turkey/duck/goose

At the rank of the "course," the primary class "entrée" has secondary classes "meat dish" and "poultry dish." Each of these two secondary classes carries a grammatical system whose terms are formal items. But this system accounts only for simple structures of the class "entrée," those made up of only one member of the unit "helping." The class "entrée" also displays compound structures, whose additional elements have as exponents the (various secondary classes of the) classes "cereal" and "vegetable." We will glance briefly at these:

Unit: Course, Class: entrée

Elements of primary structure	J, T, A ("joint," "staple," "adjunct")
Primary structures	J JT JA JTA (conflated as J((T)(A)))
Exponents of these elements (primary classes of unit "helping")	J: 1 (flesh)
	T: 2 (cereal)
	A: 3 (vegetable)
Secondary structures	(various, involving—among others— secondary elements $J_{a,b}$, $T_{a,b}$, $A_{a,b}$)
Exponents of secondary elements (systems of secondary classes of unit "helping")	J_a: 1.1 (meat ⎱systems as at M in
	J_b: 1.2 (poultry)⎰ meal structure
	T_a: 2.1 (potato)
	T_b: 2.2 (rice)
	A_a: 3.1 (green vegetable*)
	A_b: 3.2 (root vegetable*)

And so on, until everything is accounted for either in grammatical systems or in classes made up of lexical items (marked *). The presentation has proceeded down the rank scale, but shunting is presupposed throughout: there is mutual determination among all units, down to the gastronomic morpheme, the "mouthful."[8]

This advances considerably the analysis of our family eating patterns. First, it shows how long and tedious the exhaustive analysis would be, even to read. It would be more taxing to observe and record. Our model of ethnographic thoroughness for a microscopic example should not be less exact than that practiced by anthropologists working in exotic lands. In India social distinctions are invariably accompanied by distinctions in commensality and categories of edible and inedible foods. Louis Dumont's important work on Indian culture, *Homo Hierarchicus*, discusses the purity of food as an index of hierarchy. He gives praise to Adrian Mayer's detailed study of the relation between food categories and social categories in a village in Central India.[9] Here twenty-three castes group themselves according to the use of the same pipe, the provision of ordinary food for common meals, and the provision of food for feasts. Higher castes share the pipe with almost all castes except four. Between twelve and sixteen castes smoke together, though in some cases a different cloth must be placed between the pipe and the lips of the smoker. When it comes to their food, a subtler analysis is required. Castes which enjoy power in the village are not fussy about what they eat or from whom they receive it. Middle range castes are extraordinarily restrictive, both as to whom they will accept food from and what they will eat. Invited to family ceremonies by the more powerful and more ritually relaxed castes they puritanically insist on being given their share of the food raw and retire to cook it themselves in their own homes.[10] If I were to follow this example and to include all transmission of food from our home my task would be greater. For certainly we too know situations in which drink is given to be consumed in the homes of the recipient. There are some kinds of service for which it seems that the only possible recognition is half or even a whole bottle of whiskey. With the high standards of the Indian research in mind, I try now to identify the relevant categories of food in our home.

The two major contrasted food categories are meals versus drinks. Both are social events. Outside these categories, of course, food can be taken for private nourishment. Then we speak only of the lexical item itself: "Have an apple. Get a glass of milk. Are there any sweets?" If likely to interfere with the next meal, such eating is disapproved. But no negative attitude condemns eating before drinks. This and other indices suggest that meals rank higher.

Meals contrast with drinks in the relation between solids and liquids. Meals are a mixture of solid foods accompanied by liquids. With drinks the reverse holds. A complex series of syntagmatic associations governs the elements in a meal, and connects the meals through the day. One can say: "It can't be lunchtime. I haven't had breakfast yet," and at breakfast itself cereals come before bacon and eggs. Meals in their sequence tend to be named. Drinks sometimes have named categories: "come for cocktails, come for coffee, come for tea," but many are not named events: "What about a drink? What shall we have?" There is no structuring of drinks into early, main, light. They are not invested with any necessity in their ordering. Nor is the event called drinks internally structured into first, second, main, sweet. On the contrary, it is approved to stick with the same kind of drink, and to count drinks at all is impolite. The judgment "It is too early for alcohol" would be both rare and likely to be contested. The same lack of structure is found in the solid foods accompanying drinks. They are usually cold, served in discrete units which can be eaten tidily with fingers. No order governs the choice of solids. When the children were small and tea was a meal, bread and butter preceded scones, scones preceded cake and sweet biscuits. But now that the adult-child contrast no longer dominates in this family, tea has been demoted from a necessary place in the daily sequence of meals to an irregular appearance among weekend drinks and no rules govern the accompanying solids.

Meals properly require the use of at least one mouth-entering utensil per head, whereas drinks are limited to mouth-touching ones. A spoon on a saucer is for stirring, not sucking. Meals require a table, a seating order, restriction on movement and on alternative occupations. There is no question of knitting during a meal. Even at Sunday breakfast, reaching for the newspapers is a signal that the meal is over. The meal puts its frame on the gathering. The rules which hedge off and order one kind of social interaction are reflected in the rules which control the internal ordering of the meal itself. Drinks and their solids may all be sweet. But a meal is not a meal if it is all in the bland-sweet-sour dimensions. A meal incorporates a number of contrasts, hot and cold, bland and spiced, liquid and semi-liquid, and various textures. It also incorporates cereals, vegetables, and animal proteins. Criticism easily fastens on the ordering of these elements in a given case.

Obviously the meanings in our food system should be elucidated by much closer observation. I cut it short by drawing conclusions intuitively from the social categories which emerge. Drinks are for strangers, acquaintances, workmen, and family. Meals are for family, close friends, honored guests. The grand operator of the system is the line between intimacy and distance. Those we know at meals we also know at drinks. The meal expresses close friendship. Those we only know at drinks we know less intimately. So long as this boundary matters to us (and there is no reason to suppose it will always matter) the boundary between drinks and meals has meaning. There are smaller thresholds and half-way points. The entirely cold meal (since it omits a major contrast within a meal) would seem to be such a modifier. So those friends who have never had a hot meal in our home have presumably another threshold of intimacy to cross. The recent popularity of the barbecue and of more elaborately structured cocktail events which act as bridges between intimacy and distance suggests that our model of feeding categories is a common one. It can be drawn as in figure 1. Thus far we can go on the basis of binary oppositions and the number of classes and subclasses. But we are left with the general question which must be raised whenever a correspondence is found between a given social structure and the structure of symbols by which it is expressed, that is, the question of consciousness. Those who vehemently reject the possibility of a meal's being constituted by soup and pudding, or cake and fruit, are certainly not conscious that they are thereby sustaining a boundary between share-drinks and share-meals-too. They would be shocked at the very idea. It would be simplistic to trace the food categories direct to the social categories they embrace and leave

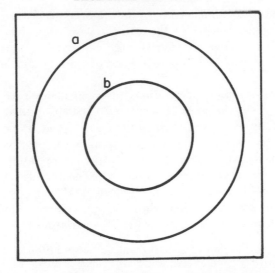

Figure 1. Social universe (a) share drinks; (b) share meals too.

it at figure 1. Evidently the external boundaries are only a small part of the meaning of the meal. Somewhere else in the family system some other cognitive activity is generating the internal structuring.

We can go much further toward discovering the intensity of meanings and their anchorage in social life by attending to the sequence of meals. For the week's menu has its climax at Sunday lunch. By contrasting the structure of Sunday lunch with weekday lunches a new principle emerges. Weekday lunches tend to have a tripartite structure, one element stressed accompanied by two or more unstressed elements, for example a main course and cold supporting dishes. But Sunday lunch has two main courses, each of which is patterned like the weekday lunch—say, first course, fish or meat (stressed) and two vegetables (unstressed), second course, pudding (stressed), cream and biscuits (unstressed). Christmas lunch has three courses, each on the same tripartite model. Here we stop and realize that the analogy may be read in the reverse sense. Meals are ordered in scale of importance and grandeur through the week and the year. The smallest, meanest meal metonymically figures the structure of the grandest, and each unit of the grand meal figures again the whole meal—or the meanest meal. The perspective created by these repetitive analogies invests the individual meal with additional meaning. Here we have the principle we were seeking, the intensifier of meaning, the selection principle. A meal stays in the category of meal only insofar as it carries this structure which allows the part to recall the whole. Hence the outcry against allowing the sequence of soup and pudding to be called a meal.

As to the social dimension, admission to even the simplest meal incorporates our guest unwittingly into the pattern of solid Sunday dinners,

Christmases, and the gamut of life cycle celebrations. Whereas the sharing of drinks (note the fluidity of the central item, the lack of structuring, the small, unsticky accompanying solids) expresses by contrast only too clearly the detachment and impermanence of simpler and less intimate social bonds.

Summing up, syntagmatic relations between meals reveal a restrictive patterning by which the meal is identified as such, graded as a minor or major event of its class, and then judged as a good or bad specimen of its kind. A system of repeated analogies upholds the process of recognition and grading. Thus we can broach the questions of interpretation which binary analysis by itself leaves untouched. The features which a single copious dish would need to display before qualifying as a meal in our home would be something like those of the famous chicken Marengo served to Napoleon after his victory over the Austrians.

Bonaparte, who, on the day of a battle, ate nothing until after it was over, had gone forward with his general staff and was a long way from his supply wagon. Seeing his enemies put to flight, he asked Dunand to prepare dinner for him. The master-chef at once sent men of the quartermaster's staff and ordnance in search of provisions. All they could find were three eggs, four tomatoes, six crayfish, a small hen, a little garlic, some oil and a saucepan . . . the dish was served on a tin plate, the chicken surrounded by the fried eggs and crayfish, with the sauce poured over it.[11]

There must have been many more excellent meals following similar scavenging after the many victories of those campaigns. But only this one has become famous. In my opinion the reason is that it combines the traditional soup, fish, egg, and meat courses of a French celebratory feast all in a *plat unique*.

If I wish to serve anything worthy of the name of supper in one dish it must preserve the minimum structure of a meal. Vegetable soup so long as it had noodles and grated cheese would do, or poached eggs on toast with parsley. Now I know the formula. A proper meal is A (when A is the stressed main course) plus 2B (when B is an unstressed course). Both A and B contain each the same structure, in small, a + 2b, when a is the stressed item and b the unstressed item in a course. A weekday lunch is A; Sunday lunch is 2A; Christmas, Easter, and birthdays are A + 2B. Drinks by contrast are unstructured.

To understand the categories we have placed ourselves at the hub of a small world, a home and its neighborhood. The precoded message of the food categories is the boundary system of a series of social events. Our example made only oblique reference to costs in time and work to indicate the concerns involved. But unless the symbolic structure fits squarely to some demonstrable social consideration, the analysis has only begun. For the fit between the medium's symbolic boundaries and the boundaries between categories of people is its only possible validation. The fit may be at different levels, but without being able to show some such matching, the analysis of symbols remains arbitrary and subjective.

The question that now arises is the degree to which a family uses symbolic structures which are available from the wider social system. Obviously this example reeks of the culture of a certain segment of the middle classes of London. The family's idea of what a meal should be is influenced by the Steak House and by the French *cuisine bourgeoise*. Yet herein is implied a synthesis of different traditions. The French version of the grand meal is dominated by the sequence of wines. The cheese platter is the divide between a mounting crescendo of individual savory dishes and a descending scale of sweet ones ending with coffee. Individual dishes in the French sequence can stand alone. Compare the melon course in a London restaurant and a Bordeaux restaurant. In the first, the half slice is expected to be dusted with powdered ginger and castor sugar (a + 2b) or decorated with a wedge of orange and a crystallized cherry (a + 2b). In the second, half a melon is served with no embellishment but its own perfume and juices. A + 2B is obviously not a formula that our family invented, but one that is current in our social environment. It governs even the structure of the cocktail canapé. The latter, with its cereal base, its meat or cheese middle section, its sauce or pickle topping, and its mixture of colors, suggests a mock meal, a minute metonym of English middle-class meals in general. Whereas the French pattern is more like: $C^1 + B^1 + A^1/A^2 + B^2 + C^2$, when the cheese course divides A^1 (the main savory dish) from A^2 (the main sweet). It would be completely against the spirit of this essay to hazard a meaning for either structure in its quasi-environmental form. French families reaching out to the meal structure of their cultural environment develop it and interact with it according to their intentions. English families reach out and find another which they adapt to their own social purposes. Americans, Chinese, and others do likewise. Since these cultural environments afford an ambient stream of symbols, capable of differentiating and intensifying, but not anchored to a stable social base, we cannot proceed further to interpret them. At this point the analysis stops. But the problems which cannot be answered here, where the cultural universe is unbounded, can usefully be referred to a more closed environment.

To sum up, the meaning of a meal is found in a system of repeated analogies. Each meal carries something of the meaning of the other meals; each meal is a structured social event which structures others in its own image. The upper limit of its meaning is set by the range incorporated in the most important member of its series. The recognition which allows each member to be classed and graded with the others depends upon the structure common to them all. The cognitive energy which demands that a meal look like a meal and not like a drink is performing in the culinary medium the same exercise that it performs in language. First, it distinguishes order, bounds it, and separates it from disorder. Second, it uses economy in the means of expression by allowing only a limited number of structures. Third, it imposes a rank scale upon the repetition of structures. Fourth, the repeated formal analogies multiply the meanings that are carried down any one of them by the power of the most weighty. By these four methods the meanings are enriched. There is no single point in the rank scale, high or low, which provides the basic meaning or real meaning. Each exemplar has the meaning of its structure realized in the examples at other levels.

From coding we are led to a more appropriate comparison for the interpretation of a meal, that is, versification. To treat the meal as a poem requires a more serious example than I have used hitherto. I turn to the Jewish meal, governed by the Mosaic dietary rules. For Lu Chi, a third century Chinese poet, poetry traffics in some way between the world and mankind. The poet is one who "traps Heaven and Earth in a cage of form."[12] On these terms the common meal of the Israelites was a kind of classical poem. Of the Israelite table, too, it could be said that it enclosed boundless space. To quote Lu Chi again:

> We enclose boundless space in a square-foot of paper;
> We pour out deluge from the inch-space of the heart.[13]

But the analogy slows down at Lu Chi's last line. For at first glance it is not certain that the meal can be a tragic medium. The meal is a kind of poem, but by a very limited analogy. The cook may not be able to express the powerful things a poet can say.

In Purity and Danger[14] I suggested a rational pattern for the Mosaic rejection of certain animal kinds. Ralph Bulmer has very justly reproached me for offering an animal taxonomy for the explanation of the Hebrew dietary laws. The principles I claimed to discern must remain, he argued, at a subjective and arbitrary level, unless they could take account of the multiple dimensions of thought and activity of the Hebrews concerned.[15] S. J. Tambiah has made similarly effective criticisms of the same shortcoming in my approach.[16] Both have provided from their own field work distinguished examples of how the task should be conducted. In another publication I hope to pay tribute to the importance of their research. But for the present purpose, I am happy to admit the force of their reproach. It was even against the whole spirit of my book to offer an account of an ordered system of thought which did not show the context of social relations in which the categories had meaning. Ralph Bulmer let me down gently by supposing that the ethnographic evidence concerning the ancient Hebrews was too meager. However, reflection on this new research and methodology has led me to reject that suggestion out of hand. We know plenty about the ancient Hebrews. The problem is how to recognize and relate what we know.

New Guinea and Thailand are far apart, in geography, in history, and in civilization. Their local fauna are entirely different. Surprisingly, these two analyses of animal classification have one thing in common. Each society projects on to the animal kingdom categories and values which correspond to their categories of marriageable persons. The social categories of descent and affinity dominate their natural categories. The good Thailand son-in-law knows his place and keeps to it: disordered, displaced sex is reprobated and the odium transferred to the domestic dog, symbol of dirt and promiscuity. From the dog to the otter, the transfer of odium is doubled in strength. This amphibian they class as wild, counterpart-dog. But instead of keeping to the wild domain it is apt to leave its sphere at flood time and to paddle about in their watery fields. The ideas they attach to incest are carried forward from the dog to the otter, the image of the utterly wrong son-in-law. For the Karam the social focus is upon the strained relations between affines and cousins. A wide range of manmade rules sustain the categories of a natural world which mirrors these anxieties. In the Thailand and Karam studies, a strong analogy between bed and board lies unmistakably beneath the system of classifying animals. The pattern of rules which categorize animals correspond in form to the patterns of rules governing human relations. Sexual and gastronomic consummation are made equivalents of one another by reasons of analogous restrictions applied to each. Looking back from these examples to the classifications of Leviticus we seek in vain a statement, however oblique, of a similar association between eating and sex. Only a very strong analogy between table and altar stares us in the face. On reflection, why should the Israelites have had a similar concern to associate sex with food? Unlike the other two examples, they had no rule requiring them to exchange their womenfolk. On the contrary, they were allowed to marry their parallel paternal first cousins. E. R. Leach has reminded us how strongly exogamy was disapproved at the top political level,[17] and within each tribe of Israel endogamy was even enjoined (Deuteronomy 36). We must seek elsewhere for their dominant preoccupations. At this point I turn to the rules governing the common meal as prescribed in the Jewish religion. It is particularly interesting that these rules have remained the same over centuries. Therefore, if these categories express a relevance to social concerns we must expect those concerns to have remained in some form alive. The three rules about meat are: (1) the rejection of certain animal kinds as unfit for the table (Leviticus 11), (2) of those admitted as edible, the separation of the meat from blood before cooking (Leviticus 17:10), (3) the total separation of milk from meat, which involves the minute specialization of utensils (Exodus 23:19; 34:26; Deuteronomy 14:21).

I start with the classification of animals whose rationality I claim to have discerned. Diagrams will help to summarize the argument. First, animals are classified according to degrees of holiness (see figure 2). At

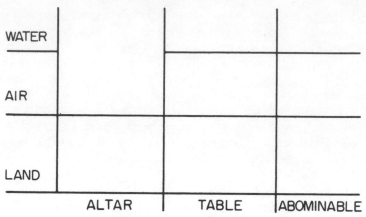

Figure 2. Degrees of holiness.

the bottom end of the scale some animals are abominable, not to be touched or eaten. Others are fit for the table, but not for the altar. None that are fit for the altar are not edible and vice versa, none that are not edible are sacrificeable. The criteria for this grading are coordinated for the three spheres of land, air, and water. Starting with the simplest, we find the sets as in figure 3.

Water creatures, to be fit for the table, must have fins and scales (Leviticus 13:9-12; Deuteronomy 14:19). Creeping swarming worms and snakes, if they go in the water or on the land, are not fit for the table (Deuteronomy 14:19; Leviticus 11:41-43). "The term swarming creatures

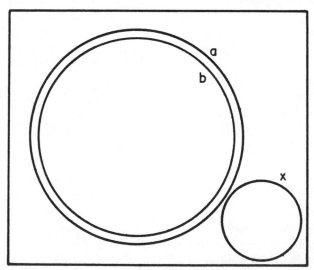

Figure 3. Denizens of the water (a) insufficient criteria for (b); (b) fit for table; (x) abominable: swarming.

(*shéreç*) denotes living things which appear in swarms and is applied both to those which teem in the waters (Genesis 1:20; Leviticus 11:10) and to those which swarm on the ground, including the smaller land animals, reptiles and creeping insects."[18] Nothing from this sphere is fit for the altar. The Hebrews only sanctified domesticated animals and these did not include fish. "When any one of you brings an offering to Jehovah, it shall be a domestic animal, taken either from the herd or from the flock" (Leviticus 1:2). But, Assyrians and others sacrificed wild beasts, as S. R. Driver and H. A. White point out.

Air creatures (see figure 4) are divided into more complex sets: set (a), those which fly and hop on the earth (Leviticus 11: 12), having wings and two legs, contains two subsets, one of which contains the named birds, abominable and not fit for the table, and the rest of the birds (b), fit for the table. From this latter subset a sub-subset (c) is drawn, which is suitable for the altar—turtledove and pigeon (Leviticus 14; 5:7-8) and the sparrow (Leviticus 14:49-53). Two separate sets of denizens of the air are abominable, untouchable creatures (f), which have the wrong number of limbs for their habitat, four legs instead of two (Leviticus 9:20), and (x), the swarming insects we have already noted in the water (Deuteronomy 14:19).

The largest class of land creatures (a) (see figure 5) walk or hop on the land with four legs. From this set of quadrupeds, those with parted hoofs and which chew the cud (b) are distinguished as fit for the table (Leviticus 11:3; Deuteronomy 14:4-6) and of this set a subset consists of the domesticated herds and flocks (c). Of these the first born (d) are to

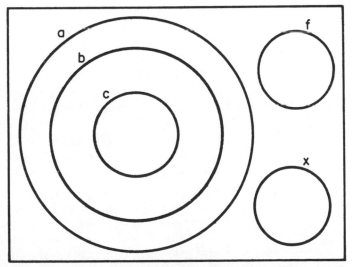

Figure 4. Denizens of the air (a) fly and hop: wings and two legs; (b) fit for table; (c) fit for altar; (f) abominable: insufficient criteria for (a); (x) abominable: swarming.

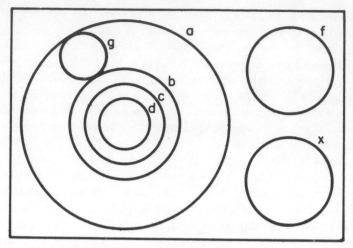

Figure 5. Denizens of the land (a) Walk or hop with four legs; (b) fit for table; (c) domestic herds and flocks; (d) fit for altar; (f) abominable: insufficient criteria for (a); (g) abominable: insufficient criteria for (b); (x) abominable: swarming.

be offered to the priests (Deuteronomy 24:33). Outside the set (b) which part the hoof and chew the cud are three sets of abominable beasts: (g) those which have either the one or the other but not both of the required physical features; (f) those with the wrong number of limbs, two hands instead of four legs (Leviticus 11:27 and 29:31); (x) those which crawl upon their bellies (Leviticus 11:41-44).

The isomorphism which thus appears between the different categories of animal classed as abominable helps us to interpret the meaning of abomination. Those creatures which inhabit a given range, water, air, or land, but do not show all the criteria for (a) or (b) in that range are abominable. The creeping, crawling, teeming creatures do not show criteria for allocation to any class, but cut across them all.

Here we have a very rigid classification. It assigns living creatures to one of three spheres, on a behavioral basis, and selects certain morphological criteria that are found most commonly in the animals inhabiting each sphere. It rejects creatures which are anomalous, whether in living between two spheres, or having defining features of members of another sphere, or lacking defining features. Any living being which falls outside this classification is not to be touched or eaten. To touch it is to be defiled and defilement forbids entry to the temple. Thus it can be summed up fairly by saying that anomalous creatures are unfit for altar and table. This is a peculiarity of the Mosaic code. In other societies anomaly is not always so treated. Indeed, in some, the anomalous creature is treated as the source of blessing and is specially fit for the altar (as the Lele pangolin), or as a noble beast, to be treated as an honorable adversary, as the

Karam treat the cassowary. Since in the Mosaic code every degree of holiness in animals has implications one way or the other for edibility, we must follow further the other rules classifying humans and animals. Again I summarize a long argument with diagrams. First, note that a category which divides some humans from others, also divides their animals from others. Israelites descended from Abraham and bound to God by the Covenant between God and Abraham are distinguished from all other peoples and similarly the rules which Israelites obey as part of the Covenant apply to their animals (see figure 6). The rule that the womb opener or first born is consecrated to divine service applies to firstlings of the flocks and herds (Exodus 22:29-30; Deuteronomy 24:23) and the rule of Sabbath observance is extended to work animals (Exodus 20:10). The analogy by which Israelites are to other humans as their livestock are to other quadrupeds develops by indefinite stages the analogy between altar and table.

Since Levites who are consecrated to the temple service represent the first born of all Israel (Numbers 3:12 and 40) there is an analogy between the animal and human firstlings. Among the Israelites, all of whom prosper through the Covenant and observance of the Law, some are necessarily unclean at any given time. No man or woman with issue of seed or blood, or with forbidden contact with an animal classed as unclean, or who has shed blood or been involved in the unsacralized killing of an animal (Leviticus 18), or who has sinned morally (Leviticus 20) can enter the temple. Nor can one with a blemish (Deuteronomy 23) enter the temple or eat the flesh of sacrifice or peace offerings (Leviticus 8:20). The Levites are selected by pure descent from all the Israelites. They represent the first born of Israel. They judge the cleanness and purify the uncleanness of Israelites (Leviticus 13, 14). Only Levites who are without bodily blemish (Leviticus 21:17-23) and without contact with death can enter the Holy of Holies. Thus we can present these rules as sets in figures 7 and 8. The analogy between humans and animals is very clear. So is the analogy created by these rules between the temple and the living body. Further analogies appear between the classification of animals according to holiness (figure 2) and the rules which set up the analogy of the holy temple with its holier and holier inner sanctuaries, and on the other hand between the temple's holiness and the body's purity and the

Under the Covenant		
Human	Israelites	others
Nonhuman	their livestock	others

Figure 6. Analogy between humans and nonhumans.

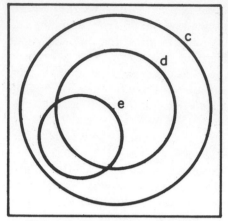 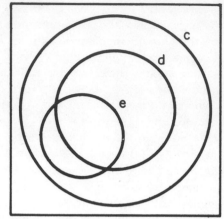

Figure 7. The Israelites (c) under the Covenant; (d) fit for temple sacrifice: no blemish; (e) consecrated to temple service, first born.

Figure 8. Their livestock (c) under the covenant; (d) fit for temple sacrifice: no blemish; (e) consecrated to temple service, first born.

capacity of each to be defiled by the self-same forms of impurity. This analogy is a living part of the Judeo-Christian tradition which has been unfaltering in its interpretation of New Testament allusions. The words of the Last Supper have their meaning from looking backward over the centuries in which the analogy had held good and forward to the future celebrations of that meal. "This is my body . . . this is my blood" (Luke 22:19-20; Mark 14:22-24; Matthew 26:26-28). Here the meal and the sacrificial victim, the table and the altar are made explicitly to stand for one another.

Lay these rules and their patternings in a straight perspective, each one looking forward and backward to all the others, and we get the same repetition of metonyms that we found to be the key to the full meaning of the categories of food in the home. By itself the body and its rules can carry the whole load of meanings that the temple can carry by itself with its rules. The overlap and repetitions are entirely consistent. What then are these meanings? Between the temple and the body we are in a maze of religious thought. What is its social counterpart? Turning back to my original analysis of the forbidden meats we are in a much better position to assess intensity and social relevance. For the metonymical patternings are too obvious to ignore. At every moment they are in chorus with a message about the value of purity and the rejection of impurity. At the level of a general taxonomy of living beings the purity in question is the purity of the categories. Creeping, swarming, teeming creatures abominably destroy the taxonomic boundaries. At the level of the individual living being impurity is the imperfect, broken, bleeding specimen. The sanctity of cognitive boundaries is made known by valuing the integrity of the physical forms. The perfect physical specimens point to the perfectly bounded temple, altar, and sanctuary. And these in their turn point to the hard-won and hard-to-defend territorial boundaries of the Promised Land. This is not reductionism. We are not here reducing the dietary rules to any political concern. But we are showing how they are consistently celebrating a theme that has been celebrated in the temple cult and in the whole history of Israel since the first Covenant with Abraham and the first sacrifice of Noah.

Edmund Leach, in his analysis of the genealogy of Solomon, has reminded us of the political problems besetting a people who claim by pure descent and pure religion to own a territory that others held and others continually encroached upon.[19] Israel is the boundary that all the other boundaries celebrate and that gives them their historic load of meaning. Remembering this, the orthodox meal is not difficult to interpret as a poem. The first rule, the rejection of certain animal kinds, we have mostly dealt with. But the identity of the list of named abominable birds is still a question. In the Mishnah it is written: "The characteristics of birds are not stated, but the Sages have said, every bird that seizes its prey (to tread or attack with claws) is unclean."[20] The idea that the unclean birds were predators, unclean because they were an image of human predation and homicide, so easily fits the later Hellenicizing interpretations that it has been suspect. According to the late Professor S. Hooke (in a personal communication), Professor R. S. Driver once tried out the idea that the Hebrew names were onomatopoeic of the screeches and calls of the birds. He diverted an assembly of learned divines with ingenious vocal exercises combining ornithology and Hebrew scholarship. I have not traced the record of this meeting. But following the method of analysis I have been using, it seems very likely that the traditional predatory idea is sufficient, considering its compatibility with the second rule governing the common meal.

According to the second rule, meat for the table must be drained of its blood. No man eats flesh with blood in it. Blood belongs to God alone, for life is in the blood. This rule relates the meal systematically to all the rules which exclude from the temple on grounds of contact with or responsibility for bloodshed. Since the animal kinds which defy the perfect classification of nature are defiling both as food and for entry to the temple, it is a structural repetition of the general analogy between body and temple to rule that the eating of blood defiles. Thus the birds and beasts which eat carrion (undrained of blood) are likely by the same reasoning to be defiling. In my analysis, the Mishnah's identifying the unclean birds as predators is convincing.

Here we come to a watershed between two kinds of defilement. When the classifications of any metaphysical scheme are imposed on nature, there are several points where it does not fit. So long as the classifications remain in pure metaphysics and are not expected to bite into daily life in the form of rules of behavior, no problem arises. But if the unity of God-head is to be related to the unity of Israel and made into a rule of life, the difficulties start. First there are the creatures whose behavior defies the rigid classification. It is relatively easy to deal with them by rejection and avoidance. Second there are the difficulties that arise from our biological condition. It is all very well to worship the holiness of God in the perfec-tion of his creation. But the Israelites must be nourished and must repro-duce. It is impossible for a pastoral people to eat their flocks and herds without damaging the bodily completeness they respect. It is impossible to renew Israel without emission of blood and sexual fluids. These prob-lems are met sometimes by avoidance and sometimes by consecration to the temple. The draining of blood from meat is a ritual act which figures the bloody sacrifice at the altar. Meat is thus transformed from a living creature into a food item.

As to the third rule, the separation of meat and milk, it honors the pro-creative functions. The analogy between human and animal parturition is always implied, as the Mishnah shows in its comment on the edibility of the afterbirth found in the slaughtered dam: if the afterbirth had emerged in part, it is forbidden as food; "it is a token of young in a woman and a token of young in a beast."[21] Likewise this third rule honors the Hebrew mother and her initial unity with her offspring.

In conclusion I return to the researches of Tambiah and Bulmer. In each case a concern with sexual relations, approved or disapproved, is reflected on to the Thailand and Karam animal classifications. In the case of Israel the dominant concern would seem to be with the integrity of territorial boundaries. But Edmund Leach has pointed out how over and over again they were concerned with the threat to Israel's holy calling from marriages with outsiders. Foreign husbands and foreign wives led to false gods and political defections. So sex is not omitted from the meanings in the common meal. But the question is different. In the other cases the problems arose from rules about exchanging women. In this case the con-cern is to insist on not exchanging women.

Perhaps I can now suggest an answer to Ralph Bulmer's question about the abhorrence of the pig. "Dr. Douglas tells us that the pig was an un-clean beast to the Hebrew quite simply because it was a taxonomic an-omaly, literally as the Old Testament says, because like the normal domes-tic animals it has a cloven hoof, whereas *un*like other cloven-footed beasts, it does not chew the cud. And she pours a certain amount of scorn on the commentators of the last 2,000 years who have taken alternative views and drawn attention to the creature's feeding habits, etc." Dr. Bulmer would be tempted to reverse the argument and to say that the other animals are prohibited as part of an elaborate exercise for rationalizing "the prohibition of a beast for which there were probably multiple reasons for avoiding. It would seem equally fair, on the limited evidence available, to argue that the pig was accorded anomalous taxonomic status because it was unclean as to argue that it was unclean because of its anomalous taxonomic status."[22] On more mature reflection, and with the help of his own research, I can now see that the pig to the Israelites could have had a special taxonomic status equivalent to that of the otter in Thailand. It carries the odium of multiple pollution. First it pollutes because it defies the classification of ungulates. Second, it pollutes because it eats carrion. Third, it pollutes because it is reared as food (and presumably as prime pork) by non-Israelites. An Israelite who betrothed a foreigner might have been liable to be offered a feast of pork. By these stages it comes plausibly to represent the utterly disapproved form of sexual mating and to carry all the odium that this implies. We now can trace a general analogy between the food rules and the other rules against mixtures: "Thou shalt not make thy cattle to gender with beasts of any other kind" (Leviticus 19:19). "Thou shalt not copulate with any beast" (Leviticus 18:23). The common meal, decoded, as much as any poem, summarizes a stern, tragic religion.

We are left the question of why, when so much else had been forgotten[23] about the rules of purification and their meaning, the three rules governing the Jewish meal have persisted. What meanings do they still encode, unmoored as they partly are from their original social context? It would seem that whenever a people are aware of encroachment and danger, dietary rules controlling what goes into the body would serve as a vivid analogy of the corpus of their cultural categories at risk. But here I am, contrary to my own strictures, suggesting a universal meaning, free of particular social context, one which is likely to make sense whenever the same situation is perceived. We have come full-circle to figure 1, with its two concentric circles. The outside boundary is weak, the inner one strong. Right through the diagrams summarizing the Mosaic dietray rules the focus was upon the integrity of the boundary at (b). Abominations of the water are those finless and scaleless creatures which lie outside that boundary. Abominations of the air appear less clearly in this light because the unidentified forbidden birds had to be shown as the widest circle from which the edible selection is drawn. If it be granted that they are predators, then they can be shown as a small subset in the unlisted set, that is as denizens of the air not fit for table because they eat blood. They would then be seen to threaten the boundary at (b) in the same explicit way as among the denizens of the land the circle (g) threatens it. We should therefore not conclude this essay without saying something more positive about what this boundary encloses. In the one case it divides edible from inedible. But it is more than a negative barrier of exclusion. In all the cases we have seen, it bounds the area of structured relations. Within that area rules apply. Outside it, anything goes. Following the argument we have established by which each level of meaning realizes the others which share a common structure, we can fairly say that the ordered system which is a meal represents all the ordered systems associated with it. Hence the strong arousal power of a threat to weaken or confuse that category. To take our analysis of the culinary medium further we should study what the poets say about the disciplines that they adopt. A passage from Roy Fuller's lectures helps to explain the flash of recognition and confidence which welcomes an ordered pattern. He is quoting Allen Tate, who said: "Formal versification is the primary structure of poetic order, the assurance to the reader and to the poet himself that the poet is in control of the disorder both outside him and within his own mind."[24]

The rules of the menu are not in themselves more or less trivial than the rules of verse to which a poet submits.

I am grateful to Professor Basil Bernstein and to Professor M. A. K. Halliday for valuable suggestions and for criticisms, some of which I have not been able to meet. My thanks are due to my son James for working out the Venn diagrams used in this article.

REFERENCES

1. Michael A. K. Halliday, "Categories of the Theory of Grammar," *Word, Journal of the Linguistic Circle of New York,* 17 (1961), 241-291.

2. The continuing discussion between anthropologists on the relation between biological and social facts in the understanding of kinship categories is fully relevant to the understanding of food categories.

3. Roland Barthes, *Système de la mode* (Paris: Editions Seuil, 1967).

4. Claude Lévi-Strauss, *The Raw and the Cooked: Introduction to a Science of Mythology,* I (London: Jonathan Cape, 1970). The whole series in French is *Mythologiques:* I. *Le Cru et le cuit,* II. *Du Miel aux cendres,* III. *L'Origine des manières de table* (Paris: Plon, 1964-1968).

5. Roman Jakobson and Claude Lévi-Strauss, "Les Chats de Charles Baudelaire," *L'Homme,* 2 (1962), 5-21.

6. Michael Riffaterre, "Describing Poetic Structures: Two Approaches to Baudelaire's *Les Chats,*" *Structuralism,* Yale French Studies 36 and 37 (1987).

7. Claude Lévi-Strauss, *The Savage Mind* (London: Heidenfeld and Nicholson, 1966; Chicago: University of Chicago Press, 1962, 1966).

8. Halliday, "Categories of the Theory of Grammar," pp. 277-279.

9. Adrian C. Mayer, *Caste and Kinship in Central India: A Village and Its Region* (London: Routledge, 1960).

10. Louis Dumont, *Homo Hierarchicus: The Caste System and Its Implications,* trans. M. Sainsbury (London: Weidenfeld & Nicholson, 1970; French ed., Gallimard, 1966), pp. 86-89.

11. See under "Marengo," *Larousse Gastronomique* (Hamlyn, 1961).

12. A. MacLeish, *Poetry and Experience* (London: Bodley Head, 1960), p. 4.

13. *Ibid.*

14. Mary Douglas, *Purity and Danger: An Analysis of Concepts of Pollution and Taboo* (London: Routledge, 1966).

15. Ralph Bulmer, "Why Is the Cassowary Not a Bird? A Problem of Zoological Taxonomy Among the Karam of the New Guinea Highlands," *Man*, new ser., 2 (1967), 5-25.

16. S. J. Tambiah, "Animals Are Good to Think and Good to Prohibit," *Ethnology*, 7 (1969), 423-459.

17. E. R. Leach, "The Legitimacy of Solomon," *Genesis as Myth and Other Essays* (London: Jonathan Cape, 1969).

18. S. R. Driver and H. A. White, *The Polychrome Bible, Leviticus,* v.l.fn. 13.

19. Leach, "Legitimacy of Solomon."

20. H. Danby, trans, *The Mishnah* (London: Oxford University Press, 1933), p. 324.

21. *Ibid.,* p. 520.

22. Bulmer, "Why Is the Cassowary Not a Bird?" p. 21.

23. Moses Maimonides, *Guide for the Perplexed,* trans. M. Friedlander (London: Routledge, 1904; first ed., 1881).

24. Roy Fuller, *Owls and Artificers: Oxford Lectures on Poetry* (London: Andre Deutsch, 1971), p. 64.

FRANK E. AND FRITZIE P. MANUEL

Sketch for a Natural History of Paradise

A REVEALING way to examine the psychic life of Judeo-Christian civilization would be to study it as a paradise cult, isolating fantasies about another world as they found expression in sacred texts, in commentaries upon them, and in their secular adaptation. Grand enterprises of Western man, among them the propagation of Christianity, the Crusades against Islam, millenarian revolts during the Reformation, the overseas explorations of the sixteenth century, and the settlement of the American continent, drew sustenance from the body of this myth. In visions of paradise terrestrial and celestial, men have been disclosing their innermost desires, whether they thrust them backward into the past, projected them forward into the future on earth, or raised them beyond the bounds of this sphere. As in dreams, men displaced themselves in time and space and compressed their manifold wishes into an all-embracing metaphor—the "golden race" of Hesiod, the "garden eastward in Eden" of Genesis, the "World to Come" of the rabbis, the "city of the living God" of the Epistle to the Hebrews, the "ineffabile allegrezza" of Dante's *Paradiso*.

Academic documentation of the paradisaical state over the centuries is now almost complete, a bold assertion. But anyone who today embarks upon this perilous journey will of necessity have to change his mentors along the route. Unlike that more fortunate Florentine seeker after paradise, he will find no lone Vergil, Matelda, and Beatrice waiting for him at appointed stations. Instead, for every portion of the way he will have to choose from among a clamorous throng of guides all of whom pretend to a preeminent knowledge of the terrain. At some crossroads the guides are friendly competitors, like those professors of literature who treat of the golden age and an earthly paradise in the Renaissance poets and have a way of tossing garlands to one another, though not without a concealed thorn here and there. At other points where new discoveries have recently been made—the scrolls in the Qumran caves—rival scholars heave great boulders from the desert and engage in such bitter learned disputation that the traveler is bewildered and must find a path through the wasteland of apocalyptic literature on the messianic age virtually without assistance.

In the beginning paradise was a myth with all the ambiguities of a myth; in time it became a religious belief in Israel and eventually a theological doctrine in Judaism and in Christianity. Like all orthodoxies it was then subject to imaginative deviations that strayed far from the dogma of the ecclesiastical establishments. Toward the end of the Middle Ages paradise ceased to be speculative alone and became enmeshed with action programs, often of a violent revolutionary character. As simple religious faith in the existence of paradise waned, the unconscious material of the original myth was preserved in a literary genre, the utopia, and in a political form, the movement. Today even among those who no longer believe in paradise in an elementary sense residues remain—last vestiges about to become extinct or seeds waiting for the moment to germinate.

The Myth of the Golden Age

Somewhere on the slopes of Mount Helikon, perhaps in the ninth century before Christ, a Boeotian poet-farmer composed a great epic of Greek rural life known as *Works and Days*. The myth of the five races of descending excellence introduced early in his poem is the *locus classicus* for a vision of a "golden generation of mortal people" who lived when Kronos was king in heaven and spent their days in feasting and merrymaking. On the meaning and significance of Hesiod's lines there is no unanimity; nor is there agreement about the personality or even the existence of the poet. The verses have been conjectured to be a collection of songs of Boeotian bards, a theology, or an intricate counterpoint of moral principles. There are convincing indications that the myth of the metallic races had earlier origins in the East, in Indian lore. Whatever its prehistory, Hesiod's golden race, transformed and embroidered by poets and philosophers, persists through Greek and Roman literature until it culminates in famous passages of the *Eclogues* of Vergil and the *Metamorphoses* of Ovid.

In the opening verses of Hesiod's description, many elements of a paradise of calm felicity, a dream of happiness that will endure in the West until the end of the eighteenth century, are already present. The abode of the golden race had no name, but it was a serene and tranquil place where food grew without cultivation and the curse of labor had not yet fallen upon mankind—a dramatic contrast with the unremitting toil of the iron men. The earth gave forth fruit of itself, *automate*, a fantasy that will often be renewed in the paradisaical imagination. The golden ones, in a state of eupsychia, led a life free from violence, pain, and grief—a pastoral idyl. Evils of old age were outside their ken, and so were the terrors of dying: in their golden well-being they glided into death as if they were falling asleep.[1] The female and sexuality are destined to play a perplexing role in paradise. While the golden race was beloved of the gods, they knew no women; their generation antedated the events narrated in the myth of Pandora, though in the present arrangement of Hesiod's poem the misogynist tale of the gods' vengeful creation of woman, the origin of evil, is placed before the myth of the races.

For Hesiod himself, twilight had descended upon the age of the heroes. The tone of life was melancholy and there was a pervasive atmosphere of decline. Hunger had become a familiar in the house of the Boeotian farmer. The barons who ruled his destiny were venal and rapacious, and Hesiod saw little hope in the future, for it was his misfortune to have been born one of the wretched men of the iron age. Bickering and strife, suffering and travail, were their daily lot, and the gloom was only rarely relieved by "good things mixed with the evils." Through a curious though not uncommon historical dialectic, the dark world of Hesiod gave birth to its opposite. The polarizing character of the paradisaical state, announced from the outset of this history, will remain part of its underlying structure: the innocence of Eden and the guile of the serpent, heaven and hell, the horrors of this world and the glories of the messianic age and of the millennium, the utopia of Athens and the dystopia of Atlantis, the happiness of the noble savage and the discontents of civilization. The antithetical nature of paradise, the coupling with a negation, may betray its primitive origin, like those words that signify their converse too when they appear in dreams.

In antiquity, the metamorphoses of Hesiod's golden race vied in number with those of the gods. The conditions of life for the golden race were constantly modified to harmonize with changing philosophical and religious preconceptions as the myth passed through the Greek and Roman literary worlds, until eventually it was reduced to a matter-of-fact account of a historical epoch in the beginning of things. During intermediate stages along the way, mythic and historical components became inseparably intermingled. At some point difficult to determine, but surely by Hellenistic times, Hesiod's five races were completely supplanted by four ages (the race of heroes was dropped) and the golden race became a golden age.

Early in the fifth century B.C. the Agrigentine poet Empedocles, in a fragment appropriately preserved in a treatise on vegetarianism written by the Neoplatonist Porphry eight hundred years later, added abstinence from blood among men and animals to the attributes of a world anterior to and even more perfect than the reign of Kronos in the golden age. In Empedocles' mystic cycle of Love and Strife, the primordial epoch corresponds to a time when Strife is yet unborn. Kupris, who in this fragment is Aphrodite and the cosmic force of Love, reigns a solitary goddess honored with animal offerings, not in the flesh, not in life-destroying ritual sacrifice, but merely with their images.[2]

The vision of man in a primitive state of nature in Rousseau's *Discourse on Inequality*, its most noteworthy modern envelopment, was, we gather from his notes, inspired by the work of Dicaearchus of Messana, a pupil of Aristotle who spent most of his life at Sparta. His universal history of culture, the first ever written, is preserved in a summary by Porphyry in that same treatise to which we owe the fragment from Empedocles on the primitive reign of Love, and came to Rousseau circuitously through excerpts in Saint Jerome.[3] Dicaearchus completely demythicized the golden age and reduced it to plain historical reality. Virtually all the physical and moral qualities that distinguish Rousseau's state of nature have an antecedent in this Hellenistic portrait of the first generations, an age extolled as the best life ever enjoyed by men, when they were truly like unto the gods. They ate little —no heavy foods—and never sickened from being loaded down with foul matter. The arts had not yet been invented, and men thrived, without care, on the spontaneous fruits of nature. Both in Dicaearchus and in Rousseau the acorn sufficed the peaceful primitives. There was no conflict or emulation among them because there was nothing of value about which to contend. To the later multiplication of desires Dicaearchus, a true forerunner of Rousseau, imputed all the evils that had beset mankind.

The Romans dreamed of the happiness of the reign of Saturn, whom they identified with Kronos, and in the Saturnalia enjoyed, if only for a brief moment and in a debauched form, a revival of the golden age. In Roman literature the epithet "golden" was rather consistently applied to a historical period instead of a mythic race. Far better known than the Greek poets, Ovid and Vergil are the pivotal figures in the transmission of the myth to the Middle Ages. Beginning with the Renaissance, Ovid's *Metamorphoses* was one of the most popular schoolbooks in Europe; and his portrayal of the golden age in Book I, which filled out Hesiod's spare text, was the definitive form in which the myth was infused into Western culture. For all his rich embellishments of the *aurea aetas,* Ovid did not disguise his close kinship with Hesiod; but the atmosphere has become heavily scented with the primitivist nostalgia of an oversophisticated society. "Golden was that first age, which, with no one to compel, without a law, of its own will, kept faith and did the right. There was no fear of punishment, no threatening words were to be read on brazen tablets; no suppliant throng gazed fearfully upon its judge's face; but without judges lived secure . . . There was no need at all of armed men, for nations, secure from war's alarms, passed the years in gentle ease. The earth herself, without compulsion, untouched by hoe or plowshare, of herself gave all things needful. And men, content with food which came with no one's seeking, gathered the arbute fruit . . . Anon the earth, untilled, brought forth her stores of grain, and the fields, though unfallowed, grew white with the heavy, bearded wheat. Streams of milk and streams of sweet nectar flowed, and yellow honey was distilled from the verdant oak."[4] As one moves on from Ovid through time, this literary rendering of a paradisaical state becomes ever more laden with ornaments until in Milton's Garden of Eden before the Fall, a virtual catalogue of attributes garnered from all times and places, the very exuberance of detail oppresses one with a sense of the impending doom.[5]

The stage scenery of the human imagination can readily be shoved about and the same props reassembled in different sequences. Many Western thinkers have joined the notion of a primitive golden age with a promise that the happy epoch now vanished will be reborn. While Hesiod's epic reflected an age of social disintegration and looked backward, the fortunate human condition of the age of Kronos could be translated into the future. In *The Divine Institutes* the church father Lactantius prophesied: "Those things shall come to pass which the poets spoke of as being done in the reign of Saturnus."[6] Paradisaical fantasy, like the unconscious world of our nightly existence, is not very insistent on precise chronology. Early in the nineteenth century Henri Saint-Simon stood Hesiod's mythic conception on its head and proclaimed: "The imagination of the poets placed the Golden Age in the cradle of mankind, in the ignorance and brutality of early times. It is rather the Iron Age that should be relegated there. The Golden Age of the human species is not behind us, it is before us."[7]

At intervals in the Hellenic world the central theme of the golden age was joined by the satellite myths of Elysium, Blessed Isles, Fortunate Isles, enchanted gardens. Elysium, which first appears in the *Odyssey,* is said to be a survival from Minoan religion. It is a death-free, comfortable retreat for heroes in a place that is neither Olympus nor Hades.[8] In Hesiod, when Kronos was overthrown by his son Zeus he was banished to the Isles of the Blessed to rule over the heroes there. Paradisaical climates are equally temperate in all times and places, eternal spring for the Eskimos, gentle zephyrs for the Greeks. The stream of the ocean is common to versions of the Elysian myth in both the *Odyssey* and *Works and Days,* though only in Hesiod is the haven explicitly an island. The human fetus, too, is an island, and in their island paradises men have often expressed a longing for the protective fluid that once surrounded them. In most paradises the maternal symbols are compelling and the idea need not be labored. Gardens, islands, valleys have reappeared with constancy through the ages. There is free feeding, security, peace, and plenitude, no rivalry. The vagueness of Homer's language in locating Elysium "at the end of the earth" gave exegetes an opportunity for play and they shifted its site about until Porphyry and Plutarch landed it on the moon, another female.

On occasion the themes of a golden age and Elysium crisscross with an otherworldly Orphic doctrine of Hades and the common man's Cokaygne utopia of Attic comedy. By the time of Pindar, a Theban of the fifth century before Christ who became the philosophical poet of Orphism, the population of Elysium had radically changed. In Homer, the next world had been located in two distinct regions, the dark underground Hades across the River Styx to which most men repaired as shades and the exclusive Elysium reserved for the immortal heroes. Under Orphic influence this division was modified by a doctrine of punishments meted out for breaches of the laws of the gods and by a belief in the transmigration of souls through successive existences and purifications until the final translation of a select group to the Blessed Isles. The cooling ocean breezes of this Orphic paradise of the pure recall Homer and Hesiod, but the environment has been newly enriched. Radiant trees and flowers of gold blaze all about and the blessed ones entwine their arms and crown their heads with chaplets. In a threnody related to Pindar's Second Olympian Ode, the immortal souls are more sportive than in the passive Homeric Elysium: "Some there delight themselves with feats of horsemanship and the athlete's practisings. Some with draught-play, others with the music of lyres."[9]

While in the *Phaedrus* Plato accepted into his own myth of the soul an Orphic doctrine, not unlike Pindar's, of three incarnations and a final release of the soul for the philosopher without guile or the philosophical lover, he was bitterly scornful of other Orphic promises of the afterlife in Elysium. In the second book of the *Republic,* speaking through the mouth of Adeimantus, he denounced the contemptible materialist rewards some Orphic poets in the name of the gods dangled before those who lived in justice and piety, and he mocked Musaeus and his son Eumolpus for their song of the alcoholic gratification in the next world that awaited righteous initiates into the mysteries: "They conduct them to the house of Hades in their tale and they arrange a symposium of the saints; where, reclined on couches and crowned with wreaths, they entertain the time henceforth with wine, as if the fairest meed of virtue were an everlasting drunk."[10] This paradise of vulgar delights was repugnant to Plato the censor, who would expel the poets from the city—even Homer and Hesiod—for prating about physical pleasures as a recompense for upright conduct.

The common folk of fifth-century Athens had a wish-fantasy of a sensuous paradise that was far closer to the Orphic poets than to Plato's philosophical haven of the soul. Among the manuscripts brought to Italy from Constantinople in the fifteenth century was a long-winded dialogue called the *Deipnosophists,* variously translated as *Banquet of the Learned* and *The Gastronomers.* Its author, Athenaeus, who flourished about A.D. 200, was a Graeculus born in Naucratis, Egypt. If Plato's is the utopia of the soul, these long, turgid discourses are a repository of fantasies of appetitiveness. The characters of the *Deipnosophists,* attending a symposium at the house of a rich landowner in Alexandria, instead of discussing lofty philosophical ideas in the Socratic manner, while away their time quoting from the whole corpus of Greek literature as far back as the eighth or ninth century before Christ on gastronomy, sexual behavior, medicine, law, and music, and reporting on customs associated with sensate pleasure throughout the world. The result is a Greek anthology of sorts, a pedantic display of learning that has acquired historical importance because many of the literary citations have survived nowhere else.

Excerpts from Greek comedy in the sixth book of the *Deipnosophists* reflect popular paradisaical imaginings in the latter half of the fifth century before Christ. In *The Miners* of the poet Pherecrates, a character who may be Persephone paints a sensuous paradise in the nether world for a comrade whose mouth salivates at the prospect of roast thrushes "craving ingurgitation" by ghostly lips. Emphasis is upon the spontaneous production of vast quantities of food and drink and their consumption; sexual desires are but lightly alluded to. The gluttony of the dead is an occasion for black humor, and the richness of their diet drives Persephone's interlocutor to call for immediate transfer to Elysium-in-Hades.[11] Greek fantasy skipped the early machine age and went directly to automation: cooking utensils and the victuals themselves respond to voice command. According to Telecleides in *The Amphictyons*, no one had to prepare food in the age of Kronos

> Since black loaves and white at men's lips used to fight
>> each asking the hungry to take it
> If they liked their bread fine; and as for the wine,
>> it filled ev'ry brook; and the fishes
> Came perfectly willing and did their own grilling
>> and served themselves up on the dishes.[12]

For the poets of the old comedy, the golden age was neither a venerated sacred myth nor a true history, but a subject of merriment. Through a process of adaptation, plays that were initially satires on the golden age and Orphic Hades became an integral part of the paradisaical myth, just as Lucian's works, written in mockery of classical utopias, served as a rich source for the local color and equipment of scores of modern ideal societies from Thomas More on. Set in another frame, the free consumption of wine that an Athenian artisan hankered after could assume a mystical, or Christological, significance. The daydream of a life in which every extravagant appetite is instantaneously appeased—aptly named the Cokaygne utopia after its reappearance in the *fabliau* of the Land of Cokaygne ("little cake") in early fourteenth-century France and England—has had an extraordinary vitality. Even the promise of green pastures in paradise paled before the robust reality of the medieval ballad-maker's Cokaygne west of Spain. In paradise there is only water to quench man's thirst; but in Cokaygne water is reserved for washing, while great rivers run with oil, milk, honey, and wine, and roast geese fly about advertising "Gees al hote, al hot."[13] Many of the same conceits, down to minute details, have been repeated not only in Attic comedy, English mummers' plays, and popular fables, but in Judaic and Christian descriptions of paradise, in legends of the Holy Grail, in the paintings of Breughel, and in nineteenth-century European and American ballads like *The Big Rock Candy Mountains,* with their streams of alcohol trickling down and their "lake of stew and of whisky too."[14] Whether the images were diffused in a literary form and through oral transmission or whether they are part of a collective gastronomic unconscious remains an insoluble question that nourishes the academic mind.

The marked preponderance of oral over sexual pleasures is a characteristic of the Jewish as well as the Greek popular fancies of paradise, which may either throw light upon their infantile character or bear witness that bread and wine have always been the heaven of the poor and the hungry. Of the three great religions, only Islam's Koran graces the couches of the elect in the future Gardens of Delight with damsels "restrained in glance, wide-eyed, as if they were eggs [or pearls], well-guarded."[15] The women depicted in the earthly paradises of the Renaissance epics, still deeply Christian in spirit, are, like Lilith, dangerous creatures. In the West paradise and sexual love have rarely coexisted.

A Garden Eastward in Eden

A parallel stream to the Greek golden age, the canonical version of paradise proper, an account of the Garden of Eden in chapter 2 of Genesis, has been recognized, at least since the eighteenth century, as a composite of separate texts one or more of which was written around the ninth or possibly the eighth century before Christ by priests of Israel—about the same time as Hesiod. Contemporary criticism, no longer content with attempts to isolate and date the discrete versions of Genesis—the Jahavist, the Elohist, the Priestly, and the other creations of the learned imagination— conceives of each of them as itself an embodiment of traditions going back much further in the religion of Israel, so that the date of final redaction loses some of its significance. While there was a time in the late nineteenth and early twentieth centuries when it was fashionable to view all elements of the biblical Garden of Eden as derivative from fragments of epic literature in the cultures of the Tigris-Euphrates Valley of the third and second millennia before Christ, the weight of biblical studies today is rather on the uniqueness and complexity of the myth in Genesis, and there is a tendency to underplay "origins" suggested by the reading of cuneiform texts. The Near Eastern myths nonetheless remain an integral part of the history of the paradisaical state, even if they no longer explain away the novelty of the biblical invention. Both are related to the oldest cultural stratum of Mesopotamia.[16]

The tablet of a Sumerian poem inscribed sometime before 1500 B.C. tells of the purity and peace of the mythic land of Dilmun, provided with water by Enki, and of the health and agelessness of its inhabitants. The place is described in a series of negatives that simultaneously conjure up before the mind's eye the spectacle of the evils of this world. "In Dilmun the raven utters no cries, the ittidû-bird utters not the cry of the ittidû-bird, the lion kills not, the wolf snatches not the lamb, unknown is the kid-devouring wild dog . . . The dove droops not the head, the sick-eyed says not 'I am sick-eyed,' the sick-headed says not 'I am sick-headed,' its old woman says not 'I am an old woman,' its old man says not 'I am an old man.' "[17] In the Akkadian Epic of Gilgamesh, for which versions exist from the second millennium, Utna-pishtim, survivor of the deluge, was made immortal and was settled with his wife "far away at the mouth of the rivers." After conquering the scorpion-people who guard the gate, Gilgamesh himself penetrates a beautiful garden whose trees, shrubs, and vines are all of precious stones—the carnelian and lapis lazuli bearing fruit lush to behold—and there Siduri dwells.[18] Rare stones and minerals—gold, bdellium, and onyx—reappear in Genesis and are even more common in an "Eden the garden of God" in Ezekiel—the sardius, topaz, carbuncle, diamond, beryl, onyx, jasper, sapphire, emerald—and in apocalyptic and Midrashic paradises. Are these merely signs of wealth and prosperity or do the gems recall the first glistening objects riveted upon the nursing infant, its mother's eyes?

While reasonable similarities can be found, there now is grave doubt whether the Sumerian epic of paradise, first published by S. H. Langdon in 1915, and Sumerian tablets relating to the Fall of man are tales of paradise in the sense of Genesis at all.[19] The first is considered to be a myth of the divine couple Enki-Ninhursag; the second, a story of the disobedience of man who failed to perform the work he owed the gods. Of the gardens appearing in the Gilgamesh epic, many are abodes of the gods, not terrestrial paradises for man; and the paradisaical land where Utnapishtim was borne to immortality is more like Hesiod's Isles of the Blessed and Homer's Elysium than a Garden of Eden. There may be, it is allowed, a number of para-disaical images in the "cedar mountain, abode of the gods, throne-seat of Irnini," and in the garden of Siduri, and the Babylonian story of creation, the *Enûma Elish* ("When Above"), is probably mirrored in biblical cos-mogony; but the identification of proper Hebrew names in Genesis with Sumerian words is now questioned, and so is the origin of the Fall in the Babylonian-Assyrian Adapa myth where a man squanders his chances to gain immortality. After a long period during which the higher criticism found virtually everything in the biblical paradise in texts of the Sumerian, Babylonian, and Assyrian world, the newest scholarship finds very little. But whatever the sources of the lines in Genesis, one stands in awe before the vast sea of commentary and hundreds of imaginative elaborations which over a period of almost 3,000 years have surrounded this handful of verses, as each generation read into them its own ever-renewed fantasy of a garden in the beginning of things. Were much of this literature not so tiresome, it could in and of itself provide the leitmotiv for a history of Western con-sciousness.

In the Hellenistic and Roman periods, tales of primitive peoples living in a paradisaical condition in the wilderness beyond the borders of civility were the products of a restless, discontented urban imagination. Soon enough this sophisticated primitivism incorporated the imagery of the myth of the golden age and the Judaic and Christian Garden of Eden. When new lands were discovered and explored, their primitive inhabitants were per-ceived in the light of the Greek and Hebrew myths, which psychically pre-determined what Europeans saw. Primitivism has an almost uninterrupted history from its inception through episodes of the Alexander legend and travel reports from the Hyperboreans, islands beyond the gates of Hercules, tribes on the Roman marches, and, in the Middle Ages, from the mysterious East. The search for the realm of Prester John, which captured the imagination of the late medieval world, is at once Christian paradisaical and primitivist.[20] This stream of thought finally becomes dominant, during the period from the sixteenth through the eighteenth centuries, in the myth of the noble savage with its syncretism of paradisaical longings and the exaltation of the virtues of uncivilized man. Missionaries were quick to see the Indians as living in either a golden age or a terrestrial paradise, but this episode is dependent for the strength of its impact upon revolutionary transformations in Jewish and Christian conceptions of paradise. By the time Europeans set forth in ships to cross the Atlantic and the Pacific and trekked over the vast continental expanses of America, always in quest of an earthly paradise, that dream had for many centuries been suffused with religious feelings of great potency—a historical continuum that is sometimes ignored by those who blithely write of the "rêve exotique" of the seventeenth and eighteenth centuries as an independent creation of that period.

The Shaping of Belief in the Talmud and the Midrash

The word paradise was not used by the Jews in the canonical writings of the Bible. The spread of conceptions of an ideal future state in another world as a reward for the righteous is usually postponed by scholars until after the Babylonian captivity, Persian influences being the supposed stimulus to the introduction of these beliefs. As anyone who has immersed himself in academic literature on paradise knows, whenever novelty intrudes there is an initial temptation to trace it back to the "East." The original Persian *pairidaēza* seems to denote a surrounding (*pairi* = Greek *peri*) wall made of a sticky mass *(daēza)* like clay or dough—an etymology to which, as Freudians of sorts, we are naturally partial, since it is more womb-like than the blander "royal park." In Persian mythology the oxhorn tree with a surrounding wall and vegetation rises from the world-wide sea of Vouru Kaša and is similar to the world mountain, a frequent Eastern location for the paradisaical garden.[21] The paradise of the other world also has a parallel in the Zoroastrian doctrine of aeons, known in the West through crude summaries in Herodotus and Plutarch. The final *apatiyārakīh* has been translated as "state-of-no-more-being-contested" and the Song to the Sōšyant (Savior) about resurrection and eternal life has been reconstructed to read: "Astvatrta will set forth from the water Kansaviya the champion of AhuraMazdāh and his other companions, that they make humanity frašam, not-aging, not-decaying, not-rotting, ever-living, ever-flourishing. When the dead will rise up, the reviver, the imperishable will come, he will make humanity frašam, please God!" Frašam means beyond "the last day of history, when the world has finished its ninth round, when time stops and eternity begins."[22]

While the Hebrew word *pardes* (garden), also of Persian origin, appears in a number of places in the post-exilic books of the Old Testament, the first use of the Greek *paradeisos* to translate *Gan Eden* (Garden of Eden) is in the Septuagint begun in the third century before Christ. In Greek and Latin Christianity this was the term employed for both the Garden of Eden and a future otherworld, and it was diffused into all European languages. The rabbinic texts of the Talmud never adopted the word paradise, and held to the phrases Garden of Eden, this world, the Days of the Messiah, and the World to Come to define the major divisions of time. As Jerusalem came to occupy a central role in the life of the Jews, this model of urban perfection, related to an idealization of the reigns of David and Solomon and symbolically represented by the Temple, became another equivalent of the paradisaical state and the origin of the idea of a heavenly Jerusalem.

At one time the messianic age of the Old Testament prophets referred solely to a future tribal or ethnic triumph of Israel over her neighboring enemies and was devoid of miraculous or unnaturalistic epiphanies; and only after the return from Babylon do universalist overtones keep insinuating themselves until the Days of the Messiah became a kind of wonder-laden prolegomenon to a final Judgment and an otherworldly paradise. Those curious about the origins of so radical a conception as the idea of a Messiah can turn to hypotheses about the recrudescence in an abstract form of a primitive ritual of the death and resurrection of a king-god whose being sustains his people. There is also a suggestive study of the dying Messiah as an archetype by a member of the Jungian school. And if these explanations fail to satisfy, one can always turn to the East.[23]

The nature of the Days of the Messiah and of the events that would precede and follow them enjoyed no general consensus in the sixty-three tractates of the oral law of the Talmud, whose interpretations of Scripture range over a period of almost a thousand years until their final codification in two different versions, the Babylonian and the Jerusalem, in the fifth and sixth centuries A.D. The eleventh chapter of the Tractate Sanhedrin in the Babylonian Talmud is devoted to the determination of who has a part in the World to Come. After an opening manifesto in its Mishnah—a division of the Talmud that incorporates the opinions of an early generation of rabbis known as the *Tannaim* and was already fixed by about A.D. 200—that "all Israel" has such a portion, the rabbis withdrew substantially from this open-ended promise. Certain grave sinners were denied entry, "he who maintains that the resurrection is not a Biblical doctrine, the Torah was not divinely revealed, and an Epiḳoros" (an adherent of the Epicurean philosophy and by extension one who led a dissolute life).[24] Ordinarily there was in the Talmud an underlying contrast between *Olam Haze*, this world, and *Olam Haba*, the World to Come, but that amphibious period on earth known as

the Days of the Messiah continually intervenes to complicate matters tem-
porally; nor is there any agreement about the substantive relationship of
the World to Come with the paradise of Adam and Eve in the beginning
of things, though there are doctrines of prefiguration to account for the
resemblance of the two states. At intervals in the history of the Jews there
has been a powerful resurgence of belief in the reign of the Messiah in this
world, usually accompanied by a conviction that the epoch was imminent
or had in effect already dawned. Faith in the advent of the Messiah was
probably most intense in Judaea in the second century before Christ during
the persecutions of the Seleucids, in the age of Bar Kochba's uprising against
the Romans, and during the mid-seventeenth-century messianic movement
of Shábbethai Zevi which gripped Jewish communities throughout the
world; but in some form trust in a messianic age at an unknown future time
is one of the constants of post-exilic Judaic religion.

Some Talmudic schools issued stringent admonitions against those who
presumed to compute the precise time of the coming of the Messiah, condemning them as propagators of disbelief. In the Tractate Sanhedrin Rabbi
Samuel ben Naḥmani is reported to have said in the name of Rabbi Jonathan: "Blasted be the bones of those who calculate the end. For they would
say, since the predetermined time has arrived, and yet he has not come, he
will never come."[25] But such imprecations did not prevent other rabbis from
making rough estimates of the three periods into which human existence on
earth was destined to be apportioned: "The world is to exist six thousand
years. In the first two thousand there was desolation; two thousand years
the Torah flourished; and the next two thousand years is the Messianic era;
but through our many iniquities all these years have been lost."[26] Judah the
Protector, in a flight of fancy, reckoned the duration of the messianic age at
365,000 years. Rabbi Joḥanan held that the son of David "will come only in a
generation that is either altogether righteous or altogether wicked."[27]

As for the nature of the other world, Talmudic opinion is equally in-
conclusive. Disputations about the resurrection of the dead, intimately related to paradisaical conceptions of the World to Come, rocked Judaic sects
in the last centuries before the Christian era, the Sadducees and the Samari-
tans denying the validity of any such doctrine. Corrupted texts led to the
perpetuation of many frivolous problems related to the resurrection, like the
saucy question "Queen Cleopatra" is reputed to have posed for Rabbi Meir
as to whether the dead arise naked or in their garments.[28] The birth of
Christianity made the whole problem of the coming of the Messiah and an
otherworldly paradise an extraordinarily sensitive one in Judaic thought, as
the rabbis found it imperative to demonstrate that the resurrection of the
dead was first foretold in the Books of Moses and was not in any way related to Christian revelations. The proper manner of distinguishing a true
from a false Messiah became critical for traditional Judaism and a vast body
of law grew up to make the identification at the appropriate moment.

There are many examples of loose Talmudic usage of the terms World to Come and Days of the Messiah, both of which were occasionally embraced by an even vaguer one, the Future to Come (*le-atid lavo*). In some texts the World to Come quite clearly refers to the plenitude of the paradise-like Days of the Messiah on earth, not to an otherworldly state. A *baraitha* (an opinion reported without the name of its authority) in Tractate Baba Bathra tells of the diversified crops that will then be allotted to everyman: "[In] this world [should] a man possess a cornfield he does not possess an orchard; [should he possess] an orchard he does not possess a cornfield, [but] in the world to come there will be no single individual who will not possess [land] in mountain, lowland, and valley."[29] Patently this is not the other world. Similar promises dating from the period of the *Tannaim* in Tractate Kethuboth remind one of the winey paradise of Attic comedy: "In this world there is the trouble of harvesting and treading [of the grapes], but in the world to come a man will bring one grape on a wagon or a ship, put it in a corner of his house and use its contents as [if it had been] a large wine cask . . . There will be no grape that will not contain thirty kegs of wine."[30] In the compilation known as the *Pesikta Rabbati* Rabbi Judah makes a valiant attempt to distinguish among the three stages of time by remarking upon the growing complexity of the harp that will be used in each one—there were seven strings in the harp of the Temple, there would be eight in the Days of the Messiah, and ten in the World to Come.[31] Obviously quantity is to be transmuted into quality. In other Talmudic passages the Days of the Messiah recall in a measure the ease of Hesiod's golden age when the earth yielded fruit *automate*. "There will be a time when wheat will rise as high as a palm-tree and will grow on the top of the mountains . . . the Holy One, blessed be He, will bring a wind from his treasure houses which He will cause to blow upon it. This will loosen its fine flour and a man will walk out into the field and take a mere handful and, out of it, will [have sufficient provision for] his own and his household's maintenance."[32]

From the period of the Talmud on, there was always a conservative body of opinion that strove to minimize the distinction between this world and the messianic age. Samuel in Babylon of the third century A.D. maintained: "This world differs from the Messianic era only in respect of the servitude of the Diaspora."[33] Under the Sassanian dynasty there was a concerted attempt to bank the fires of messianism. For many, even the World to Come after the resurrection would mean a continuation of the benign activities of this world.[34] Often there is a deliberate decision to stand silent on the otherworldly paradise. Rabbi Ḥiyya ben Abba said in Rabbi Joḥanan's name: "All the prophets prophesied [all the good things] only in respect of the Messianic era; but as for the world to come, 'the eye hath not seen, O Lord, beside thee, what he hath prepared for him that waiteth for him.'"[35] Even the patriarchs Abraham, Isaac, and Jacob, though as a rule well informed on the future of things, were according to some rabbis kept in the dark about the next world. And that nineteenth-century grandson of two rabbis, Karl Marx, remained in the same laconic tradition when it came to being circumstantial about his world to come.

It has been surmised that the reserve of the Talmud with respect to the *Olam Haba* is a reaction against the profuseness of Christian prophecy. But unincorporated Midrashim ascribed to individual rabbis, which represent a more popular layer of thought and are often of a later date, are more fulsome in pictorial detail. As in the Hellenic world there are class preferences in the representation of heaven. The otherworldly paradises of the common man's imagination allow for rather grand oral pleasures—the eating of Leviathan, for example, which God created with this ulterior purpose in mind. In popular Midrashic paradise there will be much feasting, drinking, joyousness, and each fruit will have a savor different from the next; the problem of sameness in heaven is resolved as 15,000 tastes are provided and as many perfumes. David will sing and say prayers, the angels will dance before the faithful. In the *Seder Gan Eden,* a Midrash where Mohammedan influences may be at play, "sixty angels stand on the head of each and every just man and urge him to eat honey with joy because he occupied himself with the Torah and to drink wine preserved in the grape from the six days of creation."[36] There are grand canopies to cover the heads of the elect and magnificent buildings for their habitation. Thomas Aquinas was later troubled about the age of a man at the time of resurrection. In the Midrash there are four transformations a day—childhood, youth, adulthood, and old age— as the whole of the epigenetic cycle, with joys appropriate to each state, is recapitulated. All men in heaven are as beautiful as Joseph and Rabbi Johanan were said to have been.

Of the few virtuous men who while yet in this world were vouchsafed a visit to paradise—such as Simon ben Yohai and Joshua ben Levi—all brought back the report of a play of blinding light from gems and precious metals. The tradition penetrated deep into Ethiopia where the pious hermit Gorgorios under the guidance of the angel Michael was shown the heavenly temple, a vision still preserved by the Jewish Falasha in the twentieth century: "There was in it a white sea pearl which shone brightly. Its light was brighter than the light of the sky. It was made of a shiny pearl and of pure gold, and the crown on its top was made of a green pearl like an emerald, adorned with three white pieces of silver that shone with so brilliant a light that no eye could look at it."[37] In paradise, as in the beginning, there shall be light.

In addition to oral, visual, auditory, and olfactory satisfactions—touch is excluded—the inhabitants of Judaic paradise are engaged in a major pursuit not featured in other heavens, the constant study of the Torah. This holds for both the Days of the Messiah and the *Olam Haba* in the Talmud, the Midrash, and the medieval Hebrew philosophical tradition. One underlying distinction between the two future worlds and this world resides in absolute freedom from material necessity, which permits a greater concentration on the Torah, in marked contrast with the relentless harassment by Satanic forces and Gentile persecution to which Israel is subjected in this world. In a number of popular Midrashic paradises God himself is director of studies; he finally unravels mysteries and explains the reasons for commandments whose meaning is now obscure, such as the dietary laws. In the various heavenly mansions each subdirector of studies is especially suited to guide the particular inmates. According to the *Midrash Konen* ("Of the Correct Order"), which has the most complete account, the Garden of Eden of the World to Come is divided into various classes of the just, and each occupies a separate structure.[38] Gathered in groups of families and tribes, they distribute their time between learning and praising God. The divine effulgence is enjoyed by each according to his deeds and his devotion to the study of the Torah in this world, a hierarchy of merit that has its parallel in the paradises of Augustine and Dante.

Finally, there can be discerned in the Talmud and the Midrash the beginnings of a mystical tradition on paradise that is different from both the sober and reticent rabbinic one and the earthy sensate one of the people. Its esoteric speculations and secret doctrines culminate in the Kabbala; but that contemplative paradise of which certain just men have a glimmer in this world partakes of the mystery of all Gnostic doctrine and can only be communicated to adepts—which excludes most readers of *Dædalus*. Though analysis of *Merkaba* symbolism, the vision of the divine chariot, is beyond my scope, the Kabbalist conception of alternative world orders, far superior to the one in which we languish, is reserved for the period of its full-blown development in the thirteenth century.

The Underthought of the Garden of Eden

In the first century of the Christian era the Garden of Eden was subject to a form of interpretation that came to be sanctioned by both Judaism and Christianity. In Hellenic culture it had long been accepted that myth had a *hypnoia*, an underthought, and that the literal sense was not the most profound one. Similarly, the oral law in Judaism was based upon the conviction that the commonsensical reading of the Scriptures yielded only one of a number of possible meanings. There were set rules for uncovering ancillary ideas and the secret, as contrasted with the overt, significance of each word and letter in the Bible.

Philo Judaeus of Alexandria, where at least half a million Jews lived in the first century, adopted the methodological tools of the rabbis in his commentary on Genesis, but he wrote in Greek and the spirit that animated him was often as Platonic as it was Hebraic. The precise relationship between some Midrashic interpretations of Scripture and the reading that Philo first designated as "allegorical" and passed on to the church fathers is much in dispute. When rabbis said that the four rivers of the Garden of Eden repre-sented the four world kingdoms which were to be, did they use an allegorical method in Philo's restricted philosophical sense? Whatever way one resolves this learned debate with its delicious evasive compromises—calling Mid-rashic readings "foresteps of allegory"—Philo's pivotal position in the his-tory of allegorizing in Judeo-Christian thought has been firmly established.[39]

While Philo did not depart from the Jewish tradition that accepted the biblical narrative as true in a literal sense, he left no doubt about his pref-erence for an interpretation of the Garden of Eden in the spirit of Platonic philosophy: the fruits of the garden were the virtues of the soul and the working of the garden the observance of the divine commandments. Many church fathers, though with different purpose, followed in his path: Origen, Irenaeus, and Cyprian made Eden an allegorical prefiguration of the church. "Of Paradise," Philo wrote in *Questions and Answers on Genesis,* "so far as the literal meaning is concerned, there is no need to give an explicit interpre-tation. For it is a dense place full of all kinds of trees."[40] Since it was on earth it ought to be somewhere, but Philo was unconvinced by the location generally assigned to the Garden of Eden in the Armenian mountains. "In that place there is no Paradise, nor are there two sources of the river. Unless perhaps Paradise is in some distant place far from our inhabited world, and has a river flowing under the earth."[41] Clearly he was more comfortable with the Garden as an allegory for wisdom or knowledge of the divine and the human and of their causes. "God sows and plants earthly excellence for the race of mortals as a copy and a reproduction of the heavenly . . . By the rivers his purpose is to indicate the particular virtues. These are four in number, prudence, self-mastery, courage, justice. The largest river of which the four are effluxes is generic virtue which we have called goodness."[42]

Once the Garden of Eden was opened up to symbolic interpretations, the method could induce the most untoward associations. To see the Gar-den as a typology for the future paradise in heaven was an easily acceptable extension of the meaning of Genesis; but soon Gnostics of the first century, flirting with Judaic and Christian tradition, resorted to extravagant fantasy. Simon Magus, the most notorious of the Gnostic heretics who perverted the doctrine of Christ and "foolishly and knavishly paraphrased the law of Moses," claimed that the Garden of Eden was not a real place but an alle-gory for the womb. Saint Hippolytus (A.D. 170–236), author of *The Refuta-tion of all Heresies,* our hostile source for Simon Magus' opinions, left an argument so congested with analogies between Genesis and the physiologi-cal state of a fetus in utero that it is often impossible to ascertain where the views of the heretic leave off and those of the bishop begin. While we despair of an accurate translation of his tract, it is of more than passing interest that a first-century Gnostic established a connection between the Garden of Eden and a womb. "Moses, says Simon, has given allegorically to the womb the name Paradise, if we ought to rely on his statement. If God forms man in his mother's womb—that is, in Paradise—as I have said, then let the womb be Paradise and the after-birth Eden, 'a river flowing forth from Eden, for the purpose of irrigating Paradise.' This river is the navel. This, he says, is divided into four branches; for on either side of the navel are placed two arteries, which serve as conduits for breath, and two veins, which serve as channels for blood."[43] Simon Magus' insight will be applauded by disciples of the Jungian school of psychoanalysis. For Carl Jung paradise was the positive aspect of the archetypal mother and he assimilated it to cognate symbols representing the goal of a longing for redemption, such as the Kingdom of God and the Heavenly Jerusalem.[44] Understandably, Jung has more to say about paradise and the millennium than Freud, who on clinical grounds was reluctant to stress universal symbols in the dreams of his patients—one looks in vain for paradise in his collected works.

Symbolic interpretations of the Garden of Eden have been many and varied. Ancient Hermetic writings saw it as the head rather than the womb. Church fathers said that it meant *serenitas mentis*, the *Zohar* that it connoted woman. Protestant commentators from the sixteenth through the eighteenth centuries were especially skillful in evading the literal meaning of the words of Genesis and discovering in them a hidden, abstract philosophical significance consonant with their own moral principles. By the seventeenth century, it was not uncommon to identify the historical origin of man's sense of guilt with Adam's discovery of his sexual nature in Eden, and on the basis of superficial auditory resemblances, the garden where Adonis and Venus cavorted was equated with the Garden of Eden. Adrian Beverland's *Peccatum originale* (1679) read every word in Genesis as a sexual "hieroglyph." The apple was *amoris symbolum, donare* was equivalent to *coire*, and *ramus, flos*, and *arbor* to *membrum virile*.[45] Most attempts at symbolic interpretation—and their authors included men of the stature of Immanuel Kant, whose *Conjectures on the Beginnings of Human History* (published in the *Berlinische Monatsschrift*, January 1786) transformed the narrative of Genesis into a hypothetical account of the birth of reason and free will—have had brief lives and leave one with the feeling of *suum cuique*. One major body of speculation on Genesis, however, the Kabbala of the thirteenth century, made a deep and lasting impress on Western thought.

Jewish Apocalyptic and Christian Millenarianism

By the beginning of the Christian era the Greek and the Judaic clusters of ideas on paradise were generally accessible in writing or through oral tradition to literate persons of the eastern Mediterranean, and elements from improbable sources were constantly cropping up in alien contexts. There are parallel visions in Jewish and Christian apocalyptic, as there are in patristic writings and Talmudic accounts of the messianic age and para-

dise. By now it is well established that personal relationships existed between Jewish and Christian seminarians in the same cities of Syria during
the early Christian centuries, and the adaptation of Talmudic and Philonic
exegesis on the Garden of Eden and paradise in the works of church fathers
can be amply documented.

That strange body of literature categorized during the last hundred
years as "Jewish apocalyptic" was composed from about the second century
B.C. to A.D. 150 by visionaries who assumed the identities of personages
from an earlier epoch to lend credibility to their prophecies. They are a
treasury of conceptions of an earthly paradise that is to accompany the messianic age, not always distinguishable from an otherworldly paradise. In the
seventeenth century Uriel da Costa, a tragic rebel who was expelled from
the Amsterdam synagogue, was the first to point out that the one complete
canonical work of Jewish apocalyptic, the Book of Daniel, was not written
during the reign of Nebuchadnezzar, King of Babylon, as the text itself pretends, but was produced later under the Seleucid hegemony by the Pharisees
to buttress their belief in a Messiah and in the resurrection of the dead.
Apocalyptic passages in other books of the Old Testament, as well as those
not included in the canon like the Book of the Secrets of Enoch, the
Book of Jubilees, Sibylline Oracles, Testament of the Twelve Patriarchs, II
Baruch, and IV Ezra, have been the subject of passionate scholarly inquiry
for more than a century since Friedrich Lücke pioneered *Apokalyptikforschung* in the early 1830's. The texts as they have survived—sometimes only
in Slavonic, Syriac, or Greek translation—are now thought to be composites
of manuscripts from different periods and their identification and dating
is a major enterprise. The discovery of the Dead Sea scrolls in 1947 has
excited a renewed interest in the subject, vastly enriched the literature of
Hebrew apocalyptic, and lent another dimension to our understanding of
the spiritual world into which Christianity was born. In a new interpretation
of apocalypticism, origins have very recently been pushed back to the
sixth century before Christ and the mythic material of Jewish apocalyptic has
been related to a recrudescence of "old Canaanite" mythic lore—without,
to be sure, eliminating from its later development Iranian, Mesopotamian,
and Greek borrowings.[46]

We cannot dispel the mysteries that still shroud the relations between
Jewish and Christian apocalyptic or judge between the "oriental" and Canaanite origins of the grotesque animal symbols of the apocalypses. Whether
the predictions of the visionaries represent a sharp break with ancient Jewish belief or are an outgrowth of Old Testament prophecy and whether the
apocalypses were normative or not in the centuries after Christ during which
Talmudic Judaism was taking form are questions that have not been
resolved. We stand in that period at a parting of the ways in the history of paradise. One branch moves in the direction of a legalistic, matter-
of-fact, and philosophic statement that will finally rigidify into dogma in

the synagogue and the church; the other will lead a more turbulent existence as it wanders through dark and mysterious caverns. Apocalyptic and mystical paradises with their marvelous predictions of heaven on earth and their poetic raptures about life in the other world were always suspect to the authorities, but they were never uprooted.

The bare elements of Jewish apocalyptic are clear enough. The paradisaical reign of a messianic king is foretold after the destruction of the enemies of Israel and probably of all evil in great and dreadful clashes. Vials of wrath are poured upon the unrighteous. In manuscripts from Qumran the final contest has a mild Zoroastrian cast: "When the children of Perversity are shut up then Wickedness shall retire before Righteousness as darkness retires before the light, and as smoke vanishes and is no more, so shall Wickedness appear like the sun."[47] The imagery of conflict in other works of Jewish apocalyptic, as in the most terrifying apocalypse of all literature, the Revelation of Saint John, is crowded with monsters, fornicators, prostitutes, whores of Babylon, crawling things of uncleanness—the innocence of the Garden of Eden has been polluted for the visionaries, and vengeance is theirs. Howls of rage precede the rebirth of the kingdom of virtue. The evocation of an imminent messianic era is far more vivid and dramatic, more tinged with the miraculous, more sibylline and cryptic, than the rather grave, sparse utterances of the Talmud. In Sanhedrin, 'Ulla, dismayed at the prospect of slaughter and devastation that would herald the appearance of the Messiah, cried out: "Let him come, but let me not see him."[48] Apocalyptic shows no such abhorrence of destructive fantasies; it revels in them.

The messianic age that follows the holocaust is an amalgam of paradisaical fantasies reminiscent of both the golden age nostalgia in Hesiod and Ovid and the "messianic" prophecies of the Old Testament. Peace will prevail, an earthly Sabbath that prefigures the eternal Sabbath of the World to Come. The enemies of Israel having been driven from the holy places, there will be friendship among the kings of the earth. For men there will be inner serenity and freedom from care, no unwilling engagement with practical things, and no forced labor. "The reapers shall not grow weary. Nor those that build be toilworn. For the works shall of themselves speedily advance."[49] Sin, corruption, punishment, and tribulation will be banished, as demons are either eliminated or subjugated. (Apocalyptic literature develops a complicated demonology and an equally intricate angelology.) There will be no more blind, poor, or hungry, no sadness or illness —birth itself will be painless—no mourning and no sighing, no tempests. In the latter half of the first century, II Baruch told of what shall come to pass in the end of the days: "And disease shall withdraw, And anxiety and anguish and lamentation pass from amongst men, and gladness proceed through the whole earth . . . And judgments, and revilings, and contentions, and revenges, And blood, and passions, and envy, and hatred, And whatso-

ever are like these shall go into condemnation when they are removed."⁵⁰
These euphoric prophecies from the tongues of men in extreme anguish have
been models for the apocalypse ever since.

In apocalyptic literature there is no one Messiah type, but a spectrum
from the plain to the wonder-working to the son of God. In Jewish apocalyptic he is a king of the House of David, or a priest, or a priest-king, or in
the Qumran texts the Rightful Teacher. Fission takes place and he can become more than one; there are Messiahs ben Joseph, ben Ephraim, ben
Menashe, Messiahs called Moses and Aaron. The Hebrew Book of Enoch
has two messianic ages in succession, each preceded by a cataclysmic
struggle. In the middle of the second century A.D. Phoenicia and Palestine
were still literally swarming with Messiahs each proclaiming the advent of
the new age in his own person, often with words of fire and brimstone.
Origen in his *Contra Celsum* has quoted Celsus' pastiche of a messianic
sermon, a distillation of apocalyptic modes: "I am God; I am the son of
God; or, I am the divine spirit; I have come because the world is perishing,
and you shall see me returning again with heavenly power. Blessed is he
who now does me homage. On all the rest I will send down eternal fire,
both on cities and on countries. And those who know not the punishments
which await them shall repent and grieve in vain; while those who are
faithful to me I will preserve eternally."⁵¹ The juxtaposition of aggression
against enemies and the outpouring of love for true followers and believers,
with promises of ineffable joy in victory, is a pattern of rhetoric for which
Jewish apocalyptic provided a prototype much used through the centuries,
often against the Jews themselves.

The Danielic prophecy of what would succeed the destruction of the
Fourth Monarchy, the Apocalypse of John, probably written during the
persecutions of Nero and Domitian, and a variety of Sibylline Oracles of
Judaic origin all fed the Christian millenarian spirit of the early centuries
after Christ. In a strict sense, millenarianism, or chiliasm, was originally
limited to a prophetic conviction, derived from a commentary on the fourth
verse of the twentieth chapter of the Apocalypse of John, to the effect that
Christ would reign for a thousand years on earth. The pivotal events of the
transition to the days of the millennium were depicted in well-worn images
of catastrophe: during a time of troubles empires crumble, there are titanic
struggles of opposing armies, vast areas of the world are devastated, nature
is upheaved, rivers flow with blood. On the morrow, good triumphs over
evil, God over Satan, Christ over Antichrist. As existential experience the
millennium of early Christianity is the counterpart of the Days of the Messiah
in much of Jewish apocalyptic. The bout of violence reaches a grand climax,
and then and only then is there peace—primitive priapic scenes are the
inescapable analogy.

However similar the spectacles of devastation, the angelology and
demonology, the animal symbolism, and the homilies on the reign of justice

on earth, the belief in Jesus separates Christian from Jewish apocalyptic. For Christians the Messiah has already come and expectations concentrate on a second coming; for Jews the messianic age, whatever its attributes, is a part of the future. The Qumran texts enormously improve our knowledge of the perfect order of the Essene communities in which these ideas grew and they enrich our comprehension of the background of Christianity, illuminating the flow of religious ideas throughout the Near East; but in the Qumran literature the Messiah has not yet become a heavenly savior. After the birth of Christ the barrier between those who believed that the Messiah had appeared and those who still awaited him was insurmountable. The paradisaical fantasies of Judaism and Christianity drifted apart but, as we shall see, not as radically as might be expected; both matured into orthodoxies and acquired heterodoxies.

Sabbatical millenarianism in the early Christian church developed a specific form of eschatology. A literal exegesis of the Psalmist's wonderment that a thousand days are as one day in the eyes of the Lord facilitated the reading of Genesis as at once an account of creation as it had actually happened and a prefiguration of the seven-thousand-year history of the world. The early church fathers Papias, Irenaeus, Justin, Tertullian, and Lactantius were all millenarians of this sort. Irenaeus, a second-century bishop of Lyons, was one of the first to divide world history into seven millennia, the last of which would be the reign of Christ on earth. Church fathers of the second century committed to the doctrine of the millennium were adroit in adapting images and rhetorical devices from the Talmud, Jewish apocalyptic, and popular fantasies. In his diatribe *Against the Heresies* Irenaeus prophesied in language that recalls the speaking victuals of Hades in Attic comedy: "The days will come in which vines shall grow, each having ten thousand branches and in each branch ten thousand twigs, and in each twig ten thousand shoots, and in each one of the shoots ten thousand clusters, and on every one of the clusters ten thousand grapes, and every grape when pressed will give five and twenty metretes of wine. And when any one of the saints shall lay hold of a cluster, another shall cry out 'I am a better cluster, take me; bless the Lord through me.' In like manner [the Lord declared] that a grain of wheat would produce ten thousand ears, and that every ear should have ten thousand grains, and every grain would yield ten pounds of clear, pure, fine flour."[52] In the *Divine Institutes* Lactantius, after foreseeing the enemies of Christ condemned to perpetual slavery, rhapsodized over the millennium in turns of phrase borrowed from the pagan poets: "The earth will open its fruitfulness, and bring forth most abundant fruits of its own accord; the rocky mountains shall drop with honey; streams of wine shall run down, and rivers flow with milk."[53]

The particular form of the world-week idea depended upon whether a millennium was conceived literally as a thousand calendar years or was a conventional term signifying an indefinite period of time, and upon whether the reign of Christ was interpreted materially or symbolically. Sabbatical millenarianism raised ominous questions. Was the seventh millennium to be an earthly kingdom like the golden age of the poets under Saturn, as Lactantius held, or did the Last Judgment end the world at the close of the sixth? Justin's seventh millennium was still of this world, though it was characterized by a complete cessation of sexual activity. Would there be a new creation on the eighth day?

Saint Augustine put the quietus on millenarianism as an official church doctrine, and the growth of ecclesiastical power in the Roman Empire coincided with a decline of this belief. For Augustine the dominion of Christ, the last of the epochs, had already begun; and the eternal Sabbath that was to follow the end of the sixth period was not of this earth. Christian millenarianism, however, was never extirpated and its recrudescence as heresy is continual, if sporadic, among Manichaeans, Messalians, Paulicians, Bogomilians, Patarians, and Albigensians, until its spectacular outburst in the age of the Reformation.

The Paradise of the Establishment

Unlike many rabbis of the Talmud, the church fathers unhesitatingly poured forth detailed expositions of how men would feel in the otherworldly paradise. While Talmudic depictions, such as they are, tend to be preoccupied with admission requirements, external arrangements, and the doings of the blessed, the church fathers dwell on the psychic state of the inner man. Saint Augustine, perhaps the greatest psychologist of religious life, has presented a subtle projection of his own deep needs and desires in a portrayal of paradise in the final chapter of the *City of God*. There is no equivalent in Judaism until the *Zohar*.

The felicity of the otherworldly paradise will be total, Augustine tells us; no conceivable good will be lacking. Conversely, it will not be tainted by any evil. Since heaven is freedom from labor, there will be nothing to prevent man from consecrating all his efforts to the praise of God. "Nam quid aliud agatur?"[54] God has promised Himself as the reward and loving Him is an activity that can go on without end, without alloy, without weariness. The whole human being will now be free to dwell on God since those bodily organs that on earth are devoted to the necessities of life will no longer be absorbed with such functions. We do not now understand the true nature and purposes of many parts of the body, surely not the meaning of their rhythms and proportions and harmonies. These will first be discovered to us in paradise and will then become available for laudation. If Augustine has moments of doubt about his capacity to define the power of movement that bodies will possess in heaven, he knows that their appearance both at rest and in motion will be beautiful. But these delights of the physical body are as nothing compared to the harmony that will prevail between body and spirit. Everything will be fitting. Neither body nor spirit will do contradictory things and the conflict raging in the breast of everyman in this world will subside. In heavenly paradise there are no inner spiritual wars, and no one will suffer opposition either from himself or from others. Had Augustine but foretold the end of alienation, the portrait of psychic wholeness would have stood complete for all time. Or perhaps only in Augustine's heaven can alienation from God the Father, the original terror of the religious man and the source of worldly feelings of alienation, be wiped away with transports of mutual love.

There will still be free will, though not freedom to sin; an intellectual remembrance of the bygone ills of the soul, without a sensible experience of their pain, even as a doctor knows the diseases of his patients. Paradise means the reign of eternal peace, the great Sabbath without evening. "There we shall rest and we shall see; we shall see and we shall love; we shall love and we shall praise. Behold what shall be in the end without end! For what is our end but to arrive at that Kingdom which has no end?"[55]

Commentators have signaled the communal nature of being in Augustine's heavenly state, *socialis*, whereas this world is *privatus*. His homilies use words like *familia, societas, consortium,* and *patria communis* to convey the prevailing spirit.[56] The *Enarrationes in Psalmos* keeps dilating upon the community of heavenly joys: "Commune spectaculum habebimus Deum; communem possessionem habebimus Deum; communem pacem habebimus Deum."[57] The painful privatization of man that a late Roman understood so well comes to an end as creatures are joined in everlasting harmony.

Despite the union of all men in the love of God, Augustine's heaven will not be an egalitarian society: a hierarchy of merit obtains, though Augustine cannot foresee precisely how the different degrees of honor and glory will be awarded. Whatever the system of distribution, it will have the unique quality, inconceivable in this world, of arousing no envy. And why should there be? Do archangels envy angels? The finger does not seek to be the eye when both members are consonant parts of the body. The gift of contentment, to desire no other than one has, is the supreme virtue of the heavenly condition.

There are of course less attractive aspects to paradise in some of the earlier church fathers, when the triumph of Christianity was still far from assured and its enticements had to compete with the cruel and debased pleasures of the Roman arena. Abrasive Tertullian had reserved the blessedness of direct reception into paradise immediately after death for martyrs only. "The sole key to unlock Paradise is your own life's blood."[58] Ordinary Christians would have to remain in safekeeping in a Hades until the day of the Lord. Other passages in Tertullian bear out Nietzsche's contention that much of the Christian otherworldly paradise is the invention of a slave-man's *ressentiment* and a fantasy of vengeance against his masters. The *De Spectaculis* comes to a climax in a vivid apostrophe: "What a city, the

New Jerusalem! How vast the spectacle that day, and how wide! What sight shall wake my wonder, why my laughter, my joy and exultation? As I see all those kings, those great kings, welcomed (we are told) in heaven, along with Jove, along with those who told of their ascent, groaning in the depths of darkness. And the magistrates who persecuted the name of Jesus liquefying in fiercer flames than they kindled in their rage against the Christians! . . . Such sights, such exultation—what praetor, consul, quaestor, priest, will ever give you of his bounty? And yet, all this, in some sort, are ours pictured through faith in the imagination of the spirit . . . I believe things of greater joy than circus theatre or amphitheatre or any stadium."[59]

From among the schoolmen, perhaps the opinion of Saint Thomas Aquinas will suffice to show that orthodox institutional Christianity from Augustine on lived for hundreds of years with a fairly constant official view of the otherworldly paradise. With the same skill that he refuted gentile heresies Aquinas dismissed those who held to a millenarian reign of Christ on earth. Firmly fixed in the central tradition of the church, he knew that there was to be one Last Judgment, without intermediary paradisaical ages. But what would existence be like after the universal raising of the bodies, the good and the evil, and their summons before Christ?

In the Aquinian drama there is an initial movement of souls to their designated areas in heaven and hell immediately upon the separation of the soul from the body. But the Last Judgment, conducted by Christ and his assessors, is an event of a different order. The evil bodies are condemned to eternal suffering because their souls are set forever against God, while the good souls rejoin their bodies for a life everlasting—resurrected at their best age, the age of the young Christ. We are assured in the *Summa contra Gentiles* that bodies will retain all their physical characteristics male and female, as well as the organs for ingestion, even though they will be of no practical utility since neither generation nor corruption will take place and there will be no purpose in copulation or eating. Bodies will be totally submissive to souls and not have refractory wills of their own, and souls will be interested only in the contemplation of God.[60] Aquinas was repelled by what he considered the sensate paradises of the Mohammedans and the Jews, with their pleasures of venery and eating. Though the resurrected are not ghosts or spirits, their joys are wholly spiritual. More than five hundred years later, a mad French genius, Auguste Comte, in painting the future of humanity translated Aquinian heaven into nineteenth-century biological language. In the earthly paradise of his Religion of Humanity, the ape of Catholicism, he foresaw a new man nourished solely on odors (a compromise with the total spiritualization of Aquinas) and procreation through female parthenogenesis without the intervention of a male seed. Sexuality remains for centuries the forbidden fruit of maternal paradises, celestial and earthly.

The major philosopher of medieval Judaism, Moses Maimonides, was

as inimical to any miraculous Days of the Messiah as Aquinas was to millenarian doctrines—was to be expected from a stalwart of the Judaic
establishment, Aquinas' opposite number. For Maimonides the Days of the
Messiah, since it had long traditional sanction, was a necessary state before
the World to Come; but like some Talmudic rabbis he did the next best
thing to eliminating it entirely when he reduced it to a natural part of this
world's time, distinguished from the rest primarily by the termination of
Israel's exile and subjection.[61] Maimonides interpreted the prophecy of
Isaiah in a naturalistic manner as a promise of the reign of a Judaean King-
Messiah, and the lying together of the lion and the lamb became an allegory
for a future age when the Gentiles, likened to wild beasts, would stop their
vexation of Israel. "Think not," he wrote in *Hilkhot Melakhim* (*The Laws
of Kings*), "that in the Days of the Messiah any terrestrial custom will be
nullified, or that there will be any novelty in creation; but the world will
pursue an ordinary course . . . The [great] desire of the Sages and the
prophets was not for the Days of the Messiah, not that they might rule over
the whole world . . . or eat and drink and make merry, but that they might
be accounted worthy of life in the World to Come."[62]

The Deviations: Kabbala and Joachite Prophecy

If Maimonides epitomized conservative medieval Judaism, there was
that other world of the Kabbala, rich with an inheritance of Gnostic and
Midrashic traditions and fertile with inventions on all aspects of creation—a
world that lay open to those who risked entry into the mystical garden.[63]
The doctrines of the Kabbala were given their magnificent canonical form
in the *Zohar* (*The Book of Splendor*), whose basic text is believed to have
been written by Moses de Leon in pseudo-Aramaic sometime after 1275
and represents an ingathering of Kabbalist traditions that had been accumulating in Germany, Provence, and Catalonia. What most Christians
came to know of the Kabbala in the Renaissance and in the seventeenth
century were the allegorical interpretations in the *Zohar*, and from this
canon stemmed the great Jewish efflorescence of Kabbalist thought in the
sixteenth century associated with the name of Isaac Luria of Safed. The
commentary on Genesis with which the *Zohar* opens identifies Adam and
Eve as the Father and the Mother; the Garden as the Shekinah (Divine
Radiance and Female Principle) on earth; Eden as the supernal Mother;
and the man as the Central Column. "The Shekinah was to be his planta-
tion, his spouse who was never to depart from him and was to be his proper
delight. Thus God at that time planted Israel as a holy shoot, as it is written, 'the branch of my planting, the work of my hands, in which I glory.'"
In the presence of paradisaical images of this character, whose full meaning was revealed only to initiates, the medieval Kabbalist lived. An entire
section of the *Zohar* called the "Rav Mithivtha" is a visionary journey through

future paradise and a discourse by one of the heads of the celestial academy on the destinies of the soul in the other world. The décor is traditional: glistening columns, rivers of floating pearls, fragrant reservoirs. There is more attention paid to the fortunes of just women than in Talmudic paradise, and though males and females are segregated during the day, the souls of spouses are allowed to embrace at midnight.[64]

The Kabbalistic allegorist in this world had access to a vision of the *Merkaba*, the throne-chariot of God, and could in anticipation absorb something of the odor of those secrets and mysteries of the upper world that strictly speaking belonged to the messianic age and were preserved there for the time to come.[65] The effect of ritual action here below on celestial and cosmic reality forged mystery relationships that were subversive of traditional rabbinic performance. In Kabbala each ritual served a function in the eternal order; it was not an individually limited act but had cosmic consequences, and without it a lack would have been created in the universe. A pious human deed effected a change leading to the final redemption of Israel and the coming of the paradisaical world.

A part of the existing text of the *Zohar* known as the "Raya Mehemna" (Faithful Shepherd) is a very late thirteenth-century interpolation written in imitation of the rest of the work; it is of inferior literary quality with none of the glorious imagery that distinguishes the original composition. While the anonymous author still honors the traditional centrality of the law, he is seriously troubled by the nettlesome problem of the role assigned to the 613 commandments in the Days of the Messiah, when human nature will have changed. Are not all prohibitions and precepts made supererogatory by a spiritual revolution in mankind? Instead of living under the rule of the tree of good and evil, man will be restored to the Edenic rule of the tree of life, and the divine will be suffused through all things. The Torah will continue to be the guide, but its commandments will assume a new and more profound meaning. There are contemporary scholars who discern here the influence of the Spiritual Franciscans who preached the eternal gospel of Joachim of Fiore. The ambivalence of the Kabbalist author, the tension between his commitment to the law of the Torah and the need to envisage a spiritual transformation in the Days of the Messiah, has a manifest parallel in the Joachite prophecy of the third *status* and the new man of the Reign of the Holy Ghost. In the Middle Ages Judaism and Christianity thus continued to harbor within them deviations which promised a heaven on earth to a regenerated man, a baffling creation of the religious imagination that was forthrightly rejected by the authorities. More astonishing, both of these doctrines so interpreted written Testaments and Torahs revered as eternal and absolute that they were transcended.

An even more heterodox Kabbalist tradition was excluded from the *Zohar* and embodied in an anonymous work, probably of Catalonian origin and with roots in the school of Gerona, that was known by the year 1280 as the *Sefer ha-Temunah* (*The Book of the Image*). It had its partisans and practitioners along with the *Zohar*, and in periods of messianic possession like the mid-seventeenth century enjoyed great prestige. A late thirteenth-century commentary on the *Sefer ha-Temunah* has made a good deal of its esoteric symbolism comprehensible, though the present-day master interpreter of this text confesses that even to him the language is not always pellucid. The parallelism between the conceptions of the Catalonian Kabbalists and those of the followers of Joachim of Fiore, who died in 1202, is striking, though there is no convincing proof of any direct relationship or mutual influence between them; nor can it be demonstrated that Joachim was of Jewish descent, an accusation made during his lifetime. The two are coupled in this essay because they represent contemporaneous complex doctrines of other worlds that were in flagrant contradiction to their respective religious establishments and yet were allowed to survive. In a way the *Sefer ha-Temunah* is the more far-out.

Traditions about a plurality of worlds that would succeed one another in the course of cosmic revolutions have ancient origins—Hindu, Magian, and Greek. The idea that divinity was not restricted to one creation but would continue to fulfill itself in a whole series of creations assumed a radical form in the *Sefer ha-Temunah*, where the doctrine of aeons, or Schemittas, broke through the confines of traditional biblical chronology with its five- to six-thousand-year timespan and posited a long succession of worlds. The Schemittas are cosmic cycles with beginnings, middles, and ends, and human existence is qualitatively different in each of them—this is no Stoic doctrine of eternal recurrence. Our world is in the second Schemitta under the sign of *Gevura* (power) or *Dín* (Law) and by all odds is the worst of all possible aeons. Both the preceding one that was dominated by *Hesed* (Benevolence) and the next one under *Rachamim* (Compassion) are far superior in nature, and so will be all future worlds until the coming of the aeon of *Sabbath*. While we now live under the force of law, we can look back to a paradisaical aeon in which there were only pure souls luminous as clear water; there were then no diaspora, no transmigration of souls as punishment, no lost souls, no serpent, no evil desire, no uncleanness. In the past Schemitta worship was not regulated, but was a spontaneous effusion. Abraham, symbol of benevolence in our world, was a remnant of what all creatures once were like. This world is always a struggle with desires and our Torah is full of prohibitions that raise a barrier against them. The Torah of that former world had only commandments "to do," no "thou shalt nots." The coming aeon of Compassion will witness a return to wholeness in all things. Even the moon will not wane. There will be no families, only one great family, no death until the end of the Schemitta and then death with a kiss. The symbols of light and water are pervasive: men will lead bright and translucent lives, like the angels. They will eat manna, not grain; their sabbaths will be long; absolute equality will prevail among them.

That the Torah was one and immutable was an article of Jewish faith defended with fierce tenacity against the pretensions of the new revelations of the Christians and the Mohammedans. Along came the dauntless author of the *Sefer ha-Temunah* to posit a Torah with a new phase for each Schemiṭṭa, depending upon the character of its controlling force. Instead of one revelation, that of Mount Sinai, there are at least three: the first a Torah Kaduma, a heavenly Torah that was the paradigm, so to speak, which God looked into when he created the world; the second, the written Sinaitic Torah; and the third, a Torah which is amenable to constant transformation. When this fluid conception of the Torah is combined with a doctrine of Schemiṭṭas, a wholly different view of past, present, and future emerges that is quite alien to dominant rabbinic thought as enshrined in the Code of Maimonides. The idea that a whole new letter might be added to a future Torah is only hinted at, but the revolutionary possibility that the known Torah might be entirely revamped dismayed the orthodox. The only path to conciliation lay in the belief that each of the new Torahs was but a finite and partial revelation of the Torah Kaduma according to which the world had once been fashioned.

The complex numerology of the cycles and their duration until the fifty-thousand-year jubilee need not detain us, nor the intricate changes in the Hebrew alphabet of successive aeons. For our purposes, the most compelling aspect of this work is the combination of a paradisaical retrospect and a paradisaical prospect on a cosmic scale. Unlike similar formulae in Jewish apocalyptic, each aeon fulfills its course in a slow, natural way, and the awful, catastrophic crises of epochs of transition to the Days of the Messiah are conspicuously absent, as they are in Joachite thought. Tenderness and softness fill the spiritual atmosphere, and there is a palpable unease with the rigor of the law.

The Joachite Reign of the Holy Ghost

Toward the end of the thirteenth century the Abbot Joachim, a Calabrian monk who had known the mighty at the Norman court of Sicily, a former Cistercian who had fled to the wild mountains of San Giovanni in Fiore to found a more stringent rule, was illuminated with a vision of the true meaning of cryptic passages in the Old and New Testaments, and was inspired to write of a new historical order in which the Church of Christ would be superseded by the reign of the Holy Ghost on earth. To this day Joachim has remained under a cloud in the Catholic Church, though during his lifetime he was honored by Popes and was never declared a heretic. There are rival schools of thought on virtually every aspect of his life and teachings. Some have discovered in him the hidden inspiration of the whole of Dante's *Divine Comedy*, the clue to the enigmatic Veltro; others have transformed him into a great historical villain responsible for what they call the secularized gnosis of all modern revolutionary movements.

Joachim was heir to the exegetical, topological, allegorical, and numerological traditions on paradise, the Days of the Messiah, and the millennium that had been accumulating in the West for centuries. These he fashioned into a symbolism uniquely his own. There are three states (*status*) in progression, corresponding in their essential natures to the three persons of the Trinity; each state is in turn divisible into seven periods (*aetates*), which are named after characters from sacred history. The *Concordance of the Old and the New Testament,* one of his few authenticated works, is the mystical key to the system. Every saintly father in the first dispensation has an opposite number in the second; the saints of the third state, which is just dawning, are precursors for the *Dux* of the new age, and Joachim regards himself as a John the Baptist. Life in the world is no longer a relentless Augustinian struggle between two cities only one of which can be victorious, but a stadial ascent toward goodness and absolute love. The Reign of the Son that was born of the Reign of the Father is to give way to a new perfection in the Reign of the Holy Ghost on earth.[66]

To depict the persons of the Trinity not only as theological, but also as historical realities was a hazardous innovation when it entailed an order of excellence among them, flagrantly diminishing the position of Christ and downgrading the gospel to a prologue of an earthly state of perfection. Whether Joachim envisioned the total and absolute supersession of the clerical and sacramental church or only its spiritualization, perhaps a shift of monasticism from a peripheral to a central position, remains moot. With doctrines of renewal there is always a problem as to whether renovation can take place within the establishment or whether the order has to be completely refashioned. In all forms of messianism and millenarianism a cleavage exists between those who require a new birth, with the imagery of a return to the womb and an expulsion from it (as in the eighth-century Midrash known as the *Pirke de Rabbi Eliezar*) and those who would minimize the differences of the new and see it as a mere restoration of the old or a fulfillment of what the ancients had always intended. Joachim at no time defaulted in his personal obedience to papal authority and he may not have been aware of the profundity of the chasm between his views and the institutions of the church.

The reign of love on this earth, love from the heart, can dispense with the law of both Testaments. Judgment Day is indefinitely postponed and its awesome sting is removed by the transitional third stage of the Holy Ghost. The great expectation for which Joachim prepares the faithful is not an apocalyptic end of the world and a transcendent resolution in heaven, but a more immediate event, the appearance within a generation of the Holy Ghost on earth. As with the Greek Orthodox tradition of a benign apocalyptic emperor whose reign precedes the Second Coming of Christ, so the third state of Joachim eases the passage to the Last Judgment, rendering the break between this world and the next far less frightful than it is in Augustinian Christianity.

Joachim's numerological symbolism is an intrinsic part of his work; everywhere he finds meaning in the numbers twelve and seven and forty-two, and they serve to give arithmetic solidity to the equation of parallel periods and generations among the three states. The crucial date of the new era was 1,260 years after Christ, proved with an exegetical virtuosity that ranges from Daniel and Revelations through Judith, who waited in her widowhood three years and six months or forty-two months which contain 1,260 days—ergo the reign of the New Testament will last 1,260 years. But though the Joachite predictions and the secret numbers of the heterodox Kabbalist writings are comparable, there are also important differences between them: the Kabbalists dealt with cosmic processes, while Joachimism, however interpreted, remained absorbed with changes that occurred on earth alone.

The cumbersome Joachite apparatus is less significant than the attributes with which he clothed his three states. To their radically different characters he devoted the zeal that other mystics poured into their definition of God. The *Concordia* tells us that in the first we were under the law, in the second we were under grace, and in the third we shall be under still richer grace. The first was knowledge, the second was the power of wisdom, the third will be the fullness of knowledge. The first was spent in the submission of slaves, the second in the obedience of sons, the third in freedom. The first in suffering, the second in action, the third in contemplation. The first in fear, the second in faith, the third in love. The first in starlight, the second in dawn, the third in broad daylight. Joachim's was a rich symbolic vocabulary that had resonances for centuries after his death. The ardent longing for a new man breaks through, the man who has seen the vision of Jacob's Ladder and the heavens thrown open, when the Holy Ghost descended on earth to teach him the fullness of knowledge and to strengthen his will. "Life should be changed because the state of the world will be changed."[67] The active life immersed in dross must be replaced by the pure contemplation of spiritual man, who will also be wise, peaceful, and lovable, a man stripped of the vice of envious emulation. "We shall not be what we have been, but we shall begin to be other."[68]

From the thirteenth century on, followers of Joachim were fired by his progressionist history to preach of the new man of the Third Kingdom and of the eternal gospel. The record of the reverberations of Joachite prophecy in the later Middle Ages has recently been assembled in Marjorie Reeves's voluminous study.[69] That Joachim was a hidden force in heterodox medieval thought is proved beyond question by the inventory of his manuscripts —authentic, probable, possible, and false—that have survived in European libraries.[70] Many a thinker on the borderline of Catholic orthodoxy discovered in him a predecessor, and either adopted his writings or ascribed his own to him, so that in time there emerged within the church an amorphous body of Joachite thought, an uncondemned heresy or one that was formally denounced only in its most extravagant pretensions. The name of Joachim became a magnet that drew to it hopes of a most diverse character ranging from the aspirations of the two new monastic orders whose existence seemed to confirm his prophecy, through the Arthurian romances and the quest for the Holy Grail, to fanatical antiecclesiastical exponents of a new age beyond the church. The Joachite tradition had an active, unbroken existence well into the seventeenth century, even though the content of life in the new kingdom underwent a series of transformations and the savior changed with the soil in which the prophecy was acclimated: the *Dux* was successively an angelic pope in Italy, a reborn Charlemagne in France, a revived Frederick III in Germany, even a universal Spanish monarch who in an act of self-denial would hand over his power to the Pope—the fixed idea of Tommaso Campanella who during his interrogation by the Inquisition insisted that he was merely reviving the prophecies of Joachim.

The Common Man's Heaven on Earth

Toward the end of the Middle Ages paradise ceased to be merely a dream and became a catalyst for brazen and adventurous deeds on earth. In its Christian form the paradise fantasy is a significant component of both the millenarian resurgence in Protestantism and the voyages of discovery; in Judaism after the expulsion from Spain, Kabbalism sparked the proponents of direct action, which culminated in the popular agitations of the seventeenth century with their grand delusion of a false Messiah. Religious enthusiasts, no longer content with passively waiting for the paradise of the next world, demanded the consummation of the times, the founding of the kingdom of heaven on earth immediately. Their insurgency assumed many different shapes over the next two hundred years: the proclamation of Münster as Jerusalem by the Anabaptists; the rather parochial English millenarianism of the Fifth Monarchy men; the messianic movement of Shabbethai Zevi.

When in the fourteenth and fifteenth centuries there were popular uprisings of artisans and peasants in which religious hostility to dignitaries of the church was joined to the endemic antagonism of the poor against rich lords and burghers, where could men turn but to the Bible for a society other than the odious one they were rejecting? The rationalist utopias of the Greek philosophers were beyond their ken. Perhaps echoes from the ancient Cokaygne utopia resounded in popular folklore; but these were ephemeral compared with the paradisaical states that could be drawn from the Bible and its prophecies. The Hussites in their new capital of Tabor dreamed of a patriarchal order whose rulers would model themselves on the fathers of the Old Testament. Flemish weavers went further back, to the Garden of Eden, and demanded the nudity and simplicity of the first man, the naked truth. (A quest for the truth spiritual and the nakedness of the body have accompanied visions of rebirth down to our own day.) The Old Testament prophets were read in a fresh light as a social gospel. Ultimately, a new chosen one was discovered, Thomas Müntzer's *gemeiner Mann,* a common man, and a path was opened that led to the nineteenth-century slogan of Etienne Cabet, "Le communisme c'est le vrai christianisme."

In the period before the Reformation, millenarian beliefs and movements of social revolt had interpenetrated. The Taborites designated five cities that were to be spared in the general conflagration, and multitudes gathered in these havens to establish communal societies. Norman Cohn has shown the affinities among the visions and activities of the leaders of the *pauperes* during the Crusades, the delusions of the *pastoureaux,* the belief in the legend of Frederick's reign after his awakening from a long sleep, the doctrines of the Brethren of the Free Spirit, and the apocalypse of the Taborites.[71] Always a prophet is the charismatic leader; Antichrist and his cohorts are identified with the rich, the powerful, the Jews, the ordinary clergy; a day of reckoning with much bloodshed is foretold, to be followed by an earthly reign of the good emperor or the mystic leader or by Christ himself. The language is an admixture of the prophecies in Daniel, Revelation, and the Sibylline Oracles. In the writing of the "anonymous revolutionary of the Upper Rhine" the Holy City is transferred from Jerusalem to Mainz and the rebirth takes on a deep Germanic coloration.

Some notion of the earthly paradise instituted by the Brothers of the Free Spirit is conveyed through the testimony of John of Brünn about 1330. Initiates went through two stages: first an ascetic one, during which they surrendered all their property and became beggars; then one of absolute liberty in which they were enjoined to heed all the promptings of their new, emancipated natures on pain of falling away from their freedom. "I am of the Free Spirit, and all that I desire I satisfy and gratify. Should I seek a woman in the still of the night I satisfy my craving without any feelings of conscience or sin; for the spirit is free, and I am also a natural man. Therefore I must freely satisfy my nature by deeds."[72] In Laurence of Brezova's Hussite chronicle there is a glimpse of the Taborites wandering shamelessly about like Adam and Eve in the Garden, dancing naked, and lying with each other, all under the leadership of one they called Moses.[73] In the later history of utopias there is an alternative to the more prevalent rule of sexual regulation in a fantasy of promiscuity, but this is a comparatively rare phenomenon in Western culture.

Melodramatic stories about millenarians of the Reformation period who acted out their dreams have been told often enough. The proclamation of the king of the world in Münster, the restoration of primitive Christianity, the reinstitution of polygamy, and the abolition of the distinction between mine and thine are events that lend themselves to easy ridicule. Prophetic seizures, the advance against the bullets of the enemy armed with nothing but faith in the prophet, executions and plundering, famished men, women, and children eating grass like beasts in hope of the millennium became symbols of the deception and madness of paradisaical fantasies. The image of John of Leyden gorging himself while his followers starved in community was difficult for egalitarians to live down. When David Hume in his treatise on morals wants to dismiss communism with a phrase he has only to raise the specter of the Anabaptists.

From among a host of stereotyped millenarians, Thomas Müntzer is beginning to emerge as a unique figure, largely through the efforts of Soviet and German historians and their close analysis of his sermons, theological tracts, and purported confessions.[74] Unfortunately they have brought forth two rather contradictory interpretations. Müntzer was no ignorant peasant enthralled by a vision. Of all the activist millenarians, this preacher was the most learned in Scripture, in the fathers, in the writings of medieval prophets; he even had an acquaintance with classical literature. Despite the obvious megalomania of some of his pronouncements, there was in him a rationalist core rare among the enthusiasts, which led some Germans of the Enlightenment to claim him as a predecessor and Friedrich Engels to celebrate him as the first modern revolutionary theorist. Luther had written the princes of Saxony that Müntzer was a tool of the devil and had called for his suppression. In the *History of Thomas Müntzer* (1526) that was once attributed to Melanchthon, his doctrine is described as a lazy man's *Schlaraffenland*. "He taught that all goods should be held in common as is written in the acts of the apostles. In this way he encouraged the people so that they no longer wanted to work. If anyone wanted food or clothing he went to a rich man and demanded it as a Christian right."[75] This was the old Müntzer legend, and the evidence for much of it, a confession extorted under torture after his defeat at Frankenhausen, is rather thin. The reality is far more complex.

According to the work of the Soviet historian M. M. Smirin, Müntzer took the prophecy of Daniel that the power of the heavens would be given to the "people of the saints of the most High" to refer to the common people, and he linked the clamor for land of a peasant uprising with the promise of a heaven on earth that entailed a transformation of religious consciousness. Though he cherished the witness of the Abbot Joachim, Müntzer's Kingdom of God was not designed for a sacred monastic brotherhood but for the embattled peasants in rebellion against their masters. Müntzer established an important conjunction in world history, the union of revolutionaries with a communal ideal that recognized the unique spiritual worth of the ordinary man.

The Scriptures had set forth the truth of the new order, but—and this was the subversive part of the Müntzer dispensation—its illumination was not equally available to all men. There was superior understanding in the common man over the upper classes, whose luxurious situation blinded them to a full comprehension of the inner word. "For the stone [of the Holy Ghost] torn from the mountain [Christ] has become mighty and the poor laity and peasants see it more sharply than you do," he thundered at the princes in his sermon on Daniel.[76] Devotion to the reign of God on earth required prior emancipation from pride and self-seeking, and only those already burdened with nothing were capable of that freedom. Müntzer, who signed himself Destroyer of the Unbelievers, preached a heavenly life on earth that could be attained by bestowing the power of the sword on the whole community and by cultivating internal perfection and the *Verstand* of the poor. In Müntzer the millenarian doctrine of the earthly paradise assumed a class character, a revolutionary moment in the history of the idea. Paradise acquired a political definition.

But some West German historians reject any presentation of Müntzer as either a descendant of Joachim or a forerunner of Marx and emphasize the purely theological aspects of his teachings. The times were about to be fulfilled, Judgment Day was at hand, and he Müntzer was a Daniel redivivus come to guide those who were willing to renounce the corruptions of this world and to let the fear of God suffuse their whole being in preparation for the imminent apocalyptic event. Luther's acceptance of the external dominion of the princes alongside the Christian liberty of the inner man was for Müntzer a Satanic doctrine because it involved acquiescence in the wicked order of this life and a deflection to mere creatures of part of the *Gottesfurcht*, which should be concentrated on Him alone. The coming of His kingdom was dependent upon an active mystical participation of all the elect in the eradication of evil with the sword, and Müntzer turned to the poor artisans and peasants as the chosen ones of his Christian brotherhood because they were less contaminated by the world and did not usurp to themselves powers that belonged to God alone. One is hard put to it to discover in Müntzer's authenticated writings any promise of rich material rewards for the artisans and peasants. He prophesied the spiritual freedom to be possessed by God, a conception that harks back to mystical ideas rather than looks forward to a heaven on earth.[77]

The two academic Müntzers seem to be proceeding their respective ways without much hope of a convergence. In the history of modern utopia, however, Müntzer probably remains frozen in the role into which Engels cast him, the revolutionary before his time. If there is any common denominator to the rival interpretations, it lies in the realization that Müntzer's paradise, whether of this world or after the terrible Judgment

Day, was to be brought about by the organization of a mighty host brandishing swords against the princes of evil.

Columbus at the Parting of the Four Rivers

The church fathers debated for many centuries the question of whether an earthly paradise still existed somewhere. Although there was some sympathy for Philo's allegorical interpretation of the second chapter in Genesis, the weight of opinion favored a literal reading of the text, and excluded any skepticism about the reality of a garden from which the four rivers of Pison, Gihon, Hiddekel (Tigris), and Euphrates flowed and which still harbored a few blessed ones. But if it was an actual place and no symbol for wisdom or virtue, where was it? The Tigris and the Euphrates were easily identified; the other two rivers were not, and relating them to the Ganges and the Nile only complicated the problem of discovering a common origin. The Bible said that the Garden of Eden was to the east, a direction that shifted with the stance of the commentator and the geographical world-view of his time. Medieval maps bear witness to the widespread conviction that there was an actual place called terrestrial paradise. Usually Jerusalem was in the center of a circular mappamundi and paradise was above it, at the edge of the water in which the island of the earth floated. Well into the seventeenth century Christian scholars devoted themselves to composing treatises on the situation of Eden. Bishop Huet's in 1698 was perhaps the most famous of modern times.[78] Since then, new locations have been regularly proposed, including a recent one beneath the polar icecap.

In their descriptions of the Garden of Eden, medieval poets introduced new elements from patristic commentaries, and in the thirteenth century the romances about the search for the Holy Grail became related to the quest for an earthly paradise. The tradition that the crucifix came of a tree that had once stood in the Garden cemented the connection between a crusade for the recovery of the true cross and the longing for the terrestrial paradise. According to Lars-Ivar Ringbom's bold hypothesis, motifs and architectural forms from the Zoroastrian sacred city of Šiz, excavated in 1937, continued to influence European pictorializations of paradise throughout the Middle Ages. Khosar II, the Sassanid king, had invaded Jerusalem in A.D. 614 and carried off the cross to his own capital; in revenge, the Emperor Heraclius had sacked Šiz ten years later and retrieved it. During this movement back and forth numerous decorative details from the royal palace at Šiz were supposedly transmitted to Europe, where they reappeared in paleo-Christian churches, in hermits' visions of paradise, and in the romance of the Holy Grail by Albrecht von Scharffenberg.[79]

The belief was common in the medieval world that things physically contiguous were similar to each other. If the Nile was one of the rivers flowing out of paradise, the nearness of Ethiopia to its source made inhabitants of the region seem rather paradisaical to the Christian imagination. Penetration of the Garden of Eden itself was prohibited by the archangel with the flaming sword, but one might come upon almost blessed peoples in the areas adjacent to it. The legend of the Christian-Ethiopian Emperor Prester John was related to paradise because his lands bordered the Nile; he also answered the need for an ally on the eastern flank of Islam and fitted in with Joachite belief in the coming of an Emperor-Redeemer. In 1460, the last year of his life, Henry the Navigator still hoped to pay him a visit, and Vasco da Gama carried letters addressed to him. Pierre d'Ailly's *Imago Mundi*, which Christopher Columbus studied with great care, gathered up all the tales of Prester John. The paradisaical myth was like a web growing ever more intricate as the centuries passed and fibers that were once quite distinct became entwined.

Columbus' letter on his third voyage in 1498, when he reached the mouth of the Orinoco River and its four tributaries and then hastily withdrew in fear, exemplifies the continued force of the myth of paradise in the Western imagination well into the Renaissance.[80] It also affords at least an inkling of the unconscious psychic meaning that paradise has had for some men. The facts of Columbus' overt behavior are plain enough. According to his reckoning of elevation as he approached the Orinoco (he had been taking measurements of the North Star), he seemed to be mounting; and the turbulence of the currents at the mouths of the river indicated that the waters were running downhill from some high place. The idea that the Garden of Eden was at the highest point on earth was supported by the knowledge that it had survived the flood, which in turn was proved by the fact that the living Enoch and Elijah had been wafted there. The four rivers into which the Orinoco branched, like those of Eden, were sweet; the natives were nude, handsome, and gentle, to be expected of those living in the neighborhood of paradise. As the Book of Genesis and Ezekiel reported, there were gold and precious stones in the vicinity. And, on the basis of Columbus' calculation of his geographic position, the mountain garden was located toward the east. The arguments from authority, the descriptions in Genesis, the astronomical measurements, the evidence of his eyes, and the taste on his lips all coincided and led him to surmise that he was at the foot of the Holy Mountain. There was only one difficulty: this great elevation around the equinoctial line ran counter to the view he had accepted before he embarked on his voyages that the world was a perfect sphere. Now that he had discovered the mountain of paradise, he would have to reject d'Ailly and Aristotle and conceive of a new shape for the earth. In a burst of fantasy, he concluded that it was for the most part indeed round like a *pelota muy redonda;* but on one side it had a stalk that protruded and pointed upward toward the heavens. (He used the word *pezón,* which can be both the stalk of a fruit and a teat.) The earth was thus more like a pear than a sphere (*en la forma de una pera*), rather like a woman's breast with a nipple on it (*una teta de mujer*).

One can hardly avoid reflecting that it was in the proximity of the terrestrial paradise that this image of the nipple on the breast thrust itself into Columbus' revised theory of the earth's shape. References to the mountain of paradise as the *pezón de la pera* and the *teta de mujer* on the round breast of the earth both appear twice, in two different places in the same letter; it was no casual analogy. Columbus was manifestly in a state of disarray. He was close by the terrestrial paradise, but he knew, as he wrote to the Spanish sovereigns, that no one might enter it except with the will of God. Frightened by the forbidden paradise and the ultimate secret it held, he fled back to Hispaniola.[81]

We have the letter Columbus wrote to Ferdinand and Isabella only in a copy by Bartolomé de las Casas, but its contents jibe with the published testimony of Peter Martyr on the history of the voyages. It is replete with references to traditions on paradise in d'Ailly, the Book of Ezra, Isidore of Seville, Bede, Ambrose, and Scotus. And a mere perusal of Columbus' annotations on his copy of d'Ailly's *Imago Mundi* shows at a glance how frequently he had underlined and commented on references to Joachim of Fiore and his prophecies of a new paradisaical age.[82] Columbus always insisted that his "execution of the affair of the Indies" was a fulfillment of prophecies in Isaiah and not a matter of mere reason, mathematics, and maps. Whether the great voyages of discovery represent a need for rebirth, as a contemporary psychoanalyst has conjectured, we do not know;[83] but Columbus' strange conduct suggests that the paradise fantasy not only has power to draw men to the place related to memories of the earliest moments of happiness, but can also be inhibitory.

We are prepared to accept the idea that mother-yearning has underlain a great many of the quests for paradise, that Western images of paradise have enfolded recollections of existence in the womb or the perinatal months of life, and that some paradisaical images describing a future rebirth recapitulate the actual experience of birth. But granted that the myth of paradise as a maternal symbol has meaning, this association of ideas should not lead to simplistic reductionism. Paradise is more than a longing to reestablish the blissful union of mother and child. It is a complex state that has had a history—mythic, dogmatic, mystical, activist—and, as Nietzsche taught, only that which has no history can be defined.

The manifold uses of paradise have surely not been exhausted in this essay. We have avoided discussing its two most magnificent embodiments in Western culture, the poems of Dante and of Milton; nor have we dared undertake a study of the paradise of the painters and an inquiry into their iconography. In poetry and art the conceptions analyzed here reached a point of high tension and would require a separate and very different kind of treatment, as in the elegant studies of A. Bartlett Giamatti and Harry Levin.

Paradise Now

Once Graeco-Roman culture was assimilated by the church, paradise was, as we have seen, commonly infused with elements from the similar though distinct Greek myth of the golden age and its variants. Yet this Hellenic stream has been tributary to the main paradisaical cult: the church fathers were always quick to assert that histories of the golden age in Greek poets from Hesiod down were either literary plagiarism of the true story of the Garden of Eden, or at best prefigurations. When during the classical revival of the Renaissance the imagery of the golden age threatened to establish itself as a separate entity, poets and philosophers sharply reaffirmed the religious and historical primacy of the Christian over the pagan myth, which was denigrated as mere imitation. As the myth of paradise assumed a secular form in Thomas More's *Utopia* and hundreds of works were composed after his model from the sixteenth through the eighteenth centuries, pictorial details from the classical corpus of golden ages, cities of the sun, imaginary Hellenic societies, and ideal Greek philosopher-states were allowed to intrude. The underlying psychic force, however, remained profoundly Judeo-Christian. The most incongruous devices and fragments from Greek and Roman literature could be incorporated into paradise, without impairing its religious character. In the monastic visions of the Middle Ages, and in the romances that flowered in the thirteenth century, Celtic and Norse myths were also admitted, as Islamic motifs had been during the Crusades, but only when they could be rendered harmonious with Judeo-Christian paradise.

When plain belief in religious paradise became attenuated, utopia took over. The natural history of paradise might serve as an introduction to the history of the self-conscious, deliberately fabricated utopias of modern times, and in most of them vestiges of paradise can be discovered, like the structures of superseded forms in biological evolution. One need only be reminded that *Utopia* itself was written by a Christian martyr who achieved sainthood. There is hardly a problem related to Eden, the messianic age, or the otherworldly paradise that is not rehearsed in utopian literature. Pansophia, which underlies the serious utopias of the seventeenth century—those of Campanella, Bacon, Andreae, Comenius, and Leibniz—is still profoundly Christian and in the direct paradisaical, often mystical, tradition.

But there is also a distinction between religious paradise and modern utopia that establishes a caesura in the history of the paradise cult. The paradises of Judeo-Christian religion were brought into being by a transcendent God, and the time and nature of His Creation were dependent upon His will alone. Utopia is man-made paradise on earth, a usurpation of His omnipotence. It is a Promethean act of defiance of the existing order of the world, and though the order that is substituted usually partakes of the soft, maternal attributes of a religious paradise its founder is a bold human hero. King Utopus was a conqueror who cut the umbilical cord, a strip of land that once joined the island of Utopia to the mainland; Bacon's New Atlantis was the invention of the wise Salomon; the ruler of Campanella's City of the Sun—and solar imagery is universally masculine—was an all-knowing, all-loving, and all-powerful man; Veirasse's Severambians were defeated by King Severias who then became their monarch and lawgiver. Virtually all of the utopia-writers identified themselves with their activist heroes—More daydreamed that he was King Utopus, and Veirasse's Severias was an anagram of his own name. In Hesiod's myth, Prometheus hid the fire he stole in the hollow of a fennel stick, a marvelous advertisement of male sexual potency, and utopian authors—Bacon and Campanella and Marx—were great admirers of the Prometheus figure. The Messiahs of Judaism and Christianity may also have been prototypes for the utopian rulers; but the religious saviors were always direct emissaries of God, carrying out His will, while in the utopias, even when the fiction of a vague, otherworldly power is preserved, He is remote and the stress is on the initiative and autonomy of the earthly leader.

Were the histories of paradise and of utopia connected, the eighteenth century prior to Condorcet might paradoxically turn out to be the least paradisaical of all Christian centuries and the least utopian. The age that witnessed a great proliferation of what by any definition of the term would be called utopias did not produce a single major work in this genre— Condorcet belongs to a new generation. While the number of utopias increased, they became playful literature for the ladies, the make-believe embarkations for Cythera to whose existence no one gave credence. Few philosophes, Stoics that they were, had faith in an everlasting utopia either for themselves or for posterity. There is no article on utopia in Diderot's *Encyclopedia* and the utopian writings of Thomas More, Francis Bacon, and Tommaso Campanella are treated with a measure of contempt in that *summa* of the age. Too much of the odor of Judeo-Christian paradise still clung to utopia, and the anticlericals who were trying to cut the ties that bound them to the church either mocked utopia or were deeply ambivalent about its promises. Rousseau is the noteworthy exception to the prevailing skepticism of the philosophes, but what a fall from Judeo-Christian Eden does his hypothetical savage in the state of nature represent! And what a turbulent, passion-ridden "autre monde" is unveiled in *Rousseau juge de Jean-Jacques!* Instead of hearkening to the paradisaical commandment against the admission of the passions, the Genevan heretic would heighten and magnify all sensibility a thousandfold.

The biological and anthropological discoveries of the nineteenth and twentieth centuries completed the subversion of the Edenic myth—the further back one went the more bestial man appeared, and the idea of a heavenly paradise could no longer have a prototype on earth in the beginning of things. The earthly uchronias of the nineteenth century were thus born into a barren spiritual landscape, and their creaky character as ersatz religions is apparent. They point up how difficult is the search for a terrestrial paradise .when man is bereft of belief both in a Garden of Eden that might serve as a restorative model and a future otherworldly heaven.

But written and oral tradition on the paradisaical state is not yet extinct. There is still a paradise in the collective conscious of the West, a rich repository with myriad interconnections available to those who write fantasies or organize movements. The emotional potency of these images derives from aspects of the myth that reanimate deep-rooted psychic experiences and may kindle a hope for rebirth, for another chance. The myth, religious or secular, serves a purpose in the psychic economy, for it makes possible the continuance of living in the unease of civilization. This fantasy, as Freud thought of all religion, is perhaps unworthy of adults. But it has its consolatory role, like the narcotics whose perennial utility Freud seems to have recognized, without becoming quite as incensed about them as he was about religious narcosis. To bathe in the waters of paradise or utopia for a precious while has made existence bearable for man under the most ghastly conditions. There is even a mild gratification in reading and writing about paradise. The myth can be accepted in different degrees and be correspondingly efficacious—from the absolute faith of a Christian martyr, through the formal belief of a Jew whose funeral ritual includes a promise of immediate transfer to the Gan Eden, to the humanist utopia of More who can "wish for" the optimum republic more than he can "hope for it." There are times when, by its very divorcement from reality, the paradise myth can sustain the most heroic actions of men. Tertullian offered converts to Christianity the enjoyment of the psychic pleasures of paradise from the moment of their acceptance of the new faith, and Condorcet after him extended to all revolutionaries the secular adaptation of this beatitude in the end of his *Esquisse,* when in the shadow of the guillotine he wrote of the private Elysium which "his reason has created for itself and which his love for humanity enhances with the purest pleasures."[84]

The paradise fantasy is still alive, whether in the form of Baudelaire's "paradis artificiels" and their successors like the Paradisio Club in Amsterdam, or in revolutionary utopias, or in the survival of old-fashioned Christian millenarian religions, or in the cargo cults of primitive peoples.[85] But the unique contemporary predicament of Western civilization, with its frantic demand for paradise *now,* can be understood only against the shadowy background of those two other paradises "in the beginning" and "in the world to come" whose images grow ever dimmer. The question remains: Can paradise be anything but ephemeral when two of the three paradises—the past and the future—that composed a traditional triune have vanished and paradise has to be compressed into the fleeting present? Of the thousands of paradisaical settlements that have been founded in

Europe and America since the seventeenth century only the religious ones, which recognized the other segments of time, have exhibited any signs of longevity—which augurs ill for the lifespan of the current spate of communes in young America. For those without faith, there is probably only the reality principle or a chemical paradise. And who knows which is the bitterer?

At intervals one is seized with a desire to be free of the childish fantasy of paradise once and for all, to be rid of those Messiahs, pseudo-Messiahs, half-Messiahs, prophets and charismatic leaders, the sons of God, the ben Josephs, the ben Davids, the ben Menashes, the ben Ephraims, the world-historical personalities, who promise a heavenly kingdom on earth after an apocalyptic combat with the incarnation of evil and who in the end turn out to be as horrible in the flesh as the monsters they have slain. But if paradise was born of that mystical union between mother and child, is it not man's fate to oscillate forever between a longing for the return of that state and disillusion when it finally arrives? The flux and reflux of belief in paradise then becomes a part of the order itself, and do what you may, destroy its traditional religious foundations, abolish Eden and the world to come, paradise will reappear in a new place, still drawing its children to Joachim's reign of the Holy Ghost on earth, to the third state of Auguste Comte, to Marx's Highest Stage of Communism, to Teilhard's Noösphere, and even, caricature of caricatures, to Consciousness III.

REFERENCES

1. *Hesiod*, trans. Richmond Lattimore (Ann Arbor: University of Michigan Press, 1968, c. 1969), p. 31. An earlier version of part of this section appeared in Frank E. Manuel, "The Golden Age," in *Freedom from History and Other Untimely Essays* (New York: New York University Press, 1971).

2. H. Diels, *Die Fragmente der Vorsokratiker*, 6th ed. (Berlin: Weidmann, 1951), I, 362-363, Empedocles, Fragment 128.

3. K. Müller, ed., *Fragmenta historicorum graecorum* (Paris: A. Firmin Didot, 1841-1868), II, 233ff; Jean Jacques Rousseau, *Discours sur l'origine . . . de l'inégalité*, in *Oeuvres complètes*, Pléiade ed. (Paris: Gallimard, 1964), III, 199.

4. Ovid, *Metamorphoses*, with trans. by Frank Justus Miller, Loeb Classical Library (Cambridge, Mass.: Harvard University Press, 1960), I, 9, 11.

5. See A. Bartlett Giamatti, *The Earthly Paradise and the Renaissance Epic* (Princeton: Princeton University Press, 1966), pp. 300-303.

6. Lactantius, *The Divine Institutes*, Book VII, chap. 24, in Alexander Roberts and James Donaldson, eds., *The Ante-Nicene Fathers*, VII (Buffalo: Christian Literature Publishing Co., 1886), 219.

7. Henri de Saint-Simon, *De la réorganisation de la société européenne*, in *Oeuvres choisies* (Brussels: F. Van Meenen, 1859), II, 328.

124   FRANK E. AND FRITZIE P. MANUEL

8. Homer, *Odyssey,* trans. E. V. Rieu (Harmondsworth: Penguin Books, 1946), Book IV, 77-78.

9. Pindar, *Works,* trans. Lewis Richard Farnell, I (London: Macmillan, 1930), 333, Fragment 129.

10. Plato, *Republic,* with trans. by Paul Shorey, Loeb Classical Library (Cambridge, Mass.: Harvard University Press, 1958), I, 131.

11. *The Fragments of Attic Comedy,* ed. and trans. John Maxwell Edmonds, I (Leiden: E. J. Brill, 1957), 247, 249.

12. *Ibid.,* I, 183.

13. Quoted in A. L. Morton, *The English Utopia* (London: Lawrence and Wishart, 1952), pp. 12-13, 15.

14. *Ibid.,* p. 29.

15. *The Qur'ān,* trans. Richard Bell, II (Edinburgh: T. and T. Clark, 1939), 444, Surah XXXVII.

16. Genesis, with introduction, translation, and notes by E. A. Speiser (Garden City, N.Y.: Doubleday, 1964), p. 19.

17. "Enki and Ninhursag: A Paradise Myth," trans. S. N. Kramer, in James B. Pritchard, ed., *Ancient Near Eastern Texts Relating to the Old Testament,* 2d ed. (Princeton: Princeton University Press, 1955), p. 38.

18. "The Epic of Gilgamesh," trans. E. A. Speiser, in Pritchard, ed., *Ancient Near Eastern Texts,* pp. 95, 89.

19. See T. C. Vriezen, *Onderzoek naar de Paradijsvoorstelling bij de oude Semietische volken* (Wageningen: H. Veenman, 1937); A. Heidel, *The Gilgamesh Epic and Old Testament Parallels,* 2d ed. (Chicago: University of Chicago Press, 1949); Umberto Cassuto, *A Commentary on the Book of Genesis,* trans. from the Hebrew by Israel Abrams (Jerusalem: Magnes Press, 1961); B. Strade, "Der Mythus vom Paradies. Gen. 2, 3, und die Zeit seiner Einwanderung in Israel," *Vierteljahrsschrift für Bibelkunde,* I (1903), 267-271.

20. See Henri Baudet, *Paradise on Earth: Some Thoughts on European Images of Non-European Man,* trans. Elizabeth Wentholt (New Haven: Yale University Press, 1965); Charles L. Sanford, *Quest for Paradise* (Urbana: University of Illinois Press, 1961); E. L. Tuveson, *Millennium and Utopia* (Berkeley: University of California Press, 1949); E. L. Tuveson, *Redeemer Nation: The Idea of America's Millennial Role* (Chicago: University of Chicago Press, 1968); George H. Williams, *Wilderness and Paradise in Christian Thought* (New York: Harper, 1962).

21. Leroy A. Campbell, *Mithraic Iconography and Ideology* (Leiden: E. J. Brill, 1968), pp. 129-130.

22. Ernst Herzfeld, *Zoroaster and His World* (Princeton: Princeton University Press, 1947), I, 297, 299.

23. See Hugo Gressmann, *Der Messias* (Göttingen: Vandenhoeck and Ruprecht, 1929); S. H. Hooke, "The Myth and Ritual Pattern in Jewish and Christian Apocalyptic," in S. H. Hooke, ed., *The Labyrinth* (London: Society for Promoting Christian Knowledge, 1935); Willy Staerk, *Die Erlösererwartung in den östlichen Religionen* (Stuttgart: Kohlhammer, 1938); Jean Joseph Brierre-Narbonne, *Le Messie souffrant*

dans la littérature rabbinique (Paris: P. Geuthner, 1940); Rahel Wischnitzer, *The Messianic Theme in the Painting of the Dura Synagogue* (Chicago: University of Chicago Press, 1948); S. O. P. Mowinckel, *He That Cometh; The Messianic Concept in the Old Testament and Later Judaism,* trans. G. W. Anderson (New York: Abingdon Press, 1954); Joseph Klausner, *The Messianic Idea in Israel, from Its Beginning to the Completion of the Mishnah* (New York: Macmillan, 1955); Siegmund Hurwitz, *Die Gestalt des sterbenden Messias; religions-psychologischen Aspekte der jüdischen Apokalyptik* (Zurich: Rascher, 1958); Joseph Coppens, *Le Messianisme royal, ses origines, son développment, son accomplissement* (Paris: Editions du Cerf, 1968).

24. *Sanhedrin,* trans. H. Freedman (London: Soncino Press, 1935), II, 601, 602.

25. *Ibid.,* p. 659.

26. *Ibid.,* p. 657.

27. *Ibid.,* p. 663.

28. *Ibid.,* p. 607.

29. *Baba Bathra,* II, trans. Israel W. Slotki (London: Soncino Press, 1935), p. 503.

30. *Kethuboth,* II, trans. Israel W. Slotki (London: Soncino Press, 1936), pp. 721-722.

31. *Pesikta Rabbati. Discourses for Feasts, Fasts, and Special Sabbaths,* trans. W. G. Braude (New Haven: Yale University Press, 1968), I, 415.

32. *Kethuboth,* II, 721.

33. *Sanhedrin,* II, 613.

34. *Ibid.,* pp. 614, 615.

35. *Ibid.,* p. 670.

36. *Seder Gan Eden,* in Adolf Jellinek, ed., *Bet ha-Midrasch,* II (Jerusalem: Wahrmann, 1967), 52.

37. Wolf Leslau, *Falasha Anthology* (New Haven: Yale University Press, 1951), pp. 84-85.

38. Ḥayyim Jacob Slucki, ed., *Midrash Konen* (Vilna, 1836).

39. H. A. Wolfson, *The Philosophy of the Church Fathers,* 2d ed. (Cambridge, Mass.: Harvard University Press, 1964), I, 38.

40. Philo, *Questions and Answers on Genesis,* trans. Ralph Marcus, Loeb Classical Library (Cambridge, Mass.: Harvard University Press, 1953), Philo Supplement I, 4.

41. *Ibid.,* p. 8.

42. *Philo,* with trans. by F. H. Colson and G. H. Whitaker, Loeb Classical Library (Cambridge, Mass.: Harvard University Press, 1929), I, 175, 189.

43. Hippolytus, *Philosophumena ou Réfutation de toutes les hérésies,* trans. A. Siouville (Paris: Rieder, 1928), II, 22-23; see also *Refutationis omnium haeresium,* ed. and trans. L. Duncker and F. G. Schneidewin (Göttingen: Dieterich, 1859), p. 245, and *The Ante-Nicene Fathers,* V (Grand Rapids: Eerdmans, 1951), 77.

126 FRANK E. AND FRITZIE P. MANUEL

44. Carl Jung, *The Archetypes and the Collective Unconscious*, in *Collected Works*, IX, Part I (London and New York: Routledge and Kegan Paul, 1959), 81.

45. Adrian Beverland, *Peccatum originale* (Leiden: D. à Gaesbeeck, 1679), pp. 33, 35, 37, 38. See also Martin Metzger, *Die Paradieserzählung; die Geschichte ihrer Auslegung von J. Clericus bis W. M. L. DeWette* (Bonn: H. Bouvier, 1959).

46. Frank M. Cross, "New Directions in the Study of Apocalyptic," in Robert W. Funk, ed., "Apocalypticism," *Journal for Theology and the Church*, 6 (New York: Herder and Herder, 1969), 165.

47. A. Dupont-Sommer, *The Essene Writings from Qumran*, trans. G. Vermès (Oxford: Basil Blackwell, 1961), p. 327. On the general question of apocalyptic, see Joshua Bloch, *On the Apocalyptic in Judaism* (Philadelphia: Dropsie College, 1952); Harold Henry Rowley, *The Relevance of Apocalyptic: A Study of Jewish and Christian Apocalypses from Daniel to the Revelation*, rev. ed. (New York: Association Press, 1963); Harold Henry Rowley, *Jewish Apocalyptic and the Dead Sea Scrolls* (London: Athlone Press, 1957); Krister Stendahl, ed., *The Scrolls and the New Testament* (New York: Harper, 1957); Frank M. Cross, *The Ancient Library of Qumran and Modern Biblical Studies* (Garden City, N.Y.: Doubleday, 1958); Dietrich Rössler, *Gesetz und Geschichte: Untersuchungen zur Theologie der jüdischen Apokalyptik und der pharasäischen Orthodoxie* (Neukirchen Kreis Moers: Buchhandlung des Erziehungsvereins, 1960); Johann Michael Schmidt, *Die jüdische Apokalyptik: die Geschichte ihrer Erforschung von den Anfängen bis zu den Textfunden von Qumran* (Neukirchen-Vluyn: Neukirchener Verlag des Erziehungsvereins, 1969); André Feuillet, *L'Apocalypse: état de la question* (Paris: Desclée de Brouwer, 1963); Joseph Schreiner, *Alttestamentlich-jüdische Apokalyptik: eine Einführung* (Munich: Kösel-Verlag, 1969); G. R. Driver, *The Judaean Scrolls* (Oxford: Basil Blackwell, 1965).

48. *Sanhedrin*, II, 665.

49. II Baruch, 74 (1), in R. H. Charles, ed., *The Apocrypha and Pseudepigrapha of the Old Testament in English* (Oxford: Clarendon Press, 1913), II, 518.

50. II Baruch, 73 (2, 4), *ibid.*, II, 518.

51. *Origen against Celsus*, Book VII, chap. 9, in *The Ante-Nicene Fathers*, IV (Grand Rapids: Eermans, 1951), 614.

52. *Irenaeus against Heresies*, Book III, chap. 33, in *The Ante-Nicene Fathers*, I (Grand Rapids: Eermans, 1950), 563.

53. *The Divine Institutes*, Book VII, chap. 24, in *The Ante-Nicene Fathers*, VII (Buffalo: Christian Literature Publishing Co., 1886), 219.

54. St. Augustine, *De Civitate Dei*, ed. J. E. C. Welldon (London: Society for Promoting Christian Knowledge, 1924), II, 642.

55. *City of God*, Book XXII, chap. 30, trans. J. W. C. Wand (London: Oxford University Press, 1963), p. 416.

56. Emilien Lamirande, *L'Eglise céleste selon Saint Augustin* (Paris: Etudes Augustiniennes, 1963), p. 245.

57. *Enarrationes in psalmos*, 84, 10, in *Corpus Christianorum. Series Latina* (Turnhout: Brepols, 1966), XXXIX, 1170.

58. Tertullian, *A Treatise on the Soul*, in *Ante-Nicene Fathers*, III (Buffalo: Christian Literature Publishing Co., 1885), 231.

59. Tertullian, *Apology. De Spectaculis*, with trans. by T. R. Glover, Loeb Classical Library (London: W. Heinemann, 1931), pp. 297-301.

60. St. Thomas Aquinas, *Summa Contra Gentiles*, trans. English Dominican Fathers, IV (London: Burns, Oates and Washbourne, 1929), 300-303.

61. Moses Maimonides, *Hilkhot Teshuvah*, chap. 9, 2, in *Mishneh Torah;* a Latin translation of this section was published under the title *Canones poenitentiae* (Cambridge: The University Press, 1631).

62. Moses Maimonides, *Hilkhot Melakhim*, chap. 12, 1-4, in *Mishneh Torah* (Vienna: Schmid and Busch, 1842), Part VIII, 166.

63. The treatment of Kabbala is based on the works of Gershom G. Scholem: *Major Trends in Jewish Mysticism* (Jerusalem: Schocken, 1941); "Zum Verständnis der Messianischen Idee in Judentum," *Eranos Jahrbuch*, 28 (1959), 193-239; *Ursprung und Anfänge der Kabbala* (Berlin: De Gruyter, 1962); *The Kabbala in Gerona* (in Hebrew), ed. Y. Ben-Shlomo (Jerusalem: Student Union of Hebrew University, 1964); *Jewish Gnosticism, Merkabah Mysticism, and Talmudic Tradition* (New York: Jewish Theological Seminary of America, 1960); *The Kabbala of the Sefer ha-Temunah and of Abraham Abulafia* (in Hebrew), ed. Y. Ben-Shlomo (Jerusalem: Akadmon, 1965); *On the Kabbalah and Its Symbolism*, trans. Ralph Manheim (New York: Schocken, 1965). See also J. F. Baer, "The Historical Background of the Raya Mehemna," *Zion*, 5 (1939), 1-44, for parallels with a Joachite commentary on Jeremiah written ca. 1240.

64. *The Zohar*, trans. Harry Sperling and Maurice Simon (London: Soncino, 1931), I, 101. The "Rav Mithivtha" covers folios 116b through 174a of vol. III of the Mantua edition of 1559.

65. Scholem, *Major Trends in Jewish Mysticism*, pp. 88-89.

66. Joachim of Fiore, *Liber côcordie. Novi ac Veteris Testamenti, nunc primo impressus & in luce editus* (Venice, 1519). This view of Joachim is more fully treated in Frank E. Manuel, *Shapes of Philosophical History* (Stanford: Stanford University Press, 1965).

67. *Ibid.*, p. 21, column c.

68. Joachim of Fiore, *Psalterium decem cordarum abbatis Joachim* (Venice, 1527), p. 260, column a.

69. Marjorie Reeves, *The Influence of Prophecy in the Later Middle Ages* (Oxford: Clarendon Press, 1969).

70. Francesco Russo, *Bibliografia Gioachimita* (Florence: L. S. Olschki, 1954), pp. 13-62.

71. See his *The Pursuit of the Millennium*, 2d ed. (New York: Harper Torchbooks, 1961).

72. Quoted by Gordon Leff, *Heresy in the Later Middle Ages* (Manchester: Manchester University Press, 1967), I, 373.

73. Theodora Büttner and Ernst Werner, *Circumcellionen und Adamiten* (Berlin: Akademie-Verlag, 1959), pp. 81-82.

74. See M. M. Smirin, *Die Volksreformation des Thomas Münzer und Der Grosse Bauernkrieg*, trans. Hans Nichtwiess, 2d ed. (Berlin: Dietz, 1956); Thomas Müntzer, *Schriften und Briefe*, critical ed. Günter Franz, with collaboration of Paul Kirn (Gütersloh: Gütersloher Verlagshaus Gerd Mohn, 1968).

75. *Historie Thomä Müntzers* (1526), in Otto Brandt, *Thomas Müntzer. Sein Leben und seine Schriften* (Jena: Diederichs, 1933), p. 42.

76. Thomas Müntzer, *Auslegung des anderen Unterschieds Danielis*, in *Schriften und Briefe*, p. 236.

77. See H.-J. Goertz, *Innere und äussere Ordnung in der Theologie Thomas Müntzers* (Leiden: E. J. Brill, 1967), pp. 146-147.

78. P. D. Huet, *Tractatus de situ paradisi terrestris* (Amsterdam: Boom, 1698).

79. Lars-Ivar Ringbom, *Graltempel und Paradies: Beziehungen zwischen Iran und Europa im Mittelalter* (Stockholm: Wahlström and Widstrand, 1951). See also Howard Rollin Patch, *The Other World, According to Descriptions in Medieval Literature* (Cambridge, Mass.: Harvard University Press, 1950); Elisabeth Peters, *Quellen und Charakter der Paradiesesvorstellungen in der deutschen Dichtung vom 9. bis 12. Jahrhundert* (Breslau: M. and H. Marcus, 1915).

80. Christopher Columbus, *Descubrimento del continente americano: relación del tercer viaje*, ed. facsim. de la carta enviada a los reyes, según el texto manuscrito por Bartolomé de las Casas (Madrid: Bibliotheca Americana Vetustissima, 1962).

81. Harry Levin, *The Myth of the Golden Age in the Renaissance* (Bloomington: Indiana University Press, 1969), pp. 183-184, has a similar treatment of the incident. Other sections of this essay inevitably touch on materials of his excellent book, though I believe our underlying conception differs.

82. Pierre d'Ailly, *Imago Mundi*, with annotations by Christopher Columbus (Boston: Massachusetts Historical Society, 1927); a photostat of the manuscript in the Biblioteca Colombina in Seville.

83. William G. Niederland, "River Symbolism," *The Psychoanalytic Quarterly*, 26 (1957), 71-72.

84. M. J. A. N. de Caritat, Marquis de Condorcet, *Esquisse d'un tableau historique des progrès de l'esprit humain*, 4th ed. (Genoa: Yves Gravier, 1798), p. 359.

85. See Vittorio Lanternari, *The Religion of the Oppressed: A Study of Modern Messianic Cults*, trans. Lisa Sergio (New York: Knopf, 1963); Sylvia L. Thrupp, ed., *Millennial Dreams in Action: Studies in Revolutionary Religious Movements* (New York: Schocken, 1970).

JUDITH N. SHKLAR

Subversive Genealogies

GENEALOGIES ARE rarely accurate. Their most usual purpose is, after all, to discover eminent ancestors, and a sense of veracity is not likely to inhibit such an enterprise. Social pretensions are too important to let the truth interfere with them. The Homeric heroes who boasted of divine ancestors to secure "sanction for aristocratic privilege," were neither the first nor the last noblemen to embellish their family trees. Indeed Homer's thoroughly aristocratic gods were no less prone to display their pedigrees.[1] However, if divine ancestors are the ultimate source of honor, it ineluctably follows that vulgar and disreputable ones are an intolerable disgrace. The traditional vocabulary of insult reveals nothing more clearly. To abuse a man's relatives and ancestors is the surest way of impugning his dignity and of assaulting his social position. That is why genealogies can serve as readily to destroy as to enhance claims to social supremacy.

Political theorists have often noted the rebellious possibilities of genealogies. For the search for origins need not be limited to families. Inquiries into the beginnings of regimes may lead to a god who engendered a royal house, but they can, and often do, uncover fratricides and worse. Such diverse thinkers as Hobbes and Burke entirely shared Kant's opinion that "The origin of the supreme authority is . . . not open to scrutiny by the people who are subject to it, that is the subjects should not be overly curious about its origins as though the right of obedience due it were open to doubt . . . these are pointless questions that threaten the state with danger if they are asked with too much sophistication."[2] In short, the search for origins will be subversive, especially if pursued by men of subtle intelligence.

If Hobbes was right in his belief that "there is scarcely a commonwealth in the world, whose beginnings can in conscience be justified," it is clear that curiosity about the origins of public authority is inevitably dangerous, as is all history, certainly the "most effectual seeds of death of any state."[3] It must always be rebellious in intent. That may well be an exaggeration. Ancestor worship is a reverent reversion to origins. It is because origins can glorify that they can also defame. To recognize the destructive pos-

129

sibilities of genealogy one must also appreciate the pride in noble ancestors, as Hesiod certainly did.[4] But the fears of the philosophers are, in any case, justified. Since Hesiod's day the myth of origins has been a typical form of questioning and condemning the established order, divine and human, ethical and political. The myth of creation that Hesiod devised out of the depth of resentment has been a model for writers of similar inspiration. His imitators in antiquity were legion, and in the modern age both Rousseau and Nietzsche, to name the most notable, used creation myths to express their unlimited contempt for their world. The enduring hold of this myth on the politically disaffected imagination is itself interesting. It may even illuminate our understanding of how political imagery is transmitted from age to age, how it continues to mold the memory of each literate generation, and how we are brought to political self-awareness by myths.

Although it is always called a creation myth, Hesiod's *Theogony* only describes the family tree of the gods. Birth, either parthenogenetic or by copulation, accounts for the divine population. The gods and the cosmos itself are self-evolving and not the products of a creative act or series of such acts, such as occur in the Book of Genesis.[5] Chaos (Void) simply "came to be" and then Earth and Eros appeared.[6] All subsequent deities are procreated in one way or another by these and their offspring. Moreover, the *Theogony* is less concerned with etiology, that is the "causes" of natural phenomena and forces, than with the organization of powers and of functions among the gods. Older, more nature-oriented myths were also myths of order and evaluation, but only incidentally.[7] In Hesiod the political order among the gods is the central theme and the offices of rulership are clearly dissociated from the cosmic order.[8] He was already far removed from nature worship in any form, nor were his myths recorded as part of an established order of ritual practices. He was a self-consciously original poet who wrote to instruct and entertain.[9] Hesiod was justifiably proud of his spiritual independence. To him, and to him alone, the Muses, who so often lied, had chosen to speak the truth.

Hesiod's awareness of his own powers of insight served to intensify his dissatisfaction with his actual condition as a mere "shepherd of the wilderness."[10] His other poem, *Works and Days*, is an exhaustive inventory of complaints against the state of mankind in general and his own situation especially. Known throughout antiquity as "the helot's poet," Hesiod speaks in the unmistakable tones of men who have every reason to resent their condition. The harsh natural world, the inherent inner hardness of men in general, and the specific burdens of the wretched and powerless peasantry combined to make bitterness his great poetic theme. The injustice and suffering that marked his own life led him to reflect upon the origins of the powers that rule over mankind, just as cosmic violence in turn recalls the particular ills of daily life. His is a song of universal dissatisfaction. Social and political evil permeates the world of the deities, and men reflect that world as they suffer from it and contribute to its already abundant store of miseries.

The *Theogony* is not merely the natural genealogy of the gods. The genesis of the social order among them does not follow a natural family tree. No father rules by natural right here. Generational strife, not ancestral piety, lies at the roots of the political regime of the cosmos. Earth created Heaven (Uranos) to breed with her, but he proved a cruel parent. Afraid of his own progeny, he imprisoned some of them within their mother, Earth. "Heaven rejoiced in his evil-doing," but Earth "groaned within" and plotted with her children against their father, who had done these "shameful things."[11] Her youngest child, wily Cronos, acts against his hated "lusty sire" and cuts off Heaven's genitals. Thereafter Heaven called his presumptuous brood the Titans, "the strainers."[12] As was just, given the enormity of the crime, retribution was sure to follow. Perhaps as an explanation Hesiod tells of the birth of "hateful Doom," "black Fate and Death," "Blame and painful Woe," and of the Destinies, right after his account of the Titan's crime against Heaven. "Murky Night" gives birth to them "though she lay with none." Death and Nemesis affect only mortal men, but the others, especially the avenging destinies, certainly act upon the gods also.[13]

Heaven is avenged when Cronos' son Zeus, "father of gods and men," rises against his own father. Now Zeus is clearly not the actual father of gods and men; he is so only metaphorically, as the founder of Olympian society. He is not particularly creative, in spite of his numerous progeny. Most of the moral and natural "gods" have already been "born" by the time he appears. It is Earth who is really creative. Zeus establishes a civil order, but he does not bring its members into being. Even in his rise to power Mother Earth is his guide. It is she who takes the initiative in his early struggles, just as she led Cronos on. In introducing Zeus at once as a "father" Hesiod makes us aware again of his second, political, myth of origins, the one that deals with the creation of the Olympian order.

Cronos swallowed each of his children as they came forth from the womb of his spouse Rhea, so that none of them "should hold the kingly office amongst the deathless gods."[14] However, he was not able to escape his fate. Rhea conspired with her parents, Heaven and Earth, to save Zeus. Cronos is forced to vomit up his children and Zeus, who had grown up under Earth's protection, also sets free the other sons of Heaven whom Cronos had enchained. The results of this liberation were not, however, altogether satisfactory. For ten years there was perpetual war between the Titans who occupied Othrys and the sons of Cronos on Olympus. Finally Zeus assumed leadership of the Olympians, and with the aid of some particularly monstrous deities, and after a violent struggle, the Titans were conquered, subdued, and isolated. Prompted by Earth, the victorious gods asked "far-seeing Olympian Zeus to reign and to rule over them."[15] He begins his rule by dividing "dignities among them." Rewarding one's allies clearly is a mark of foresight in a ruler.

Heaven evidently was avenged and Cronos met the destiny that must overcome anyone who violates his father. However, Zeus's conduct is no less unfilial. His triumph in the struggle for "honors" over the Titans, and his imprisonment of his own father, Cronos, must surely be avenged. They are not. Zeus avoids Cronos' fate by a shrewd stratagem. Following the advice of Heaven and Earth, he swallows his first wife, Metis, the wise. This was the best way to avoid any challenge to his royal authority. Metis' daughter by Zeus, Pallas Athene, is born after her mother had been swallowed, so she sprang directly from Zeus' head. Without a mother, such as Earth or Rhea, she would never be able to conspire against her father. Subsequent mates appeared to pose no threat, perhaps because of their immense number. Zeus remains secure in his power thanks to his superior intelligence and the help of Heaven and Earth. Thereafter his supremacy is never questioned. Nevertheless nothing is more evident than that his rule is based on acts of violence and on outrages. His power is defined by the very fact that he evades the just retribution that sooner or later meets other rebellious sons, just as he manages to avoid the normal hostility of his children.

Zeus is an artificial father, a creator in his own right. He is the political progenitor of the new civil order among the gods and men. It is a political order that is based on his omnipotence and omniscience. At no point is it suggested that Zeus's character alters in time, or that he redeems himself in any way. He is a god to be feared and to be obeyed. Toward mankind his conduct is, moreover, ambiguous at best.[16] If he enforces retributive justice among men, there are a mass of evils in the world that express his undeviating hostility toward them. Hesiod's genealogy of the gods accounts admirably for the obvious—that we live in a world of pervasive suffering, moral and physical. Zeus "holds the aegis" and we know what he is and does and how he came to rule.

Some readers of Hesiod have wondered why he felt it necessary to explain Zeus's supremacy, since Homer had, after all, already made clear how perfectly established that dominion was.[17] Homer was certainly not much interested in the prehistory of Olympus. It is only mentioned twice in the *Iliad* and then it is of no particular significance. Poseidon grumbles that Zeus, who is his brother, should not dominate him. However, Zeus is the older of the two, and Poseidon gives in, as is apparently only right. Homer's heroes simply have no interest in investigating the genealogy of Zeus's reign, since, in fact, their own claims to prestige are based on descent from divine ancestors. They are all related to the gods. Only their mortality makes them different from the Olympians. Zeus, as befits his unique position, remains aloof from the great struggle that embroils the heroes and gods, but in Achilles he has at least a partial counterpart among the heroes.

Nor is Zeus willfully cruel. He is even moved to express pity for the tragic lot of mortal beings. The princes of the world have no reason to question the character of the Olympians, who so faithfully mirror their own ways. Hesiod, however, had ample cause to fear and resent princes who oppress peasants, and the gods who were their models and who had fashioned the iron race. He had therefore an obvious incentive to investigate their origins. If Homer's gods are amoral, happy warriors, the heroes did not mind. Hesiod, however, looked for justice and did not find it among the rulers of men and of gods.

The politics of the gods are typically palace politics, with the confusion of personal passions and general purposes, pervasive sexuality and endless intrigues. Procopius and the Duc de Saint-Simon had their precursor in Hesiod. Court history, such as this, is not mere scandal-mongering. It expresses a profound sense of moral dissonance. The restraints that are imposed upon the ruled are seen to have no effect upon the rulers, because no one can force the latter to behave. It is not that the kings of the world are subject to an ethos different from the common morality because of the demands of politics. That might readily be justified by the necessities of their office. The outraged "secret histories" of princes and their courts measure only the distance between those who must be industrious, just, and monogamous and those who are not thus constained. The distrust that these historians often arouse is less due to their readers' innocence, or to a belief that the scandals are exaggerated, than to the recognition that this is not the whole of politics, not even at court.

The extent of Hesiod's bitterness can be seen even better in his second creation myth, which deals specifically with the origins of mankind. As the *Theogony* presents a picture of palace politics, of the intrigues and quarrels of the mighty, so *Work and Days* shows us what all this means for the lower orders, especially for the humblest, the peasantry. At no time are men anything but the playthings of the gods. That much is already made evident in the *Theogony*. There we hear of Hecate and Calliope, who take an interest in men. The first protects nurslings, but for the rest distributes her favors quite arbitrarily among competitors in war and sport. The second gives eloquence to "wise princes" which helps them politically. Some men evidently receive favors from the gods which accounts for inequality in fortune and talents. However, the lot of mankind in general is not really improved by these intercessions as the story of Prometheus makes clear. Prometheus encourages men to eat the meat of a sacrificial animal that he has cleverly disguised to fool Zeus. It is prudent, of course, not to waste the meat, but Zeus cannot be deceived. Prometheus' gift of fire to men is another sign that he is indeed "kindly." But men must pay a heavy penalty for his favors. For Zeus not only punishes the presumptuous Titan, but also his hapless protégés. "In his heart he thought mischief against mortal men which also was to be fulfilled."[18] He "made an evil thing for men as the price of fire"—woman, who is nothing but trouble to men. No one can deceive Zeus.[19] It is simply not possible to go beyond the will of Zeus. Mankind's misery is the corollary of Zeus's omnipotence. In *Work and Days* this lesson is driven home relentlessly. The story of Prometheus is here embellished. It is told to explain why "the gods keep hidden from men the means of life."[20] Zeus now not only devises plagues for men, but "laughed aloud" as he does so.[21] Moreover, he does not merely send woman this time, but Pandora with her fatal jar, as a sheer, hopeless snare for his victims. Foolish Epemetheus forgets Prometheus' instructions and delivers her, as prudence is always defeated by folly and regret is the normal form of understanding. The contents of Pandora's jar are scattered among men—sorrow, disease, and misery. Only hope does not escape, because Zeus prevents it from leaving the jar. Even hope is denied men. "So there is no way to escape the will of Zeus."[22]

Prometheus' daring is not the only possible explanation for the origins of suffering. Hesiod offered an alternative: the tale of the Five Ages. In the age of Cronos the gods made a race of golden men whom they loved. These men were perfectly happy and they died as if overcome by sleep. Even now they hover about mankind as its guardians. They were succeeded by another, less successful creation of the gods, men of silver, who were simpletons. The reign of Cronos is now over and we are in the era of Zeus. He is angered by these foolish creatures, who fail to honor the blessed gods, and he puts them away. Zeus now makes all the subsequent generations, and they are terrible. First a hard of heart, fearful race of bronze is fashioned. These destroy each other. Then Zeus produces a superior, more noble and righteous race of bronze among whom are the heroes who fought at Troy. When they pass away they go to the "island of the blessed," where they live happily under the kindly rule of Cronos, now released from his bonds. The division of the men of bronze into two separate generations has puzzled many readers. Some have suggested an undue reverence for Homer's heroes. Perhaps Nietzsche was right in suggesting that Hesiod wanted to bring out both sides of heroic man, his frightfulness and his nobility of character.[23] In any case, the heroes do not endure, and are followed by Zeus's final creation, the men of iron. This is the age of history to which we all belong. Now men "never rest from labor and sorrow." There is no justice, no decency, no shame, no righteousness, and no help against evil. Such is the work of omnipotent Zeus, "the father." It is worth noting that Cronos is the creator of happy men and the guardian of the island of the blessed, while Zeus, the successful usurper, makes and rules over a deformed humanity.

At the end of the myth of the Five Ages Hesiod inserted a little fable that underlines the parallel between the order on Olympus and that which prevails on earth. One day a hawk dug his talons into the little neck of a nightingale and said, "Miserable thing, why do you cry out? One far stronger than you now holds you fast and you must go wherever I take you . . . He is a fool who tries to withstand the stronger, for he does not get mastery and suffers pain, besides his shame." This fable is addressed to "princes who themselves understand" and it is followed by a warning to his wayward brother, Perses, to "listen to right." "For violence is bad for a poor man."[24] Clearly, the princes of the world can afford to act like hawks and so does Zeus. If men act unjustly Zeus punishes them sooner or later. To that extent he is a god of justice. Before him the hawklike princes must also tremble, just as peasants are helpless. That is the sole element of positive worth in Zeus's conduct toward men. It does not, how-ever, modify his original and enduring malignity and ill-will. Zeus's omnip-otence is what really matters. That inspires overwhelming terror, and its only value is that this fear is the only restraint effective among iron men. Moreover, there are many ills from Pandora's jar beside injustice, such as disease and work. The whole world that Zeus made for man is like Hesiod's own native village "bad in winter, sultry in summer, and good at no time."[25] Avoid the anger of the gods, protect yourself against them by sacrifices and magical devices, and work incessantly and ritualistically as a substitute for hope. Such is Hesiod's final advice to us. It is the counsel of an angry and resigned man.

Creation myths have generally been treated as primitive man's science. If their political character has been noticed at all, it is usually as mirrors of historical events. The Babylonian creation myth has been described as a cosmic state, a reflection of the political experiences of that people.[26] Again, the transition from Homer's relatively easygoing deities to Hesiod's harsh ones is attributed to the anxieties generated in Greek society as it became more patriarchal and authoritarian.[27] That is, however, only one way of interpreting political literature. The political implications of these myths may well lie in the sentiments they directly express. They may just mean exactly what they say. The Greek moralists from Xenophanes onward, who chastised Homer and Hesiod for attributing immoral and wicked con-duct to the gods, evidently took their authors at their word.[28] So did Plato, who deeply disapproved of both. In the *Republic* he insisted that Hesiod's tales about Heaven and Cronos ought not to be repeated at all, or at least told only to the wise, who, presumably, would not believe them.[29] Their effect on the moral life of the less than wise was altogether clear to Plato. Foolish Euthyphro argued that since Cronos and Zeus punished their fathers, he, Euthyphro, should also neglect his filial duties and initiate criminal proceedings against his parent for a minor and justifiable act of violence.[30] Euthyphro was merely obnoxious and stupid, but lack of respect for one's parents was for Plato also one of the vices peculiar to democracy.[31] It was the mark of moral anarchy. There was therefore little doubt in his mind that Hesiod had an unsettling impact upon the self-assertive young.

Among more recent readers of Hesiod only one has shared Plato's sense of the moral disorder presented by the *Theogony*. Norman O. Brown has quite aptly compared its Zeus with Machiavelli's Romulus.[32] Zeus is also the founder of a civil society who shrinks from no crime to establish a secure political order and to ensure his own power. His justification is to be found in success, in the stability and might of his polity and of his own rule. There is, however, an important difference in the two portraits. Going to the foundations to expose the fratricide at the origin of even the greatest of republics was, for Machiavelli, a revolutionary enterprise. It showed others how it could be done and what rewards they might expect from successful imitation. It was meant explicitly to encourage conspirators and aspiring princes to forget any remaining scruples and to act as others, like Romulus, had in the past.[33] Machiavelli may have had a vision of political greatness that involved more than success acquired by all and any means, even the most vicious, but if he could not wholly admire the butcher, he certainly was not inclined to deprecate his final success in winning power.[34] The myth of foundations, or rather, the countermyth of Machiavelli, has revolution and the repetition of the creative blood bath as its object.[35] Hesiod's myth had no such designs. His response to a Zeus who was a Machiavellian prince was one of overt obedience and covert rejection more subtle than that of hawklike princes. To tell the truth is subversive in a way that violence and injustice are not. The latter may be offenses against Zeus's rule, as are excesses and failure to honor the gods. However, these punishable crimes are insignificant in comparison with Hesiod's philosophic indictment. If his is in no sense a defiant stand, it is only ostensibly an obedient one. It is surely remote from the abject submission to the God of Abraham or Job.

In the Old Testament man himself is the origin of evil. There is something inside Eve that responds to the serpent, so that it is not possible to blame that animal for the fall of man entirely. Above all, evil is not primordial, coextensive with the generation of the divine being. The God of the Old Testament is the creator of everything except evil. Man is wholly responsible for his own unhappiness. He cannot look to God, as Hesiod does, and see human evil as a mere mirroring of a cosmic pattern. Human violence is almost justified by Olympian violence. There is no occasion or possibility for a fall in this scheme. The Adamic myth, in stark contrast, is wholly anthropological. A human ancestor, a being just like us, originates evil. There is a perpetual tension, therefore, between the complete perfection of God and the radical wickedness of man. In the Christian tradition this tension crystallized in the notion of original sin. However, even without this later elaboration, the Adamic myth offers a totally different view of the origins of good and evil. A God so wholly outside the natural order, so wholly other as to be without any human features, can only receive humble obedience. And that is the response of Abraham and eventually of Job. Man cannot judge God or even comment intelligently upon his ways.

Zeus neither invites, nor receives, such submission. These two creation myths, the biblical and the Hesiodic, offer archetypal alternatives upon which subsequent speculation could and did build.[36]

The thinking that followed the Hesiodic pattern was essentially philosophic, critical, and in search of understanding rather than of moral rules. However, we may, nevertheless, speak of it as religious in the cultural sense of that term. It is a kind of religiosity peculiar to many members of a known group, the modern European men of letters and learning. The need for myths is most likely to arise for them, as for other men, when they are faced with extreme moral perplexity, when they reach the limits of their analytical capacities and powers of endurance. In the face of intellectual despair and intolerable moral tension, men tend to turn to what is called religion. The myth does not "solve" intractable ethical paradoxes, but it is the only available vehicle of expression for an overwhelming sense of such paradox.[37] It has been said that religion makes pain sufferable. That is surely true, but there are various ways of achieving that end, given the variety of religious possibilities and cultures and the various degrees of intellectual intensity among these. Hesiod's myth is only one way of coping among many. But it is an exceptionally intellectual way, a model of and for philosophy. By opening an avenue to the truth that lies at the very foundation of all experience, it appeals to minds not only in revolt against the structure of actuality, but also unable to rest with any obvious solution to its most tormenting paradoxes. The Book of Genesis is not adequate to these demands. The creation myth which solves nothing but illuminates everything answers the needs of those who seek a method for expressing anger and doubt, rather than means to assuage them. Ritual will sooner or later come to the aid of those who want remedies, who want "to do something." Philosophy is not for them. It elucidates, but does not remove intellectual distress. It is a way of living with it.

In the modern age the rejection of the notion of original sin created a host of such painful puzzles. If men were inherently good and destined for happiness, why was their historical existence so uniformly miserable? The question of the origins of universal human suffering, and the need to affix the blame anew, became tormenting again. No philosopher felt it more intensely than did Jean Jacques Rousseau. He spoke at least twice of his life's work as a tracing of "the genealogy" of the human vices. And at the root of all vices he found inequality. It was for him the source and essence of evil.[38] With this in mind it is not difficult to recognize his *Discourse on the Origins of Inequality* as a new creation myth and one that follows the Hesiodic pattern very closely.[39]

Like Hesiod, Rousseau was "the helot's poet." He also spoke for the peasants, and like the old poet he found them wronged and oppressed. In an age when inequality was almost universally accepted as necessary and just, Rousseau felt as isolated as Hesiod. If not the Muses, nature had told

him the truth, and only to him. All other writers lied.[40] It does not, therefore, matter whether Rousseau had ever read Hesiod, had become familiar
with his creation myth in one of its many Latin imitations, or had just
resorted to the same model of exposition, because it corresponded to his
own style of thought. Determined to expose the evils of actual society,
Rousseau proceeded to look for its origins and to show that inequality was
the ancestor of all other human vices. If he did not speak of his genealogy
as a myth openly, he at least did take great care to explain that he was not
writing history of any sort, either sacred or profane.[41] He had little respect
for historians in any case. As for the ethnologists of his age, some of whom
he did admire, he disposed of them by lamenting the unreliability of the
information provided by travelers and the undeveloped state of the science
of comparative anatomy. This device permitted him to construct his genealogy without directly contradicting the ethnologists in such a way as to
seem ignorant of their science.[42]

To dispose of the myth of Adam and of the belief in original sin, which
had for so many centuries served to justify social inequality as part of the
necessary order restraining and disciplining fallen mankind, Rousseau began
by simply brushing aside "supernatural information" and the sort of "facts"
supplied by Moses.[43] His most serious readers were in any case not likely
to worry about his religious conformity; they also were looking for an
alternative to the Book of Genesis. The Bible was, however, not the only
book with which Rousseau had to contend. Hobbes's *Leviathan,* with its
version of the origins of society, designed to support the whole structure
of political inequality, had also to be overcome. To this end neither revelation, history, nor ethnology would do. Moreover, psychology was a serious
obstacle as well, not least because Rousseau's own social psychology was
not altogether remote from Hobbes's. The new creation myth had therefore
to be not only prehistorical but also prepsychological. That is typical of
modern creation myths in general because the paradox of a being made
for happiness who can never reach his end requires some image of man
with a psychic structure unlike his actual self-contradictory and self-destruc-
tive character. Cosmic protest is now protest against man's ontological
status, as the one and only animal wholly at odds with himself and totally
unadapted to his environment.[44] Ill-made and badly placed, man is doomed
to be what he is, and that, surely, is enough reason for outrage.

To go behind Hobbes and anthropology one had to set aside scientific
books and their kind of facts. They have no bearing on the question at
hand.[45] To conceive of original man, as he was, is not directly possible,
since he may never have existed. Rousseau was quite candid. The notion
of a state of nature is required solely to "judge our present condition."[46]
As in any creation myth, one must go to "the real foundations of human
society" to see original man, to recognize his real needs and duties in order
to condemn the present.[47] The "veritable origins" are not the object pursued

by science, but by that art that learns directly from nature to praise our first ancestors, to criticize our contemporaries, and to terrify future generations.[48]

What does nature tell us about our admirable first ancestor? He was, apparently, a pure clod. Original man was strong, healthy, and suffered from nothing, not even death. Like Hesiod's man of gold, he dies without being aware of it. For even disease is the result of inequality. It makes some men starve, while others suffer from the effects of gluttony.[49] Original man differs from beasts only in his ability to make choices rather than to follow instinct compulsively. Man can avoid starvation by changing his diet, animals cannot. Moreover, he can perfect himself through this faculty of choice. He has potentialities which can be awakened and which can alter him. Man originally is, in short, chaos, void, but he can be activated. Without language, imagination (foresight—Prometheus) or memory (hindsight—Epimetheus) he lacks even fire.[50] Sex is casual and momentary. Whatever natural, genetic inequalities of strength, intelligence, or age exist are insignificant, since in the absence of any social relationships, they do not manifest themselves. The law of the strongest simply can have no place here. Original man is neither Hobbes's "robust child" nor Adam. He is a total stranger to virtue and vice.[51]

Originally man is, moreover, passive. Some external force must act upon him, like the Eros of Hesiod's myth, to dislodge him from his lazy inactivity. Rousseau did not, to be sure, resort to divine personifications of natural phenomena. However, his environmentalist psychology fulfills the same mythical function. What are the environmentalist's "external forces" that impinge upon man to mold him if not depersonalized gods? In either case man's victimhood, his helplessness in the face of uncontrollable powers, is manifest. Unlike Adam, original man is expelled from his Eden not through any fault of his own or of his mate. That is not the pattern Rousseau's creation myth followed.[52] Original man is compelled by some alien force to leave his mindless state. A "fortuitous combination of several strange causes," accidents which need never have occurred, somehow denature him.[53] Vulgar readers need not concern themselves with their exact nature. Certainly history is silent. Rousseau, in short, is being frank about his inventions. They are necessary to link man, the tabula rasa, to man, as he is known to us. That is a matter of moral arithmetic, the addition of stages of moral change that bring man to the final departure from nature: the establishment of the division of labor and of property.[54]

The end of harmony between natural man and the natural environment is due to hostile, sinister "accidents" in the natural order. Moreover, man's own nature includes all those potentialities which develop to render him miserable. Clearly nature is not unambiguously "good," however frequently Rousseau may insist upon its perfection. The old Hesiodic nature gods, the Titans, were, as we saw, well disposed toward man. Cronos and

Prometheus, respectively, created the golden race and gave man fire. Hecate takes some interest in our doings. The terrible war between the Titans and the Olympians which shakes the earth violently ends in a divine regime far less favorable to mortal men. Like the gods, Rousseau's nature seems to come in two generations. The first, as it operates *within* man, as his original natural state, and as a cooperative environment, seems wholly favorable to him. The succeeding nature is not. It is violent in thrusting man out of this satisfactory situation. It is positively malignant in the form of that innate capacity for perfectibility which now becomes man's chief inner driving force. Both as environment and as man's psychic structure nature is, in fact, both good and evil. The two, in short, are inherent aspects of the cosmos from the first, though this becomes evident only gradually. In any case, man suffers no fall. He is rather betrayed by the regulative forces of a world into which he, unlike the other beasts, does not fit properly. Man may be one of nature's mistakes, but he is not a sinner. There is no fall of man. To be sure, nature is not the real villain at the root of Rousseau's genealogy of evil. Society is the evil ancestor. Nevertheless nature, human and nonhuman, far from protecting man against his doom, actively propels him toward it, as did the gods in the classical past.

The first steps out of nature are due to accidents of nature. Men move to new areas, which require more adaptation. Learning begins. Such accidents as lightening or volcanoes teach men about fire. The intellectual powers required to make measurements and comparisons are awakened.[55] Men begin to recognize their kinship to each other and to enter into temporary common enterprises, such as hunting.[56] All this may take centuries. The first real revolution does not occur until the relations between the sexes undergo a fundamental change. Like Hesiod, Rousseau did not think sexual love an unmixed blessing. Moreover, it is the root of domesticity. Huts and family life follow.[57] With that the march out of nature proceeds steadily and unalterably. Work and dependencies—human chains, in short— are forged. New "accidents" contribute to changing the entire face of things.[58] The fourth age, succeeding those of nature, fire, and family huts is the last happy one. In fact it is the best of times. It is the age of villages, the age of gold. It has its faults; men are cruel, and vanity and public opinion begin to dominate them. It is also marred by the birth of inequality. Nevertheless, good and evil are in balance and men are now as well off as they possibly can be. It does not last. Again a "sinister accident" interferes and the fifth age, the age of grain and iron, dawns.[59] This is the world of history, the classical age of iron man, "the perfection of the individual and the decrepitude of the species are at hand." All latent powers are now active in each "member" of the race, which is now rushing to collective misery.

Not gold and silver, but iron and grain are the ruin of mankind. For with these come the division of labor, the application of naturally unequal talents in work and its results, wealth and poverty.[60] This is Hesiod's fifth age, that of men of iron doomed to labor and injustice. The strong and able now dominate the weak and incompetent.[61] The master needs a slave and the slave a patron, each depends on the other.[62] The final addition to this pattern is the establishment of property and of civil society. They do not alter men fundamentally in the way earlier changes did. They only ensure that they will never leave the iron age. It is like the reign of Zeus, the rule of justice. It transforms inequality and all its pains into recognized obligations. The rich, in order to escape the Hobbesian state of nature, which the division of labor and property create, impose a fraudulent contract upon the poor. The poor are tricked into accepting an order which protects the property of the rich and which seems to offer the dispossessed an escape from arbitrariness.[63] The origins of law and government have now, at last, been revealed. At their foundations are fraud and force. Not fratricide, but the manipulation of the dull and weak by the strong, secures thrones. If a Lycurgus had created states, they would certainly be different. However, that is not what actually occurs.[64] Nor do benevolent gods preside over their birth. The gods are mere inventions which the powerful use to legitimize their rule and to frighten their subjects.[65]

The conditions that give rise to political authority justify it. The vices that tend to it ensure its continuation and deterioration. That is why it will never be destroyed.[66] Genealogy is a one-way street. It is irreversible. The child cannot be the father of its parents. That is why the Hesiodic creation myth is the perfect form for expressing a specific sort of pessimism. It is the myth that expresses the outrage of those who know all the evils of the world and recognize their necessity. It permits defiance and rejection, without arousing the slightest hope or impulse to action. As Hesiod implores his brother to behave justly, so Rousseau far from believing that any return to nature was possible, called for an acceptance of justice. He did so knowing perfectly well that justice and equality are incompatible. Not even the worst regime ignores justice entirely, he argued. All reward merit and punish crime to some degree. However, a system of rewards and punishments, even when perfectly fair in its practices, ensures inequality. Distributive justice is merely the consistent administration of inequality. It remains wholly opposed to the equality of nature which knows no differences of merit.[67] Society means drawing distinctions between men, even if these need not be, though they always are, based on wealth.[68]

If Hesiod and Rousseau spoke for the peasant, their sympathies extended to mankind as a whole. Rousseau did not think the rich were really happy. We are all losers. That is why he felt pity to be so valuable a sentiment. However, one may despise the weak and scorn pity and still cling to the creation myth. Nietzsche had a far narrower range of sympathies than Hesiod or Rousseau. In fact, he scorned Hesiod as a crude poet and hated Rousseau as the incarnation of every pseudo-Christian, democratic degeneracy.[69] Yet, he also resorted to the creation myth in structuring his indictment of European culture. He certainly knew exactly what he was doing. An incomparable reader of Greek tragedies, he saw it as his life's mission to remind his impoverished historical-critical age of all that had been lost when tragic pessimism and myth had been expunged from European culture.[70] In his youth he had entertained some hope these might be revived, but that did not last.[71] What remained was his uncompromising hatred for the biblical-priestly spirit. He had known from the first that Adam and Prometheus were hostile opponents. Prometheus' story recognizes the painful and irrevocable contradiction between man and god in a way that confers dignity on sacrilege, and justifies human evil, while Adam's fall expresses a feebleness, a sense of evil as mere weakness and disgrace.[72]

What can be only inferred from Rousseau's genealogy is explicit in Nietzsche's; both shared a contempt for history, sacred and profane, as a self-justifying form of knowledge. Neither had any use for historical facts. That the author of *The Use and Abuse of History* should ever have attempted a historical account of European moral development is unthinkable. And, indeed, he did not. He wrote *The Genealogy of Morals,* not a history of values, and he wrote it with the same daring and abusive intent that inspired Hesiod and Rousseau. Even if the evils he exposed were not generally the same ones, he was at one with them in suspecting that the origins of justice were marked by hidden irregularities.

Nietzsche's *Genealogy* is meant to trace down to its remotest ancestor the present moral outlook of Europe. It is no mere mnemonic exercise, but an effort to expose the ultimate progenitors of the morality that has now revealed its final aim and nature: nihilism, the longing for nothingness. The rot sets in, as in Hesiod's myth, with the end of the heroic age, with the passing of the men of bronze, who, Nietzsche admitted, were both terrible and violent, and yet noble. They combined the character of both of Hesiod's bronze races. The men of iron are for Nietzsche the men of the age of the slave spirit triumphant. After two thousand years their exhaustion is evident, as Hesiod also foresaw, when he predicted that eventually the men of iron would be born senile. For Nietzsche's story of Prometheus is, also, never quite over and done with. Noble figures—most recently, Napoleon—do appear from time to time, but they have no enduring effect upon the overwhelming power of the priest-led slaves, who dominate Europe with only rare and brief interruptions.[73] Indeed, the metaphors that Nietzsche applied to some of the manifestations of slave morality are more reminiscent of the Babylonian creation myth *Enuma elish* than of Hesiod. A watery, passive chaos rather than divine malice seems recurrently to threaten the world of order and culture. English psychologists, whom he regarded as the chief purveyors of vulgarity, are characterized as frogs creeping around in "the swamps" and in a "mud volcano."[74] This fear of watery chaos goes well beyond Hesiod's sense that nothing in nature is ever destroyed, not even Heaven's dismembered genitals. Tiamat the primordial, passive female water deity who is overcome and must be kept down in the Babylonian myth is hauntingly revived in Nietzsche's fear of the passive, massive drift toward spiritual nothingness, and the end of all creative action. It is, however, only one of his themes. The major battle is not between the active and the passive forces of culture and nature, respectively, but between the far from passive, crafty priest class and the noble heroes.[75] The victory of the shrewd priest over the simple-minded hero is complete and total—as Zeus's over the Titans.

At the beginning of morality, as we know it, there is war, a conflict between two irreconcilable wills to power, the priestly and the noble. The priest triumphs, since like Zeus he is far more intelligent than his victim. He is certainly no slave himself. On the contrary, he is an aristrocat and formidable as such. Even if he is sick and morbid with his obsessions about the "clean" and "unclean," he alone has made man "an interesting animal," for he has made the human soul "evil." He is the inventor, the creator, the father of "evil," in fact.[76] Without him history would have been dull.[77] As dull, one would guess, as Hesiod's ages of golden and silver men were. The noble hero may be healthy and spontaneous, rather than ill and reactive, but he is not clever.[78] All epics end badly for the heroes. Who can forget the mournful sight that meets Odysseus in Hades? Culture cannot be the creation of these lovely heroic animals, and it is culture that permanently organizes the masses. In its final decay, Nietzsche saw priestly culture as an exhaustion. "We are weary of man." [79] This is not a historical decline. It is an uncovering. The heroes are pure prehistory, the Titans in whom we must believe if we are to see the meanness of actuality. There has not, since pre-Socratic Greece, been anything but priestly culture. Europe had never been adequate, and the heroes are necessary for the creation myth as a contrast, to show that this society and its justice have their origin in an abusive act, in the elimination of something infinitely valuable. It begins with destruction because its course and end must be seen as wholly ruinous manifestations. The heroes serve the same purpose as the happy ages of Hesiod and as Rousseau's original man. They exist solely to be destroyed, and so to show that the evil of the end is present at the beginning.

The second section of Nietzsche's *Genealogy of Morals* seems, at first, quite remote from this "archeology." In prehistory noble men were happy and fulfilled, while the peasants were pillaged and mistreated, as Nietzsche admitted. It ended when priests led these natural inferiors in a triumphant war against their natural masters. Such was the beginning of history, that is of Europe's slave culture. Now this theme seems to be abandoned as Nietzsche turns to the real scene of battle: within the human soul. The metaphoric personifications, or quasi-gods, are dropped. The psychic struggle is now directly revealed, without overt mythmaking. Priests and heroes drop their names, roles, and disguises. It is man's own will that is now at work. Fate is, after all, character. Rousseau had known that also. It is man's endowment, not all those "accidents," that really create "evil" and suffering. And as for Rousseau, it is memory and imagination which undo man. Mnemosyne is for Nietzsche also united with Epimetheus, regret. The evils they bring upon mankind are indeed so immense that one is surprised that Hesiod reversed the one and only ascribed idiocy to the latter. But he still believed in truth, as Nietzsche did not. Memory is now our illness and torment.[80] It is part of that will to power which drives men, not from without, but from within. That does not make it any less compelling. The will to control the future, to understand and dominate the world, the will to society, all prohibit forgetfulness. Man must be made "calculable" if he is to master the world and himself. He must make himself into a promise-making, accountable, predictable social being and all this requires the creation of memory, a profoundly painful, self-denying process. It is cruelty self-inflicted.[81] Like Rousseau, Nietzsche speaks of untold eons that must have passed to reveal this "perfectibility" so.[82] Yet both knew that this self-destruction is ever-present.

The psychic origin of justice according to Nietzsche's genealogy is cruelty. The first promise is one that allows the injured party to get his own back by exercising his cruelty upon his injurer—for the sheer pleasure of it.[83] Justice is nothing but licensed cruelty. Reflecting on the Greek gods, Nietzsche saw that they enjoyed spitefulness for its own sake. Their justice is an occasion for seeing men suffer. The pity that tragedy was said to arouse derived its "sweetness" from the cruelty of the spectacle.[84] Zeus uses Prometheus' disobedience as an occasion for enjoying the sight of the humbled Titan. "Without cruelty there is no festival."[85] Hesiod had made no bones about that either. Zeus laughs as he inflicts every misery upon his victims. The gods, Nietzsche recalled, certainly enjoyed the Trojan war. It was a play produced for their delight.[86] That, at least, gave suffering some intelligible purpose. It was not wholly pointless, since the god's at least derived some pleasure from it. Suffering is made comprehensible. One knows how it came about, why these things happen. That is not, however, a justification; quite the contrary. Unlike history, "genealogy" refers to both the past and the present simultaneously. It deals with the past that is wholly present in the offspring. That is why the prehistory of justice, its primordial cruelty, is not just a thing of the past, but something "which is present in all ages and may always reappear."[87] It is not an etiology, just an analysis, and one that does not use explanations as excuses.

The exchange of cruelties is the justice appropriate to noble equals. It cannot prevail between unequals. What is now called justice is a quite different type of cruelty. It is resentment, the anger of those who cannot fight back.[88] As long as the distinction between strong and weak was clear, punishment was a fate, not revenge or retribution, but just the sense that something had gone awry. Punishment had no rational sense, served no useful ends. It was merely an infliction.[89] Only when the strong were subdued in a civic order and Zeus's justice was internalized in the self-mutilating form of "bad conscience" was punishment rationalized. Law creates the idea of punishment as deserved, as something the guilty ought to suffer.[90] Now the nobles no longer enjoy the cruel privileges of the gods. Cooped up in cities with their erstwhile inferiors, they also must now be dominated by universal deities, such as Zeus, the juristic monopolist. Their ultimate point of degradaton is reached when that "maximum god," the Christian God, god of the guilty, finally achieves supremacy.[91] The ascetic ideal is now triumphant within us, and that is not surprising. Because its great invention, guilt, renders pain not merely intelligible, but valid. Suffering is now approved by the sufferer. History is justified. The Adamic myth that destroys the animal in man offers him considerable intellectual compensation. He has his guilt now. The priest in each of us, our bad conscience, has given us a consistent morality. Fraudulence was not what upset Nietzsche as he looked into this scheme. It was the self-destructiveness of cruelty turned inward that seemed so outrageous. For the immense intellectual advance of bringing cause and effect to bear upon the experience of suffering, the myth of pain as the consequence of sin, is a systematic repression of vitality.

The priest in the long run proves no physician to his sickly flock. At best guilt is a pain killer, a hypnotic device. When sin becomes unbearable, religion can hold out only the promise of nothingness, a mere absence of experience.[92] At best men learn to love their pain, a sort of sick voluptuousness. Nevertheless, Nietzsche held on to one hope; even the will to nothingness is still a will, a sign of life.[93] That is not very encouraging. It is not a vision of a cycle, or of a return to heroism. Nietzsche may have believed in some sort of future, but his genealogy of moral oppression gives no grounds for more positive expectations. His healthy noble animals are not only mythical beings, they are also born losers, like the Titans. They have no purpose other than to expose their destroyers, the originators of European morality, and especially of their justice.

If Nietzsche seemed to admire Hesiod's shamelessly cruel Zeus, it is only because he so greatly appreciated the tragic pessimism with which the Greek poets responded to Zeus. He recognized that Zeus was already the precursor of the biblical deity. Nietzsche found in the cruel god, and in the spirit he evoked, the contrast which he needed to reveal the indignity and sheer neurotic sickness of the Adamic myth. For him biblical religion played precisely the same part that Zeus played in Hesiod's myth. The victory of either one suffices to ensure man's humiliation. Whether it be the subjugation of the nobles by priest-led slaves and the repression of vitality by the calculating resentment in ourselves, or the defeat of the Titans by shrewd Zeus and the creation of a defective humanity, the result is the same fatality.

There are differences to be sure. For Nietzsche it was not suffering
as such that mattered, but how men bore it. That is the great difference
between his aristocratic stance and that of the two peasant-philosophers.
To Nietzsche the contrast between the noble and the priest was one between heroism and cowering guilt, between facing fate and blaming oneself. The progeny of the two reveal it also. Art is at least an acceptance of
nobility, while philosophy is the expression of priestly guile. The struggle
between Homer and Plato, poetry and philosophy, is only a battle in the
war between creativity and asceticism.[94] Why truth? It also is an assertion
of the will to power by the priestly intelligence. That it ends by exhausting
religion and even itself does not hide the fact that philosophy also is a
member of the priestly family. Philosophy and science are not alternatives
to religion; they are merely new expressions of the same ascetic principle.[95] Truth is only another priestly narcotic to evade the meaninglessness
of nature. With that Nietzsche recognized the paradox of his own efforts.
For his genealogy is also a pursuit of truth. Just as Rousseau acknowledged
his own degeneracy, Nietzsche knew himself to be in the grip of an intellectuality he derided. Both saw the inescapability of the inheritance
whose origins they had so mercilessly exposed. There is a profound self-
hatred in this creation myth and in the subversive intent that it fulfills. To
be a member of a race of iron is a doom from which no amount of understanding can deliver one. Truth is here no consolation. Adamic guilt is not
the only form of self-humiliation.

Indeed the immense energy that the Adamic myth releases derives in
no small degree from its belief that guilt can be expiated and fallen man
redeemed. Hope is not locked up in a Pandora's jar for biblical mankind.
The most Hesiod can say about the age of iron man is that he wished he
had been born before or after it, since things could not possibly be worse.
That does not imply a cyclical or any other view of history. It does not say
that anything must follow the historically known world. The genealogy
of the gods that the daughters of Mnemosyne reveal is one in which past
and present are joined. It is an account of the past as an integral part of the
present. Genealogy deals with the ever-present, indestructible actualities.
So also Rousseau and Nietzsche found monotonous repetition, not really a
cycle. Especially at the psychological level there is perpetual recurrence.
For Rousseau natural man is reborn in each child who must go through the
same stages of imperfect denaturation. The Nietzschean struggle between
asceticism and vitality is a timeless one. This theme of psychic repetition
is also evident in Freud's anthropological writings. The guilt experienced by
the first generation of sons who cannibalistically disposed of the father-
ruler of the primeval horde is relived, and in identical form, by all future
generations.

It is indeed not surprising to find a late restatement of the Hesiodic
creation myth in Freud.[96] He undertook his anthropological investigation

with the intent of exposing the roots of that "collective obsessional neurosis," religion, above all biblical belief. *Totem and Taboo,* and especially *Moses and Monotheism,* which he had the good sense to call his "Moses-novel," were inspired by a profound hatred of religion.[97] Like his Enlightenment predecessors, Freud stood before the paradox of men driven by the pleasure principle to seek a happiness that must inevitably escape them.[98] The contribution of religion to this misery of mankind was particularly revolting to him. In one utopian outburst he considered the possibility of dispelling this damaging illusion. Mostly he entertained no such expectation. Quite on the contrary, he was convinced, on Lamarkian grounds, that the guilt feelings that give rise to religion were inherited and not acquired through learning. Religious beliefs and the characteristics and rituals of religious groups were, therefore, just as unalterable as any part of man's genetic structure. It was not a matter of tradition, of ignorance, or of oppression. Moreover, the primal act, the murder of the father, was not a recurrent fantasy. It was an actual event.[99] He quite literally meant the Faustian assertion, "In the beginning was the deed," that closes *Totem and Taboo.*[100] The Jews had killed the foreign, despotic Moses and had ever since been hereditary victims of his religion and of their guilt. Like Hesiod, he had very ambiguous feelings toward this Hebrew Zeus. If he was a god-obsessed tyrant, he was also a great man and the Jews owed him all their best characteristics—pride, intellectuality, and ethical vigor.[101] Nevertheless, they, and Christendom also, could thank him for a religion which had made them far more profoundly ignorant and unhappy than they would have been without it. Moreover, these fathers, Moses among them, were oppressors and their murder is as inevitable as Cronos' and Zeus's crimes. As in the original creation myth, it is not this or that act alone that matters, but the sequence of deeds as a whole. The evil father destroyed by evil sons does not disappear, and the myth of oppression, murder, guilt is ritually repeated over and over again. In Freud's, as in Nietzsche's myth, guilt and self-punishment directly contribute to making historical life a miserable, iron one. Asceticism, justice, and half-repressed violence make man's history what we know it to be. What renders Freud's a true creation myth is its genealogical character. There actually were acts of patricide, and from these are born, in successive order, blood-stained sons who inherit all the debilities of their murderous ancestors. Nor is this analogous to original sin. As in Hesiod, man is cursed rather than guilty. For Freud guilt itself and its illusions are the curse and a hereditary one. He drew a family tree of the belief system which had made men suffer. As in Hesiod, it is man's helplessness in the face of the misery imposed by his culture that evoked a subversive genealogy, and one that, quite consistently with all of Freud's thinking, demonstrated the indestructible presence of the past.

Since the main use of the creation myth in the modern age has been polemical, one may well ask whether it has been effective. Surely it has been and still is. Reductionism remains the most powerful of all methods of polemical abuse. To destroy the prestige of a convention, nothing will do as well as to show that it *really* is not what it appears and pretends to be. If its beginnings were sordid, surely its essence cannot be worthy. To unmask is to display an ambiguous parentage at best. Since we accept the origins, that is the motives, of actions as their moral definition, it makes sense to show up these less than admirable beginnings.[102] If the motives of conduct are its roots, then reductive criticism, a tracing back to the psychic or social origins of overtly moral behavior, can be shattering. As people continue to derive their sense of their own worth to some degree from that of their families, it is likely that they will be vulnerable to attacks on their pedigrees, whether moral or social. By analogy, the origins of their personal habits, character, and beliefs will also remain sensitive to such scrutiny.[103] The art of reductive unmasking today has come to depend on a sociological and psychological vocabulary, rather than that of traditional morality. Its resemblance to subversive genealogy is, however, clear. In pragmatic terms, surely, the creation myth has proved its value as a combative weapon in repeated and unabated practice.

If tracing a man's character to its psychic roots, or a social institution to its founders, could, and still does, effectively destroy their claims to honor, then the creation myth is certainly a most enduring archetype of polemical discourse. That is, however, not all that can be said about its archetypical character. It is not merely a form of intellectual warfare. In its most comprehensive character it is an evocative reconstruction of an abiding state of mind which arises out of the sense of the terrible distance between what we work for in history and what we always get. Such states of mind are not directly observable phenomena. They must be expressed in metaphorical language to be recognized and shared by others. Without going into the vexed question of what myths always are and how they *must* function in societies, one can take it that Hesiod wrote myths to "express unobservable realities in terms of observable phenomena," and that his successors have done the same thing in order to convey, in elaborate forms, their felt discord with their surroundings.[104] These myths deal not with "things encountered" but very much with things "remembered and considered."[105] They are meant to make evident and clear what is often merely felt. Actuality is to be revealed, shown, and shown up by a review of its origins that does not delineate the causes, but the awful character of this aging world. This is neither pseudo-history nor pseudo-etiology nor primitive science. It is neither the rival nor the precursor of more rigorous forms of thought. It is psychological evocation, an appeal, with the aid of very familiar memories, to others to accept a picture of social man as a permanently displaced person.

Creation myths appeal to the memory. They are mnemonic devices.

Hesiod relied on familiar tales no less than on common experiences, and so did his successors. Within any culture there is at any time a wealth of mythical memory upon which the philosophical fable can draw to structure its message for its audience. From Mother Goose to beloved childhood stories to television commercials we have all acquired a less than half-remembered store of mythical building blocks. Among the highly educated there is, moreover, a literary memory which certainly includes the great myths of classical antiquity. The modern writer of creation myths evokes these memories in us to make us understand his particular reconstruction. That is also why their reformulations continue to interest us and to speak to us so immediately. One does not tire of Rousseau or of Nietzsche because they awaken literary and mythical memories in us which we can attach to their suggestions. We possess the "associative clusters," so that the new telling of the old myth is sufficiently familiar to be understood.[106] Yet it is also novel enough in its images and metaphors to make us rethink it. Hegel was surely right when he noted that the memory re-members, that it is a faculty that integrates thought. It acts to make us entirely conscious of ideas, states of mind, intellectual possibilities that rested in disordered and unstructured form in the recesses of our minds. When we are made to recollect them philosophically, these ideas are liberated and re-formed.[107]

The actual experiences which give these myths their emotional power are often as obvious as they are general. The sense of inferiority and its anger are common enough. Gods and men, fathers and sons, strong and weak, astute and dull, the many and the one, the rich and the poor; there are endless possible occasions familiar to all to render the subject matter of creation myths instantly stimulating. Rousseau may have exaggerated in seeing inequality as the defining character of all association. There is more to politics than inferiority and superiority, and the powerlessness of the weak. It is not an insignificant aspect of all known social history either. The harshness of justice in a dismal age, the defeat of the creator by the shrewd manipulator, the misery of self-generating guilt, all speak of and to remembered experiences of defeat. The creation myth addresses itself to these recurrent failures. They do not always afflict the least intelligent men. For them the creation myth is an archetype that acts as a model of their own experiences and as one for their own efforts at making sense of their yet unformulated ideas. They might use it to tell their own version of the myth, or they can rest content with following its many known forms. The latter is not a wholly passive rereading of completed texts. Interpretive latitude is, after all, very great in reconstructing the political literature of the past. Today, indeed, the study of the history of that literature, and of its critical remaking, has taken the place of the art of articulating present experience through older myths. However, though criticism is not able to produce new metaphors or images, it is not entirely unlike the more imaginative retellings of the past. For that also was a matter of recreation, even though far less inhibited by the sense of history and the limits of the given than is the art of interpretation. Yet both are at one in this: by appealing to our memory they stir our imagination and, above all, our will to understanding. Both bring down the barriers between past and present, and free the individual from the confines of personal and contemporary knowledge by opening to view intellectual possibilities that could not have been imagined in solitude or found among the merely living.

REFERENCES

1. M. I. Finley, *The World of Odysseus* (New York: Meridian Books, 1959), pp. 142-144. For pedigrees among Olympians, see H. P. Nilsson, *A History of Greek Religion*, trans. F. J. Fielden (Oxford: Clarendon Press, 1925), p. 148.

2. *The Metaphysical Elements of Justice,* trans. John Ladd (Indianapolis: Bobbs-Merrill, 1965), p. 84.

3. *Leviathan,* ed. Michael Oakeshott (Oxford: Blackwell, 1946), p. 463. For Burke's views, see *A Vindication of Natural Society,* in *Works* (Boston: Little, Brown, 1869), I, 9-10.

4. Hesiod's *Catalogues of Women* is a genealogy listing those women who by mating with a god founded noble families.

5. W. K. C. Guthrie, *In the Beginning* (Ithaca: Cornell University Press, 1957), pp. 27-28, 63-69, and *History of Greek Philosophy* (Cambridge, Eng.: University Press, 1967), I, 142; Werner Jaeger, *The Theology of the Early Greek Philosophers* (Oxford: Clarendon Press, 1947), p. 16.

6. *Theogony* in *Hesiod,* trans. Hugh G. Evelyn-White (Cambridge, Mass.: Harvard University Press, 1936), p. 87.

7. Thorkild Jacobsen in Henri Frankfort and others, *Before Philosophy* (Harmondsworth: Penguin Books, 1949), pp. 139-140, 162-165.

8. J-P. Vernant, *Mythe et penseé chez les grecs,* 2d ed. (Paris: Maspero, 1969), pp. 291-292. It is a point that Hegel particularly noted. See especially *Lectures on the Philosophy of Religion,* trans. E. B. Speirs and J. B. Sanderson (New York: Humanities Press, 1968), II, 229-239.

9. Frankfort and others, *Before Philosophy,* p. 250; W. K. C. Guthrie, *The Greeks and Their Gods* (Boston: Beacon Press, 1954), pp. 51-53; Werner Jaeger, *Paideia* (New York: Oxford University Press, 1939-1944), I, 54-73; Rzach, "Hesiodos," Pauly-Wissowa, *Real-Encyclopädie* (1912), XV, 1167-1240; Bruno Snell, *The Discovery of the Mind,* trans. T. G. Rosenmeyer (Cambridge, Mass.: Harvard University Press, 1953), pp. 138, 304; Friedrich Solmsen, *Hesiod and Aeschylus* (Ithaca: Cornell University Press, 1949), passim; M. L. West, ed., *Theogony* (Oxford: Clarendon Press, 1966), 1-39.

10. *Theogony,* p. 81.

11. *Ibid.,* p. 91.

12. *Ibid.*, p. 95.

13. *Ibid.*, pp. 95-96.

14. *Ibid.*, p. 113.

15. *Ibid.*, p. 143.

16. Kurt von Fritz, "Das Hesiodische in den Werken Hesiods," in Kurt von Fritz and others, *Hésiode et son influence* (Geneva: Fondation Hardt, 1962), pp. 3-47.

17. For example, M. H. James on "Mythology of Ancient Greece," in S. N. Kramer, ed., *Mythologies of the Ancient World* (Garden City, N.Y.: Doubleday, 1961), pp. 265-266. See Cedric Whitman, *Homer and the Heroic Tradition* (New York: Norton, 1965), pp. 241-248. Also Guthrie, *The Greeks and Their Gods,* p. 298; Nietzsche, *On the Genealogy of Morals,* trans. and ed. Walter Kaufmann (New York: Vintage Books, 1967), I, § 11.

18. *Theogony,* p. 119.

19. *Ibid.*, p. 121.

20. *Work and Days,* in *Hesiod,* p. 5.

21. *Ibid.*, p. 7.

22. *Ibid.*, p. 9.

23. Vernant, *Mythe,* pp. 20-22; Whitman, *Homer,* p. 43; Nietzsche, *Genealogy.*

24. *Work and Days,* p. 19.

25. *Ibid.*

26. Jacobsen, in Frankfort and others, *Before Philosophy,* pp. 139-140, 162-165.

27. E. R. Dodds, *The Greeks and the Irrational* (Boston: Beacon Press, 1957), pp. 44-46.

28. Xenophanes in Kathleen Freeman, trans. and ed., *Ancilla to the Pre-Socratic Philosophers* (Oxford: Blackwell, 1948), p. 22.

29. *Republic,* 377b-379a.

30. *Euthyphro,* 6.

31. *Republic,* 562e-563a.

32. Norman O. Brown, "Introduction" to his translation of Hesiod's *Theogony* (New York: Liberal Arts Press, 1953), pp. 21-22.

33. Niccolo Machiavelli, *The Prince,* VII; *Discourses on the First Ten Books of Livy,* I, ix, xxvi; II, xiii; III, vi.

34. *The Prince,* VIII, VI; *Discourses,* I, x.

35. See Hannah Arendt, *Between Past and Future* (New York: Viking Press, 1961), pp. 136-139.

36. Paul Ricoeur, *The Symbolism of Evil,* trans. Emerson Buchanan (New York: Harper and Row, 1967), pp. 206-278.

37. These remarks are an application of the ideas of Clifford Geertz to a very specific cultural group, the literati of Europe, which as such has "historically transmitted patterns of meaning" no less than the groups he discusses. See his remarkable monograph "Religion as a Cultural System," in Michael Banton, ed., *Anthropological Approaches to the Study of Religion* (London: Tavistock Publications, 1968), pp. 1-46.

38. *Oeuvres Complètes* (Paris: Gallimard, 1959——), Bibliothèque de la Pléiade, III, 49-50; IV, 936.

39. I cannot agree with the suggestion that the fairy tale of the Sleeping Beauty underlies Rousseau's theories, because I think it is a misreading of his texts to impute hopes of a bright future to him. In the work under discussion here he certainly makes his dread of the coming ages perfectly clear. The Sleeping Beauty joke occurs in Northrop Frye's otherwise admirable *Anatomy of Criticism* (Princeton: Princeton University Press, 1957), p. 354.

40. *Discours sur l'origine et les fondements de l'inégalité parmis les hommes*, in C. E. Vaughan, ed., *The Political Writings of Jean-Jacques Rousseau* (Oxford: Blackwell, 1962), p. 142.

41. *Ibid.*, p. 151.

42. *Ibid.*, p. 142.

43. *Ibid.*, pp. 141, 196.

44. For the most explicit statement of this see *Emile, Oeuvres*, IV, 305, 814.

45. *Discours*, pp. 138, 141.

46. *Ibid.*, p. 136.

47. *Ibid.*, pp. 136, 138-139.

48. *Ibid.*, pp. 140, 142.

49. *Ibid.*, pp. 145, 151.

50. *Ibid.*, pp. 152-153.

51. *Ibid.*, pp. 159-160.

52. The notion that Rousseau is following the biblical archetype of the fall has often been put forward, most recently by Jean Starobinski in his "Introduction" to the *Discours, Oeuvres Complètes*, III, lvii. It is, I think, wrong.

53. *Discours*, p. 168.

54. *Ibid.*, p. 169.

55. *Ibid.*, pp. 170-171.

56. *Ibid.*, pp. 171-172.

57. *Ibid.*, pp. 172-173.

58. *Ibid.*, p. 173.

59. *Ibid.*, pp. 174-175.

60. *Ibid.*, p. 176. Rousseau did have a direct precursor, Dicaearchus, a follower of Aristotle, who also saw agriculture and metallurgy as man's undoing. Guthrie, *In the Beginning*, pp. 74-76.

61. *Discours*, pp. 177-178.

62. *Ibid.*, p. 179.

63. *Ibid.*, p. 181.

64. *Ibid.*, p. 183.

65. *Ibid.*, p. 189.

66. *Ibid.*, pp. 193-194.

67. *Ibid.*, pp. 219-220.

68. *Ibid.*, pp. 191-192.

69. This opinion of Hesiod is an early one and appears in Nietzsche's lecture notes prepared for his course when he was still actively engaged in teaching, *Gesammelte Werke* (Munich: Musarion Verlag, 1922), V, 97-103. Unflattering remarks about Rousseau occur frequently in most of Nietzsche's works. A fair sample can be found in *The Twilight of the Idols*, trans. R. J. Hollingdale (Harmondsworth: Penguin Books, 1968), § 48. Here and throughout I cite sections rather than pages in Nietzsche's works. I have relied throughout on Walter Kaufmann's remarkable translations and my paraphrases follow them no less than the direct quotes. I use the paragraphs because these make it easier to follow the original German if anyone should choose to do so, and because Kaufmann does so. Additional outpourings against Rousseau are to be found in *The Will to Power*, especially §§ 94, 98-100.

70. *Birth of Tragedy*, trans. and ed. Walter Kaufmann (New York: Vintage Books, 1967), § 23.

71. "Attempt at a Self-Criticism," in *Birth of Tragedy*, § 6.

72. *Birth of Tragedy*, § 9.

73. Nietzsche, *Genealogy*, I, § 16.

74. *Ibid.*, I, §§ 1, 4.

75. *Ibid.*, I, § 6.

76. *Ibid.*, I, § 6.

77. *Ibid.*, I, § 7.

78. *Ibid.*, I, § 10.

79. *Ibid.*, I, §§ 3, 11.

80. *Ibid.*, II, § 3.

81. *Ibid.*, II, §§ 2, 3, 4.

82. *Ibid.*, II, § 1.

83. *Ibid.*, II, § 5.

84. *Ibid.*, II, § 7; also *Beyond Good and Evil*, trans. Walter Kaufmann (New York: Vintage Books, 1966), § 229.

85. *Genealogy,* II, § 6.

86. *Ibid.,* II, § 7.

87. *Ibid.,* II, § 9.

88. *Ibid.,* II, § 11.

89. *Ibid.,* II, §§ 14, 15, 23.

90. *Ibid.,* II, § 16; III, § 9.

91. *Ibid.,* II, § 20.

92. *Ibid.,* II, § 21; III, §§ 15, 17.

93. *Ibid.,* II, § 24; III, § 28.

94. *Ibid.,* III, § 25.

95. *Ibid.,* III, §§ 24, 25, 27.

96. Robin Fox, "Totem and Taboo Reconsidered," *The Structural Study of Myth and Totemism,* ed. Edmund Leach (London: Tavistock Publications, 1967), pp. 161-176.

97. Ernest Jones, *The Life and Works of Sigmund Freud* (New York: Basic Books, 1953-1957), II, 350-360; III, 349-374; Paul Roazen, *Freud: Political and Social Thought* (New York: Knopf, 1968), pp. 125-192.

98. *Civilization and Its Discontents* (London: Hogarth, 1946), pp. 26-28, 39-40.

99. *Moses and Monotheism* (New York: Vintage Books, 1967), pp. 102-114, 126-130, 167-175.

100. *Totem and Taboo* (New York: Vintage Books, 1946), p. 207.

101. *Moses,* pp. 109, 135-147, 158.

102. Nietzsche was, I believe, the first to observe that the search for moral motives was derived from the aristocratic concern with pedigrees. See *Beyond Good and Evil,* § 32.

103. That Freud was not above using psychoanalytic technique to destroy a public reputation can be seen—whatever the degree of his collaboration—in his and William C. Bullitt's *Thomas Woodrow Wilson* (Boston: Houghton Mifflin, 1967).

104. This definition, though it is evidently used very differently here, is drawn from E. R. Leach, "Genesis as Myth," in John Middleton, ed., *Myth and Cosmos* (New York: Natural History Press, 1967), p. 1.

105. Again for purposes quite different from those of their originator I have taken these phrases from Susanne K. Langer, *Philosophy in a New Key,* 3d ed. (Cambridge, Mass.: Harvard University Press, 1969), pp. 144-145.

106. Frye, *Anatomy of Criticism,* p. 102, and "The Road to Excess," in Northrop Frye and others, *Myth and Symbol* (Lincoln, Neb.: University of Nebraska Press, 1963), pp. 7-8.

107. *The Phenomenology of Mind,* trans. J. B. Baillie, 2d ed. (London: Macmillan, 1949), pp. 789-808. It is evident that this essay has throughout been informed by ideas drawn from that work and especially its closing pages. As such it could be called an effort, however insignificant, of applied Hegelian phenomenology.

REUBEN A. BROWER

Visual and Verbal Translation of Myth:
Neptune in Virgil, Rubens, Dryden

ALTHOUGH WE commonly speak of "*the* Oedipus myth" or "*the* Hercules myth," and though anthropologists refer to mythical "archetypes" or "structures," it can be said that there are no myths, only versions. To put it another way, there are only texts for interpretation, whether the text is written or oral, a piece of behavior—a dance or a cockfight—a drawing or painting, a sculptured stone, or a terracotta pot. The principle texts I have chosen for exploration here are two of them verbal, the third a painting (with some related examples in other visual media). My primary concerns in exploring each text will be with how the "same" myth—the universalizing "the" seems unavoidable—is transformed when rendered in words or in line and color and what parallels and contrasts can be observed between these different events in expression.

The present essay began in a rather casual encounter between an interest in translation and an interest in paintings of the seventeenth and eighteenth century, particularly of classical subjects. While making some comparisons between Dryden's *Aeneid* and Virgil's, I happened to remember the beautiful picture by Rubens in the Fogg Museum, *Quos ego—*, or "Neptune Calming the Tempest," which is based presumably on a well-known scene in the first book of the *Aeneid*. From that encounter, and later visions and revisions, comes this venture into the notoriously beguiling study of a "Parallel Betwixt Poetry and Painting."

In Virgil's poem, it will be remembered, Neptune rises from the sea to calm the storm in which Aeneas was shipwrecked on his voyage from Troy. Aeolus, king of the winds, acting on Juno's orders, had loosed violent gales from the south, east, and west. Neptune breaks off his denunciation of the winds, "*quos ego—*," "whom I—," in order to smooth the waves, scatter the clouds, and bring back the sun. He then rides off driving his horses and chariot beneath a cloudless sky. A glance at Rubens' picture (see figure 1) will show that the painting is strikingly like and unlike the narrative. Dryden's translation, though reasonably true to the speech and actions of the original, has revised the myth in ways that can be better understood once we are more familiar with Rubens' painting and the

155

Figure 1. Rubens, *Quos ego*——, "Neptune Calming the Tempest," Fogg Art Museum. Courtesy of the Fogg Art Museum, Harvard University, Alpheus Hyatt Fund.

transformation that has taken place there. The painting, which I refer to henceforth as the "sketch," is a beautifully executed modello for a large work, a sketch in no pejorative sense.[1] Many questions besides the primary one concerning the transformation of a myth will arise as we explore our various texts. What is the mythical action "like" in each version? What does each version tell us about the mythical thinking or imagination of the author? What does it tell us about the world in which the translation grew? And since all three artists are rendering an event in nature, what is the experience of nature that comes through to us in the Virgilian narrative, the translation, and the picture?

Translations, in whatever medium, can be best understood not only in relation to an original text but in light of the "conditions of expression" within which they were created. Dryden's version is in rimed pentameters, because that was held to be the proper measure for heroic poetry. Rubens' sketch has a pictorial rhythm common to many baroque paintings of mythological and religious subjects. Two conditions that affected Dryden and Rubens with almost equal force are the Renaissance and seventeenth-century doctrine and practice of "imitation" and the complex of literary and pictorial traditions variously referred to as "heroic" or "historical." The most important sense of imitation for the present study is not the exact copying of classical vocabulary or motifs, but that dynamic process of "assimilation," as Gombrich calls it,[2] by which a Renaissance artist remakes in his own terms what he has lovingly learned in active commerce with masterpieces of the past. Though Dryden spoke scornfully of modernizing imitation in contrast with translation, he indicates in *The Dedication of the Aeneis* that his aim has been imitation in a sense common to many of his contemporaries: "Yet I may presume to say . . . that taking all the Materials of this divine Author, I have endeavour'd to make Virgil speak such English, as he wou'd himself have spoken, if he had been born in *England,* and in this present Age."[3] Earlier in the same essay he shows that he recognized the close parallel between creative imitation in poetry and in painting:

> By reading *Homer, Virgil* was taught to imitate his Invention: That is, to imitate like him; which is no more, than if a Painter studied *Raphael,* that he might learn to design after his manner. And thus I might imitate *Virgil,* if I were capable of writing an Heroick Poem, and yet the Invention be my own: But I shou'd endeavour to avoid a servile Copying.[4]

We can sharpen our perception of what Dryden and Rubens "saw" in Virgil by considering briefly how the Greek Neptune, Poseidon, was presented in Homer and in one or two examples from the Greek arts of a later period. As Cedric Whitman has noted,[5] we have no certain illustrations of Homer's text from the Geometric vases more or less contemporary with the *Iliad* and the *Odyssey,* though there are paintings of episodes from the Trojan story not included in the Homeric poems. The contrast drawn by

Whitman between Minoan and Geometric art is most helpful for understanding Homer's representation of his gods, and of Poseidon in particular:

For the one, reality lies in the actual appearance; for the other, it lies in action
and inner nature, and there can be no question as to which view is nearer to
Homer's. Homer almost never describes anyone's actual appearance. His method
is strictly dramatic, emphasizing always deed, motive, and consequence.[6]

To all who are familiar with the vivid images of Greek vase painting
and sculpture it may be surprising to discover how little we are made to
see the gods of Homer. We have, it is true, impressions of Athena's dazzling
brightness and of the shining eyes of Zeus. But though we are told how
Poseidon took three giant strides from Samos to Aigai, the point is not the
visual image it may suggest to the modern reader, but the action as testimony of things not seen, of *numen*, divine power. In general, we see the
Homeric gods doing and suffering, not "looking." For if the heroes of the
Iliad are "godlike," the gods are like heroes. While Zeus sleeps, Poseidon
defends the Danai, leading them to battle with the usual heroic cry,
iomen, "let us go forward!" (xiv.374). He comes to the rescue of one
warrior, Antilochus; he is angry because of the death of another, Amphimachus, and enters the battle to avenge him: "A god, he strode through
mortals' struggle" (xiii.238). We hear in prophecy how he will lead the
way "with trident in hand" (xii.27) in destroying the Greek Wall. This is
the sole mention of the trident in the *Iliad*, the phrase implying that
Poseidon is using it as an instrument, as he does later in the *Odyssey*,
when angered at Ajax, son of Oïleus, "taking the trident in his mighty
hands, he struck the rock on Gyrai, and split it off" (iv.506-507). But if the
actions and emotions are manlike, the scale is gigantic. Poseidon speaks
with the voice of "nine or ten thousand men" (*Iliad* xiv.135)—though this
reminds us of Achilles' colossal shout at the trench. The epithets commonly
used of Poseidon similarly imply action on a huge scale: He is *gaioxos
ennosigaios*, one "who encircles the earth and shakes it." He is also *kyano-
chaites*, "dark (blue)-haired," an epithet also used of the mane of horses,
and perhaps suggesting the color of the sea. (Both connotations are appropriate since Poseidon is also closely associated with horses.) It is worth
noting that he is not grey-haired, no old man of the sea. Zeus is in fact
older and more powerful. But though Poseidon acknowledges Zeus's
superior strength, he reminds him that they are both equal in honor, and
that as the lot gave Hades the underworld, and Zeus the heavens, so his
share was the "grey sea." He adds that the earth and "broad Olympus" are
common property of all three, thus emphasizing both his Olympian character and his role as earth-god (xv.190-195). He is the great earth-shaker when
he steps down to Aigai, an episode that anticipates in part the scene in Virgil:

He took three long strides forward, and in the fourth came to his goal,
Aigai, where his glorious house was built in the waters'

depth, glittering with gold, imperishable forever.
Going there he harnessed under his chariot his bronze-shod horses,
flying-footed, with long manes streaming of gold; and he put on
clothing of gold about his own body, and took up the golden
lash, carefully compacted, and climed up into his chariot
and drove it across the waves. And about him the sea beasts came up
from their deep places and played in his path, and acknowledged
   their master,
and the sea stood apart before him, rejoicing. The horses winged on
delicately, and the bronze axle beneath was not wetted.

xiii.20-30[7]

There is visual splendor in these lines, but gold, it should be remembered, is not merely something beautiful to the eye, but a sign of kingliness and divinity, of the "unperishing." Equally notable is the matter-of-fact character of the narrative. The horses are "bronze-shod," as elsewhere in Homer; the lash is "well-made," and the language of harnessing, mounting, and driving is standard and formulaic; the chariot, *diphros*, is no different from those used by Homeric warriors. Miracle enters with: [Poseidon] "drove it across the waves" and "the bronze axle beneath was not wetted." But "miracle" as I have used it is a term of the Enlightenment, of a world governed by laws of nature, whereas in Homer the marvelous "occurs as it occurs," and it is recorded in the same tone in which "real" events are recorded. As there is no distinctly physical world, so there is no distinctly spiritual one. The "will of Zeus" is not *la sua volontade*, but what Zeus quite humanly wants and intends. Magic is present very often in other actions of Poseidon. He takes the form of many persons; he strikes a man with his staff and it fills him with courage; he bewitches one hero with his eyes and makes the spear stroke of another useless. These and similar actions of many gods are "just the things gods do," and the resultant effects on mortals might well have taken place without divine intervention. To say that a god caused or occasioned the behavior is not to rationalize it away, but to make the commonplace mysteriously wonderful. (As it is: how does a man suddenly become brave? why does the spear miss its mark?)

It may be said that when the Greeks represented their gods definitively in painted and sculpted images, they ran the risk of making the wonderful commonplace. The unnameable god of the Hebrews rightly forbade graven images: he was a *spiritual* divinity in a sense that Christians and Platonists well understand. It is the human that is glorified in Greek sculpture as in the Homeric poems. None of Homer's gods can compare in heroic dignity with Achilles and Hector. The well-known bronze in Athens (see figure 2), whether of Poseidon[8] or of Zeus, is majestic in stance and noble in facial expression. The impression of contained, arrested motion, as often in Greek sculpture, is the "thing"—the effortless ease of the athlete, of a *man*, not of a divinity in the Judaeo-Christian sense. (A "god" yes, but not God.) The heroic character of the figure comes out if it is compared with a

Figure 2. Poseidon/Zeus, ca. 470-350 B.C. National Museum, Athens.

Hellenistic counterpart[9]—in the overripe, sensuous handling of muscles, the melodramatic pose, the turbulent locks of hair, the absence of an implied inner life.

We can see what happens when the heroic vagueness of Homer is translated into clearly outlined figures by looking at the Poseidon of the Amphitrite Painter[10] in the Boston Museum (figure 3). Here Poseidon is shown as a slender young man in the act of attacking Polybotes, whom he has already wounded. The god, bearded, his long hair crowned with a wreath,

Figure 3. Poseidon and Polybotes, Attic red-figured Kantharos, Museum of Fine Arts, Boston. Courtesy of the Museum of Fine Arts, Boston.

seems about to run his trident into the giant's side (as he actually does in another version, in the Louvre).[11] Over Poseidon's left arm a "small wrap" falls in elegant motionless folds from beneath a pillowy mass, "the island of Nisyros (which he snapped off with his trident from the island of Cos)," and which he is about to "bring down on his opponent."[12] "What man, what god is this?" His glance is alert and amused, and his slight figure—David to Polybotes' Goliath—looks more like the quick-devising Odysseus than the great god of the *Iliad*. If Homer's Poseidon were accurately rendered, he would be of Brobdignagian proportions. A more serious version of the same scene, by the Troilus Painter,[13] shows the god going after the giant with a more violent if less well-aimed forward thrust. Both these figures, like many representations of gods on Greek vases, are barely distinguishable in size or type from the heroes or the young men leaving for wars. Their divinity is marked principally by their icons, the trident, the club of Hercules, the helmet of Athena, the drinking cup of Dionysos.

To jump from these fifth-century forms to Virgil's scene is to have a curious sensation of moving both backward and forward in time—a characteristic response to a poem that is at once a recall of the Homeric world and a prophesy of Rome's Augustan age. Postponing consideration of this mixture of impulses and motifs, let us concentrate first on picture, on scene and gesture in Virgil's account of how Neptune calmed the storm:

> Interea magno misceri murmure pontum
> emissamque hiemem sensit Neptunus et imis   125
> stagna refusa vadis, graviter commotus; et alto
> prospiciens summa placidum caput extulit unda.
> disiectam Aeneae toto videt aequore classem,
> fluctibus oppressos Troas caelique ruina.
> nec latuere doli fratrem Iunonis et irae.   130
> Eurum ad se Zephyrumque vocat, dehinc talia fatur:
>   "Tantane vos generis tenuit fiducia vestri?
> iam caelum terramque meo sine numine, venti,
> miscere et tantas audetis tollere moles?
> quos ego—! sed motos praestat componere fluctus   135
> post mihi non simili poena commissa luetis.
> maturate fugam regique haec dicite vestro:
> non illi imperium pelagi saevumque tridentem,
> sed mihi sorte datum. tenet ille immania saxa,
> vestras, Eure, domos; illa se iactet in aula   140
> Aeolus et clauso ventorum carcere regnet."
>   Sic ait et dicto citius tumida aequora placat
> collectasque fugat nubes solemque reducit.
> Cymothoe simul et Triton adnixus acuto
> detrudunt navis scopulo; levat ipse tridenti   145
> et vastas aperit syrtis et temperat aequor
> atque rotis summas levibus perlabitur undas.
> ac veluti magno in populo cum saepe coorta est
> seditio saevitque animis ignobile vulgus;
> iamque faces et saxa volant, furor arma ministrat;   150
> tum, pietate gravem ac meritis si forte virum quem
> conspexere, silent arrectisque auribus astant;
> ille regit dictis animos et pectora mulcet:
> sic cunctus pelagi cecidit fragor, aequora postquam
> prospiciens genitor caeloque invectus aperto   155
> flectit equos curruque volans dat lora secundo.

Aeneid I.124-156[14]

To read this narrative properly demands, in Henry James's phrase, "a sharper survey of the elements of Appearance" than any similar episode in Homer—Poseidon's journey in the *Iliad,* or the shipwreck of Odysseus. Virgil asks us much more often to attend to the seen thing, the picture in words, as in the memorable lines just before this passage:

apparent rari nantes in gurgite vasto,
arma virum tabulaeque et Troia gaza per undas.
118-119

Here and there are seen swimmers in the vast gulf,
arms of men, and planks, and Troy's wealth on the waves.

The first impression in the Neptune narrative is of the sea's confusion, *magno misceri murmure pontum*, the storm that the god "sees," *sensit*. Next, the waters sucked up from the lowest depths, *imis/stagna refusa vadis*, the phrase neatly placed between *Neptunus* and *graviter commotus*, "mightily stirred," so that we take the participle as describing the sea's "wild commotion" and the god's anger. (Note here and throughout the importance of descriptive adjectives—aural, visual, emotive.) Then follows the unforgettable contrast: the god "looking forth," *prospiciens*, raises his "*calm* head," *placidum caput*, from the sea's surface. "He sees," and we see, "the scattered, broken fleet," *disectam classem*. We hear of his "divine power," *numine*, and glimpse again the confusion of earth, sky, and masses of water (133-134). "Sooner done than said," the god "calms the swollen waters," *tumida aequora placat*: "he chases the clouds away and brings back the sun" (143). "The nymph Cymothoe and Triton, working together, *adnixus*, shove, *detrudunt*, the ships from the sharp rock, *acuto scopulo*." In a series of swift action verbs—like Homer's in describing Poseidon's destruction of the wall—the god "himself with his trident lifts the ships, lays open the vast sandbanks, soothes the water, and on light wheels goes gliding over the very top of the waves" (145-147). At the end Neptune is seen guiding horses and chariot with the reins, moving away against a clear sky, *caeloque invectus aperto*— one final brilliant image of light, reviving by contrast the clouds and "the black night brooding on the sea," *ponto nox incubat atra* (89), when the storm struck.

The increased emphasis in Virgil on appearance and scene, as compared with similar passages in the *Iliad*, is proof of an interest in the natural setting for its own sake rare in Greek poetry. Yet if we think of the phrase Wordsworth once used of Virgil in a disparaging contrast with Dryden, "his *eye* upon his object,"[15] we must feel that Virgil had *his* eye on much more than the event in nature. The storm is being "done up," given scenic value in a kind of mythological drama. It is surprising that so much of the simple anthropomorphism of Homer has survived: down-to-earth human actions and feelings—using the trident as a lever to heave up ships, the passionate anger of the god. But there is also some loss of the immediately magical and the divinely mysterious, some imminent separation between icon and intended religious significance. The presence of the looming Roman *fatum* is more *felt*, as everywhere in the *Aeneid*, than the imported Olympians. As often happens in translations, a retraction in one area is matched by a gain in another area of experience slighted or vaguely implied in the original. The Neptune of the *Aeneid*, this scene notwithstanding, is much less of a dramatic character than Poseidon in the *Iliad*. In nearly every episode in which Poseidon appears, he is vigorously carrying out his role as ally of the Greeks in the long drama of the Trojan war, and his will be the final act, when with Apollo he destroys the wall of the Achaeans. The gain in Virgil comes through dynamic assimilation: Virgil turns Poseidon into something new, a *literary* symbol, which bears a part, as recent critics have shown, in the imaginative order of the whole poem. The order is not Homer's, but the creation of a very different kind of poet, a poet of symbolic and lyric narration.

Before considering how Virgil's form of "proceeding" is reflected in his transformation of the Poseidon myth, let us look briefly at Neptune's speech to the winds and the related simile of the man whose wise words put a stop to an incipient uprising, *seditio* (148-153). Even when Neptune sounds most like the Greek god—as when Poseidon reminds Zeus that the three brothers born of Kronos and Rhea each got an equal share of honor "when the lots were shaken" (xv.190)—the rhetoric, the accent, and the implications are very different. Poseidon's rhetoric is familial, though saved from vulgarity by the formulaic style, but Neptune has been through a course in Roman forensics, and the tone is reminiscent of Cicero to the followers of Catiline —shrewd, but senatorial. The aposiopesis, "*quos ego—*," is the master stroke of an accomplished orator: the terrors of the incompleted sentence are more fearsome than anything he might merely *say*. Instead of a "lot," we hear of *imperium* (almost "sphere of influence"), a term reeking of Roman power and law, of the Augustan world constitution, the peculiar political achievement that Virgil's poem is celebrating. In an admirable passage, Victor Pöschl reminds us of the surprising force and extension of meaning and of the links with a larger imaginative design through Virgil's use of a political simile for "the subjection of the storm." In so doing, Virgil was "highlighting a very important sphere of the poem (namely that of the historical world)." "The connecting symbol becomes an expression of the symbolic relation between nature and politics, myth and history, which is at the heart of the *Aeneid*." In speaking of Virgil, we may refer rightly to an "order of Nature" under divine law, implying a sophisticated notion, an *idea*, of which there are only faint hints in the poetry of Homer. But we also feel that the Neptune-Aeolus myth has a new function in Virgil as a poetic symbol for the storm, locally for the actual storm, and in the larger economy of the poem for the "wave breaking against Roman destiny."[16] Or, as Brooks Otis points out in his analysis of *Aeneid* I, "the contrast [in the simile] between the *vir pietate gravis ac meritis* [the man revered for 'piety' and his services], and the *ignobile vulgus* [the common herd] armed by *furor* reveals at a stroke the human meaning of the storm."[17] In Otis' view, the storm and its calming becomes an instance of the dominant moral and thematic pattern of the *Aeneid*, the opposition of *pietas* and *furor*, enacted in countless events throughout the poem. A use of myth so easily open to thematic interpretation comes close to allegory. Though many readers will agree that Virgil does not quite cross the line between the two modes, they may at the same time feel that we are too often distracted, so to speak, from men or gods in action, from drama, to something beyond, to large values and concerns— the history and destiny of Rome, the moral and religious ideal of "piety," the dream of a harmony attainable among personal, political, divine, and natural realms of experience.

If we now recall Virgil's action-picture and turn to Rubens' sketch (figure 1), what do we see, disregarding for the moment the historical occasion of this adaptation of the original? What strikes the viewer above all is violent motion—in the waves, the horses, and the wind-tossed clouds— seen against the mellow golden light at the horizon and opening in the distant sky. The center and director of this movement is Neptune, who is stepping forward and upward in his chariot-shell, his piercing look following the line of that marvelous gesture of command toward the departing winds and the returning light. The streaming hair and beard, the twisting torso, the whole body "works" with the emotion implied in glance and gesture. The mighty right arm and the trident-thrust (exactly on the line of the forward bending knee), symbolize, like the outstretched left arm and pointing finger, power and intention—no question here of anything so practical as raising ships or splitting rocks or wounding a giant adversary. Yet the trident is no mere identifying icon or stage prop as in its decorative use by many artists, including Rubens himself on occasion. The grandly serious look, the body's total gesture, are alone sufficient: no further evidence of things seen or unseen is necessary, as in Homer and in Virgil. We are nearer to something like the imagined gesture of *Fiat lux*.

As we should expect, the pictorial element has been much enhanced. The buxom nymphs, in lighter tones of brown and pink, with faint sea-blue touches on the hair, blend below into sea-green waves, as if to blend mythical figure and its origin. The winds appear as half-seen faces and forms emerging from cloud-wind streaks, figures and clouds alike done in a range of fused colors from grey and slate blue to brownish and pinkish tones. The chariot-shell—no literal Homeric or Roman war chariot—has produced a kind of wheel with incomplete spokes sprouting "naturally" from the shell whorl. No wheels as in Virgil move lightly over the water: this wheel, such as it is, is involved in the hazy watery motion. The horses are sea horses, hippocampi, legs entangled in panic violence, vivid expressions of the sea's turbulence. These creatures could hardly be driven, nor does this god think of driving, though one nymph pulls—ineffectually—on a "pink bridle."[18] Rubens' scene is not least pictorial in over-all composition, in the manner in which violent motion is ordered and contained: the central and echoing diagonal thrusts, of which Jacob Rosenberg speaks so eloquently, the balancing of light and dark in human and animal figures, in ship and sail forms, in areas of sea and sky, the posing of definite and less definite outlines—color, line, and light so harmonized that all actors, animate and inanimate, seem to be caught up in the total natural and supernatural event.

How composition works in the two media of picture and poetry is particularly significant for defining the different reinterpretations of the Poseidon myth. "Words move in time only." In Virgil the action-picture is enmeshed in other narrative and nonnarrative contexts of metaphor, theme, and history. The painter has only one instant, at the most the brief time while the eye moves, as in viewing Ruben's sketch, from left to right, upward and downward within the frame. The shift from poem to painting is all the more striking when the artist has chosen for his moment a speech, an effective piece of rhetoric compared to another piece of rhetoric.

What happens, then, in Rubens' translation? No "calm head" rises from the water; Virgil's anticipation of the calm to come is rendered here immediately in the outstretched hand pointing toward the smoother sea and the brighter light. What was storm and darkness *before* in Virgil is in the picture storm and coming brightness here and now. Virgil's contrasts are compressed with a much more shocking effect. The overwhelming violence of the horses and waves in the foreground is countered directly above by the lovely arc of sails as the favoring breeze fills them. At one point the compactness of poetry is equaled or surpassed in picture: Virgil's *graviter commotus*, simultaneously the sea's and the god's disturbance, is rendered in Rubens' sketch by Neptune's figure moving in harmony with waves, horses, clouds, and other deities. "Consider," Burckhardt says of Rubens' rare lapses into theatricality, "how seldom his figures are shown in loud, emotional speech, how they never rant, how his hands, with all their abundance of beautiful gesture, never gesticulate."[19] In *Quos ego*—the whole body speaks, language is gesture, drama compressed to the uttermost. And with what result?—an increase in the sense of miracle, of spiritual—the word is now inevitable—power. Virgil's speech, noble as it is, makes the god himself proclaim his power, *meo numine;* and his invective is uncomfortably like scolding, as it is in Homer. To compare the marvelous act to the feat of an orator is to run the risk of bringing miracle down to political reality (a risk Virgil willingly embraced).

In Rubens we are brought closer to the unexplained wonders of Homer, but with the matter of fact "doings" left out. Hence Rubens' drama and his god are more deeply serious, splendidly and ineffably godlike. The compression and the immediacy enforce the implication of a purely spiritual power, paradoxically "out of the blood" of this warmly living god. But he is not the dark-haired youthful god of Homer or of the "Landing of Marie de Médicis,"[20] who puts his hand to the great ship, bringing it against the pier. The head of the *Quos ego*—Neptune, white-haired and bearded, with his intent eye, can scarcely be disassociated from images of God himself. We find much the same head and expression in many religious pictures by Rubens, of God in the coronation of the Virgin and in the Trinity, of saints and Old Testament patriarchs (and sometimes of elder pagan deities indistinguishable from saints and holy men of the Judaeo-Christian tradition). The contemporary audience, well-educated in religious art, would have seen and felt this association more instinctively than we do. The ease and frequency with which Rubens transforms pagan figures and motifs into Christian ones, and occasionally, Christian into pagan, has often been noted, most recently in Wolfgang Stechow's *Rubens and the Classical Tradition*.[21]

It is commonly assumed that Rubens had seen the *Quos ego*— of Marcantonio Raimondi (ca. 1480-1527/37), based on a drawing by Raphael (figure 4).[22] A look at the engraving will reenforce what I have been saying about the "spiritual" in Rubens' sketch and show the difference between more or less literal illustration or visual translation and live reworking of a poetic text. (The splendid quality of the original, the richness and warmth of contrast, and the almost excessive clarity of line are largely lost in the photograph.) Marcantonio has chosen the exact moment when the god, rising from the sea, launches his verbal attack on the winds. His lips are parted in speech, and he pulls hard on the horses' rein. Ships are seen wrecked or sinking, and a slightly earlier event is introduced—Aeneas "stretching his palms to the stars," *duplicis tendens ad sidera palmas* (I.93). No one will be tempted to use "spiritual" of this snub-nosed well-muscled strongman. The figure as a whole is less dramatically expressive than Rubens': for example, the right arm thrusting the elegant trident downward (not forward) seems comparatively weak. The hippocampi, with their oddly elongated necks and snouts, comically equine expressions, and inextricably entangled fish-tails, seem to belong to a more prehistoric age than Rubens'. The all-too human faces of the slightly sullen wind-cherubs may have given Rubens a hint for his beautifully vague cloud beings, but they are curious substitutes for Virgil's revolutionary "mob" (as Michael Putnam calls them).[23] Though well composed, the engraving has little of Rubens' composition in emotional and imaginative depth, or in subtle echoings and blendings of line and color.

But, as readers familiar with Rubens' sketch must be saying, the painter had other and more complex intentions than the engraver. The sketch was a model for a huge painting on an architectural stage erected to welcome Ferdinand Cardinal Infante of Spain on his entrance into Antwerp, April 17, 1635. Ferdinand, brother of Philip IV, had journeyed from Barcelona to serve as governor of the Netherlands in succession to Isabella, Rubens' patron and friend. Antwerp had commissioned Rubens to design a series of magnificent triumphal arches and stages to adorn Ferdinand's progress through the city.[24] Though assistants executed most of the paintings, Rubens gave the finishing touches to the large *Quos ego*—, if he did not do the whole picture (as some accounts suggest). Before the painting (now in Dresden) was turned over to the Cardinal in 1637, Rubens "again repainted" it along with the companion piece on the meeting at Nordlingen between Ferdinand of Spain and Ferdinand of Hungary.[25] The event that lay behind sketch and

Figure 4. Marcantonio Raimondi, *Quos ego—*, "Neptune Quelling the Storm," Fogg Art Museum. Courtesy of the Fogg Art Museum, Harvard University, Gray Collection.

picture was, according to a contemporary narrative, somewhat less disastrous than the shipwreck of Aeneas. Ferdinand's fleet, having sailed from Barcelona, arrived safely at Caduquès (now a semibohemian resort on the Costa Brava). "Après le temps se changea avec des tramontanes et vents contraires" it proved impossible to continue the voyage for "thirteen whole days": Then came the morning when "the sea grew calm, and with the wind [from the south] in the stern, they parted at mid-day, and the weather was so constant and favorable, that on the next morning they began to make out the coast of France."[26] At a distance of three years and many miles, this princely contretemps became to the eye of imagination the glorious event of Rubens' sketch, in which Virgil's simile was in effect reversed, the historical reality now being compared to the storm and calm of myth. In Rubens' adaptation of the Virgilian moment, the ships are seen quite unharmed, the dark hued clouds moving through and above them, and the spectral wind-face to the far right, Boreas (the wind unfavorable for sailing toward France), is pursued by southern and western winds that fill the sails of the splendid vessels now getting under way. In Virgil, it will be remembered, *all* the winds are loosed by Aeolus, and Neptune directs his wrath especially against the Southeast and West, Eurus and Zephyrus.

We are beginning to see meanings in Rubens' work that would not be apparent apart from three "translations" that his sketch underwent: the large painting by the master and his pupils, the engraving (figure 5) by a colleague, T. van Thulden, and the verbal explanation by Gevart, which accompanied the engraving in the *Pompa Introitus . . . Ferdinandi*,[27] a splendid folio memorializing and interpreting all the works of art and the various celebrations of the Cardinal Infante's entrance into Antwerp. The first shock comes when we see the Dresden version, inferior in nearly every respect to the sketch, though less obvious in its outlines and less abrupt in its transitions than the engraving. Since the commentary is based on the engraving, we may consider a few changes from the sketch, along with Gevart's interpretations. In general, we may say that everything has become terribly definite, with a loss in the effect of a hazy and mysterious mythical-natural sea change. The wind-faces have taken on the solidity of Marcantonio's cherubs, and Boreas is now an aged swimmer with fin-like wings and hands and legs like twisted forms of half-baked pastry, *brachiis in pennas desinentibus & serpentinis pedibus*, Gevart says. The whorl of the shell blending easily into the wheel has disappeared, and one nymph hangs heavily on a spoke, turning it, Gevart explains, with the help of her sisters. The suggestion of rationalizing in Rubens is crudely exposed: *Quâ re vortex marinus denotatur, qui in gyrum actus ipsam promouet. NYMPHAS autem quasi LYMPHAS, notum est.*[28] "(By [their turning of the wheel] is signified the sea's whirlpool, which being driven in a circle, carries it [the shell] forward. It is well known that we speak of 'Nymphas' as it were for 'Lymphas' [waters].)" In Rubens' sketch all three nymphs are caught up in

Figure 5. T. van Thulden, engraving after Rubens, *Quos ego—*, from C. Gevartius, *Pompa Introitus serenissimi principis Ferdinandi Austriaci Hispaniarum Infantis* (Antwerp, 1641), Houghton Library. By permission of the Harvard College Library.

the dramatic and visual movement, one looking forward with arm out-stretched, the second pointing ahead and glancing back to engage the atten-tion of her sister, who is also looking toward the god. In the engraving, the inert turner faces forward, the next nymph turns away, and the third looks coyly out at the viewer. The god's gesture has lost its full effect, since as Jacob Rosenberg notes, his hand comes uncomfortably close to the serpen-tine legs of Boreas. (Neptune's hair and beard no longer stream in the wind.) Parts, including the too accurately equipped "triremes," shatter the blended life of the whole.

Gevart's commentary brings some interesting support and some surpris-ing increments to our earlier reading of the sketch. The inscription on the title page of the *Pompa Introitus* is a bald adaptation of the Virgilian prophecy, *Aeneid* VI.851, 853:

> Tu regere imperio Belgas Germane, memento:
> Parcere subjectis et depellare superbos.

Later in the commentary, the great triumphal arch for Ferdinand[29] is com-pared with the "Arch of Titus Augustus." In another scene, the temple of Janus is adorned with sculptures of Peace and War, and Gevart offers an ap-propriate quotation (VII.601-605) that echoes Jupiter's words in *Aeneid* I.291-296, on the closing of the temple and the binding of *Furor* (a thematic echo[30] of Neptune's action in the storm scene). In the whirl of quotations from Latin and Greek authors, it is curious that Gevart never cites or refers to the "*quos ego—*" passage. When describing a Neptune on another stage, Gevart quotes in Greek the Homeric epithets for Poseidon, and comments on them with appreciation of the god's role as earth-shaker. Neptune "bears the trident, since he strikes and lashes the earth with his waves."[31] Gevart's interest in historical evidence, *historica fide*, helps us to appreciate what he and the people of Antwerp saw most vividly in Rubens' scene. An inscrip-tion below the engraving begins with *Neptuno sternente fretum*, "Neptune calming the sea," but most of the five lines are spent in praising the "noble cargo" and the ship that brought it safely over "the Tyrrhenian waters." One suspects that Rubens or his associates reread his sketch in a way to fit this more obvious emphasis, one more to the taste of a seaport town.

What then was Rubens doing in the sketch as compared with the en-graved version? Something much more complexly organized, and more subtly related to local history, to contemporary and older artistic, literary, and religious traditions. Both versions are very much of their time, but the sketch is more profoundly baroque than the painting in many features we have noted—the focus on the "moment," the strong contrasts and vio-lent movement, the diagonal thrust, and above all in the dramatic expres-siveness of Neptune's form and gesture. The effect of spontaneity in the whole is characteristic of Rubens' better sketches: "La forme surgit du pin-ceau en même temps qu' elle naît avec la pensée artistique dans l'esprit de l'artiste."[32] Behind the sketch lies a powerful mythical vision, Virgilian and Homeric and peculiarly Rubensian. If Rubens renews for us the moment of anger in the *Aeneid* and the change that followed, and if he suppresses some of the humbler actions of the god in both ancient versions, he also revives the religious mystery of divine action in Homer. He goes still further along the road toward a purely spiritual interpretation of mythical action and toward a more immediate and impressionistic expression of an event in nature, while not forgetting the human actor—a combination that allies him with Homer of the storm similes and the landscape painters of the later eighteenth and early nineteenth centuries. There is in Rubens' sketch the oddest blend of precise observation, of rationalizing (as in the treatment of the chariot-shell), and of primitive mythical vision (as in the wind-faces): "The wheel survives the myths."

But as Svetlana Alpers reminds us in her splendid Introduction to the Torre de la Parada series,[33] Rubens' alliances with the past and the future are not easily defined. His treatment of the human body as dramatically expressive is at once in line with contemporary theory and related to practices of Helenistic sculptors, whose work Rubens had so closely studied. If like Homer and "unlike Ovid, Rubens commanded a heroic style, which he could inform with a sense of real life without puncturing its ideality,"[34] he was also capable of entering into the Ovidian world of irreverence and comedy, as he did in creating the paintings for the Torre de la Parada. Here too he was also working in an earlier tradition, that of the sixteenth-century illustrators of the *Metamorphoses*.[35] Looking through some of the volumes to which Mrs. Alpers refers, we come on plates that may account for some of the departures from Virgil's text in Marcantonio and in Rubens or his colleagues. In *La Metamorphose d'Ovide figurée* (1557), a "Fin du déluge" pictures Neptune in a shell driving two hippocampi. The verses below, based on Metamorphoses I.324-344, tell how the clouds give way to "Aquilon, leur ennemi contraire." In "Vénus et Pluton," Pluto comes from the underworld in a shell-like chariot drawn by horses. In the *Metamorphoseon Libri XV* (1582), a very animated Neptune rides on a lively and amusing hippocampus[36]—a version also illustrated by Gevart from ancient coins. This continental Ovidian tradition appears in England in Franz Cleyn's "engravings for Sandys's Ovid [1632], which . . . represent a parallel effort to Rubens' works" for the Torre de la Parada. "They share with Rubens an interest in the mythological narratives as human dramas."[37]

Cleyn also illustrated the Ogilby translation of Virgil (1654),[38] a volume well known to Dryden, who spoke scornfully of the translator, though on occasion borrowing from his fairly accurate if inept version. With an eye to costs, Dryden and his publisher took over Cleyn's illustrations for the *Virgil* of 1697. Dryden's visualization of figures from Graeco-Roman mythology was almost certainly influenced by these Rubensian baroque engravings. Though Cleyn did not illustrate the *Quos ego—* episode, Ogilby's rationalizing notes on the passage—of a kind we have encountered in Gevart—are worth noting. Aeolus is referred to as the "king of the Aeolian Islands," who, famed for his ability to foretell "the change of Winds, . . . therefore was thought to have power over" the stormy weather. On the same page we are told that "the physical ground of all, is this: Tempests are begotten by the Clouds, over which *Juno* presides, they being agitated by the Winds, of which Aeolus is Lord."[39] The note on Neptune's horses is even more illuminating: "Turnebus, and others understand here, *Hippocampi*, Sea-Horses." Ogilby then quotes Statius as evidence that hippocampi have hooves in front but "trail off behind in the form of fish" (*postremi solvuntur in aequora pisces*).[40] While this fits Rubens' steeds, it does not fit Cleyn's illustration for the Neptune scene of Book V (figure 6), where the god assures Venus that the Trojan ships may pass safely on, though "one [Palinurus] must give his life for many" (815). This plate, also used in Dryden's volume, gives a much lighter-hearted impression than the *Quos ego*—illustrations, in part since Neptune is here shown in a milder mood, soothing the fears of the goddess. His erect figure and gesture dominate the scene as in Rubens, and he strides forward with dignity and strength (in spite of an awkward twist of the right flank). Neptune is not pointing with his trident, but in the act of launching it (at what?),[41] and he is holding the reins of four spirited and capering horses(?), with fin-like forefeet, though without fish tails. He is snub-nosed and crowned, his somewhat protrusive eye fixed on the goddess above. This Neptune is beneficent-looking, and seems to have the beginnings of a smile on his lips, parted perhaps in speech. From her bathlike triumphal car, Venus answers with a tender glance and a charmingly deferential gesture. The upper sky opens for her epiphany, as in Virgil, *fugiunt vasto aethere nimbi* (V.821). The god's shell (ending in a cheerful dolphin's head) has the most cunning and convincing wheel-whorl we have yet encountered. It apparently works as a paddle-wheel, something like the vortex in Gervart's note. (It may be of course that both Rubens' and Cleyn's chariots derive from a common original in illustrations of Ovid.) The lighter tone of Cleyn's scene is picked up —perhaps with a glance at Virgil's nereid band (825-826)—in three decorative mermaids gaily swimming, one with "locks blown forward in the gleam of eyes," another with a comic-book smile of flirtatious satisfaction. Not far off, a male swimmer half-emerges from the waves.

One slightly unsettling question before we turn to Dryden: was Rubens' sketch surely based on Virgil's *Quos ego*—? Not solely, as we have seen, but as the focal mythical image in a complex of historical allusions and many sorts of visual impressions. To strains noted earlier, we may now add one of Ovidian lightness—in the eager nymphs (for Virgil's lone Cymothoe) and in the lusty Triton blowing the way for the sea lord. This is Triton's usual function in both Virgil and Ovid, but not in *Aeneid* I, where with Cymothoe he is a vigorous helper in freeing ships from the rock. He is very prominent

Tum Saturnius hac   domitor maris edidit alti:
Fas omne est, Cytherea,   meis te fidere regnis,
Vnde genus ducis merui   quoque: sæpe furores
Compressi, & rabiem   tantam cœlique, marisque,
Iungit equos curru, geni   tor spumantiaque addit
Fræna feris, manibusque   omnes effundit habenas.

Henrico Dukeson Arm: Tabula merito votum

Figure 6. Franz Cleyn, "Neptune and Venus," from John Ogilby, *The Works of Publius Virgilius Maro* (London, 1654), Houghton Library. By permission of the Harvard College Library.

in the scene from *Metamorphoses* I (above), where Neptune "The wild waves calmes, his *trident laid aside*" (Sandys' translation). There is also that pink bridle held by the smiling nereid. A glint of Ovidian comedy—of Homeric and Shakespearean "relief"—enters the Renaissance *Fiat lux* of Rubens.

Dryden had access to Rubens' Olympian imagery through other channels than Cleyn's engravings, as Jean Hagstrum suggests in his interesting account of baroque pictorial elements in Dryden's odes.[42] He could hardly have avoided seeing Rubens' apotheosis of James I on the ceiling of Whitehall, although "by 1687, humidity had already been fatal to it."[43] (It is appropriate that James II "authorized a complete restoration.") The passage on Rubens in the supplement to Dryden's translation of Dufresnoy's *De arte graphica* shows some acquaintance with criticism of Rubens,[44] if not surely direct knowledge of the paintings. More to the point is the remark in his own *Parallel of Poetry and Painting*, cited by Hagstrum, on the close correspondence between pictorial posture and epic description: "The posture of a poetic figure is . . . the description of [the] heroes in the performance of such or such an action."[45] Dryden follows this with a highly pictorial account of Aeneas' "posture" before killing Lausus. It should be noted that Dryden had interrupted his *Aeneis* to do the translation of Dufresnoy, and that these notions of pictorial rendering of heroic gestures were in his mind at the time he was translating Virgil.

How does Dryden's *Quos ego*— appear in the context of the literary and pictorial traditions we have been observing in Rubens and in various writers and artists, ancient and modern? It is still the most readable and energetic version in English:

> Mean time Imperial *Neptune* heard the Sound
> Of raging Billows breaking on the Ground:
> Displeas'd, and fearing for his Wat'ry Reign,
> He reard his awful Head above the Main:
> Serene in Majesty, then rowl'd his Eyes   180
> Around the Space of Earth, and Seas, and Skies.
> He saw the *Trojan* Fleet dispers'd, distress'd
> By stormy Winds and wintry Heav'n oppress'd.
> Full well the God his Sister's envy knew,
> And what her Aims, and what her Arts pursue: 185
> He summon'd *Eurus* and the western Blast,
> And first an angry glance on both he cast:
> Then thus rebuk'd; Audacious Winds! from whence
> This bold Attempt, this Rebel Insolence?
> Is it for you to ravage Seas and Land,   190
> Unauthoriz'd by my supream Command?
> To raise such Mountains on the troubl'd Main? ⎫
> Whom I—But first 'tis fit, the Billows to restrain, ⎬
> And then you shall be taught obedience to my Reign. ⎭
> Hence, to your Lord my Royal Mandate bear,   195
> The Realms of Ocean and the Fields of Air
> Are mine, not his; by fatal Lot to me

The liquid Empire fell, and Trident of the Sea.
His Pow'r to hollow Caverns is confin'd,
There let him reign, the Jailor of the Wind: 200
With hoarse Commands his breathing Subjects call,
And boast and bluster in his empty Hall.
He spoke: and while he spoke, he smooth'd the Sea,
Dispell'd the Darkness, and restor'd the Day:
Cymothoe, Triton, and the Sea-green Train   205
Of beauteous Nymphs, the Daughters of the Main,
Clear from the Rocks the Vessels with their hands; ⎤
The God himself with ready Trident stands,   ⎬
And opes the Deep, and spreads the moving sands; ⎦
Then heaves them off the sholes: where e're he guides ⎤   210
His finny Coursers, and in Triumph rides,   ⎬
The Waves unruffle and the Sea subsides.   ⎦
As when in Tumults rise th' ignoble Crowd,
Mad are their Motions, and their Tongues are loud;
And Stones and Brands in ratling Vollies fly,   215
And all the Rustick Arms that Fury can supply:
If then some grave and Pious Man appear,
They hush their Noise, and lend a list'ning Ear;
He sooths with sober Words their angry Mood,
And quenches their innate Desire of Blood: 220
So when the Father of the Flood appears,
And o're the Seas his Sov'raign Trident rears,
Their Fury falls: He skims the liquid Plains,
High on his Chariot, and with loosen'd Reins,
Majestick moves along, and awful Peace maintains.   225

The large contrasts of Virgil's and Rubens' scene are there, though the
analogy between god and orator is less salient in this much expanded version. The rhetorical tone, which has a counterpart in Virgil, is louder and
more insistent throughout. Other stresses, emotive and visual, also have
some basis in the original, but their character can be best understood in relation to sixteenth- and seventeenth-century pictorial styles. As in Rubens
and the engravers, there is much violent movement and feeling, sharply contrasted with their opposites. There is also the continual emphasis on *seeing*
Neptune in various poses and with various looks and implied emotions. "He
reared his *awful* Head" ("awful" is Dryden's addition), yet he is also
"Serene in Majesty" (179-180). "The god himself *with ready Trident stands*"
(208). Attention is directed first to the pose, then to the action. Again, "the
Father of the Flood *appears* . . . and . . . his *Sov'raign Trident rears*"—sight
and gesture without words are sufficient: "Their Fury falls" (221-223).
Neptune is seen "High on his Chariot" (224) (as in all the pictorial versions).[46] He moves "with loosen'd Reins" (224-225), which is reasonably
close to Virgil's text (note however the descriptive "with" and the participle
for an active verb). But the final picture, "Majestick moves along," is nearer
to Rubens: this god is no mere charioteer. One line, "And first an angry
glance on both he cast" (187), though not in Virgil, is quite comparable

to the strong look of Rubens' Neptune. The line and a half added by Dryden, "then rowl'd his/Eyes Around the Space of Earth, and Seas, and Skies" (180-181) suggests something of the scale of Rubens' scene; but the "rowling" eyes are baroque with a vengeance, more grotesque than those of Cleyn's engraving. Other pictorial elements not in Virgil are added: "and the Sea-green Train/Of beauteous Nymphs, the Daughters of the Main" (205-206)—which has the effect of dimming the precise if "low" acts that follow. Dryden does mention the "Chariot," but like the painters he brushes over the awkward business of a chariot race on the water. The wheels are not mentioned, and the "finny Coursers" recall the pictorial style and the rationalizing tendency of the seventeenth-century versions and their commentators. Stock poetic diction—note also "Wat'ry Reign" and "the liquid Plains"—elevated and vaguely visual, is the verbal equivalent of the heroic descriptive style in painting. The writer makes a gesture toward picture, without giving much evidence of having *seen* anything in particular.

What probably most strikes twentieth-century readers of Dryden's lines is the heightening of the imperial and the political themes, although there are analogies in the arbitrary gesture of Rubens' god and in his many references to the historical occasion, more blatant in the painting than in the sketch. As often, Dryden adopts a note in Virgil, heightens it, and loads it with local applications. The underlining of the imperial and royal character of Neptune appears from beginning to end of the passage: "Imperial *Neptune*," "Wat'ry Reign" and "obedience to my Reign, "Majesty" and "Majestick," "my supream Command," "your Lord," "my Royal Mandate," "sov'raign." Finally, the god is the ruler who "awful Peace maintains"—language that might suit the Supreme Deity of the next century. In the grand generalizing force of this phrase and in the insistent "mys" emphasizing the royal prerogative, Dryden reflects Charles II's seriocomic obsession with the image of an absolute monarch, ruling by divine right.[47] The scornful references to "th' ignoble Crowd" are more vulgar than Virgil's, and we hear the Tories' fear and mockery of "Rebel Insolence" and "Rustick Arms." The dignity and wisdom of Virgil's "grave and Pious Man," though the translation is literal to a fault, is brought by the context down to English political realities. To define the parallels and the differences between Dryden and Rubens in this area would require a separate monograph. "The subtle adaptation of the mythological scene" in Rubens, says Rosenberg, "to the actual life of the prince shows how earnestly the Baroque humanists and artists undertook to prove the Divine support of the sovereigns."[48] Rubens is doing more than this, as we have seen, in the commanding presence of a Godlike figure who reminds us of a spiritual order perceptible in Nature and superior to kings, though the allusion confers honor on them. In Dryden's version, as in his royal odes, the strain of the royal-divine rhetoric is all too evident, as it is for some viewers (though not for the writer) in the Marie de Médicis cycle, where myth happily eclipses history.

What finally can we say about Dryden's translation of myth in relation to Virgil, Rubens, and the other texts, verbal or visual, that we have surveyed? We can hardly suppose or expect that Dryden's mythological event will reveal the complex poetic, historical, and moral ordering of Virgil's poem. That cannot be if Virgil is to "speak such *English,* as he would himself have spoken, if he had been born in *England,* and in the present Age." Resonances are lost on which larger connections depend: "pious" is not *pius* and "Fury" is not *furor.* But it should be said that in spite of these inevitable losses, Dryden's *Aeneid* as a whole carries over much of Virgil's sense of history and "destiny." The political and rhetorical accent of Dryden's lines, which has some justification in Virgil, unfortunately also inclines his version toward the values and mores of the rising Tory party in the reigns of Charles II and his brother. That Dryden attempted to *picture* the action again starts from a Virgilian quality, though the style of his verbal "painting" derives from the baroque manner of Cleyn and more generally from the Rubens tradition as it reached not the most visual of English poets. Although the "postures" of Dryden's Neptune remind us of Rubens' god, they also remind us that Dryden did not take either his visual apparatus or the divine machinery very seriously. The tendency to emphasize the pose, not the act or the *numen,* to rationalize miracle by omission or soften it by veiled poetic diction, will find a point of arrival in the picturesque gods and goddesses of decorative painters and landscapers of the eighteenth century in Italy and in England. Pope, who looked on Nature with more reverence and with a keener eye as painter and mythmaker, and who loved mythological allusions in landscape and garden, also saw their possible triviality and abuse:

> Here Amphitrite sails thro' myrtle bowers;
> There Gladiators fight, or die, in flowers;
> Un-water'd see the drooping sea-horse mourn,
> And swallows roost in Nilus' dusty Urn.

But if Ovidian irreverence, which anticipated the death of the gods, had its effect on the tradition that touched Dryden in the Cleyn engravings, if it also affected Rubens even in the noble mood of the *Quos ego—,* it did not prevent him from embracing other mythical modes and ways of seeing, even contradictory in impulse. He, too, quietly omits the more humble operations of Homer's Poseidon and Virgil's Neptune, and he subdues the literalism of "wind-men and -women," and of war chariots at sea and their human drivers. How Virgil regarded Neptune's "shovings" and "liftings" we cannot know, though at least one critic sees a "rough humor" in this and similar narratives in the *Aeneid.* What is most remarkable about Rubens is that he harmonizes both the deeper Virgilian and the Homeric visions. His *Quos ego—* bears a weight—perhaps too great a one—of historical and ideological reference: the heavens themselves, God and Nature, further the purposes of the king of Spain and his emissary. But if we return to the visual "thing," we see that without literalism, Rubens renews the Homeric vision of human figures and gestures dramatically expressing events both natural and supernatural.[49] In the way in which rushing lines, subtle harmonies of color and light, work to give a sense of how Powers are "begotten" from our sensations of the physical world, he takes us beyond Homer to where all myths begin:

> One's grand flights, one's Sunday baths,
> One's tootings at the weddings of the soul
> Occur as they occur. So bluish clouds
> Occurred above the empty house and the leaves
> Of the rhododendrons rattled their gold,
> As if someone lived there. Such floods of white
> Came bursting from the clouds. So the wind
> Threw its contorted strength around the sky.
>
> Could you have said the bluejay suddenly
> Would swoop to earth? It is a wheel, the rays
> Around the sun. The wheel survives the myths.

—Wallace Stevens, "The Sense of the Sleight-of-hand Man"[50]

REFERENCES

1. Leo van Puyvelde, *Les esquisses de Rubens* (Bâle: Les Editions Holbein, 1940), p. 57. "L'exécution . . . est aussi poussée que dans un petit tableau de chevalet."

2. E. H. Gombrich, "The Style *All-Antica:* Imitation and Assimilation," *Acts of the XX International Congress of the History of Art* (Princeton: Princeton University Press, 1963), II, 31. For this reference and other bibliographical information and for valuable advice in the preparation of this essay, I am indebted to John Abel Pinto. See his *Related Aspects of Roman Architectural Design,* unpublished honors thesis, Department of Fine Arts, Harvard College, 1970, pp. 52-53.

3. John Kinsley, ed., *The Poems of John Dryden* (Oxford: Oxford University Press, 1958), III, 1055. All quotations of Dryden's *Aeneis* are from this volume.

4. *Ibid.,* p. 1036.

5. Cedric Whitman, *Homer and the Heroic Tradition* (Cambridge, Mass.: Harvard University Press, 1958), p. 95.

6. *Ibid.,* pp. 89-90.

7. Translation by Richmond Lattimore, *The Iliad of Homer* (Chicago: University of Chicago Press, 1951).

8. The identification as a statue of Poseidon is accepted by Gisela M. A. Richter, *A Handbook of Greek Art* (London: Phaidon Press, 1959), p. 89.

9. A bronze statue of Poseidon, the Louvre, *ibid.,* p. 190.

10. For this example, the one below by the Troilus painter, and for most helpful suggestions, I am indebted to Emily E. T. Vermeule, Samuel Zemurray, Jr., and Doris Zemurray Stone Radcliffe Professor, Harvard University. For the vase by the Amphitrite Painter, see L. D. Caskey and J. D. Beazley, *Attic Vase Paintings in the*

Museum of Fine Arts (Boston: Oxford University Press, 1963), pt. III, no. 152. *98.932*, pp. 52-53, pl. LXXXV.2.

11. *Catalogue des vases peints de la Bibliothèque Nationale* (Paris: A. de Ridder, 1902), II, 429, no. 573.

12. Caskey and Beazley, *Attic Vase Painting*, p. 53, n. 10.

13. J. D. Beazley, *Attic Red-Figure Vase-Painters*, 2d ed., II (Oxford: Clarendon Press, 1963), 1643, 10 bis. For photographs of this vase, now in Williamstown, Mass., see *Masterpieces of Greek Vase Painting*, catalogue of André Emmerich Gallery, Inc. (New York, 1964), no. 24.

14. Text of F. A. Hirtzel, ed., *P. Vergili Maronis Opera* (Oxford: Oxford University Press, 1900). On Dryden's use of the text edited by Ruaeus, see J. McG. Bottkol, "Dryden's Latin Scholarship," *Modern Philology*, 40 (1943), 243-245.

15. Ernest de Selincourt, ed., *The Early Letters of William and Dorothy Wordsworth* (Oxford: Oxford University Press, 1935), p. 541, cited in L. Proudfoot, *Dryden's "Aeneid" and Its Seventeenth Century Predecessors* (Manchester: University Press, 1960), p. 196.

16. Victor Pöschl, *The Art of Vergil*, trans. G. Seligson (Ann Arbor: University of Michigan Press, 1962), pp. 22, 23, 24.

17. Brooks Otis, *Virgil: A Study in Civilized Poetry* (Oxford: Clarendon Press, 1963), p. 230 et passim.

18. Jacob Rosenberg, "Rubens' Sketch for Wrath of Neptune," *Bulletin of the Fogg Museum of Art*, X (1943), i, 14. My seeing of this detail and of much else in the sketch is indebted to Rosenberg's beautiful study.

19. Jacob Burckhardt, *Recollections of Rubens*, ed. H. Gerson, trans. Mary Hottinger (London: Phaidon, 1950), p. 73; Burckhardt's chief example is "Queen Tomyris receiving the head of the slain Cyrus," in the Boston Museum.

20. Photograph in Adolf Rosenberg, *Klassiker der Kunst* (Leipzig: Deutscheverlags-anstalt, 1905), p. 239.

21. Wolfgang Stechow, *Rubens and the Classical Tradition*, Martin Classical Lectures (Cambridge, Mass.: Harvard University Press, 1968), p. 47, and examples in chap. 3, "Transformation." Note the example of "Mary Magdalene transformed into a *Pudicitia*," p. 58.

22. The attribution of the original design to Raphael, often mentioned, appears in Adam Bartsch, *Le Peintre Graveur* (Vienna, 1803-1821), XIV, 264-269 and Henri Delaborde, *Marc-Antoine Raimondi* (Paris: Librairie de l'art, 1888), p. 146. "Elle [Marcantonio's engraving] semble avoir été faite pour servir de frontispice à une édition de l'Enéide," p. 146.

23. "Throughout his account of the winds and their doings, Virgil treats them metaphorically either as horses or as a foolish mob, part beast, part brutish man, easily misled into wreaking havoc." Michael Putnam, *The Poetry of the Aeneid* (Cambridge, Mass.: Harvard University Press, 1965), p. 11. If the equine character of the winds was recognized by Rubens and his contemporaries, the sea horses also may have been regarded as embodiments of the winds.

24. Max Rooses, *L'oeuvre de P. P. Rubens* (Antwerp: J. Maes, 1886-1892), III, 292-293.

25. *Ibid.,* p. 298; Rooses cites evidence that the whole picture was originally executed by Rubens. J. Rosenberg, "Rubens' Sketch," p. 14, says "retouched, but not executed by Rubens."

26. *Le voyage du Prince Don Fernande infant d'Espagne,* trans. from Spanish of Diego de Aedo y Gallart (Antwerp, 1635), pp. 19-20.

27. C. Gevartius, *Pompa Introitus serenissimi principis Ferdinandi Austriaci Hispaniarum Infantis* (Antwerp, 1641), pp. 19-20.

28. *Ibid.,* p. 16. The form of shell-wheel may be traditional, perhaps from early illustrations of Ovid. See above, p. 172.

29. Plate before p. 109.

30. Otis, *Virgil,* p. 230.

31. Gevartius, *Pompa Introitus,* p. 149.

32. Puyvelde, *Les Esquisses de Rubens,* p. 28.

33. Svetlana Alpers, *The Decoration of the Torre de la Parada,* in *Corpus Rubenianum Ludwig Burchard,* IX (London and New York: Phaidon, 1971). My discussion here and later is much indebted to the "Conclusion," pp. 166-173.

34. *Ibid.,* pp. 167-168.

35. *Ibid.,* pp. 80-100.

36. Page 52.

37. Alpers, *Decoration of the Torre de la Parada,* p. 93; "invented by Franz Cleyn and executed by Salomon Savery," p. 92.

38. John Ogilby, *The Works of Publius Virgilius Maro, Translated, Adorn'd with Sculpture, and Illustrated with Annotations* (London, 1654).

39. *Ibid.,* p. 168.

40. *Ibid.,* p. 171.

41. John Pinto has suggested a possible connection with Bernini's "Neptune and Triton," ca. 1620, where Neptune thrusts his trident downward, with great vigor, apparently toward the water of the fountain in which it was originally placed. See Howard Hibbard, *Bernini* (Baltimore: Penguin Books, 1965), pp. 39-43. Note, in relation to Cleyn's shell, "the trailing cloak that suddenly becomes a dolphin," p. 40. Cleyn's triton bears some resemblance to the rear view of the triton in Bernini's group, and possibly to the triton of the Piazza Barberini.

42. Jean Hagstrum, *The Sister Arts* (Chicago: University of Chicago Press, 1958), pp. 197-208.

43. Puyvelde, *Les Esquisses de Rubens,* p. 287.

44. W. Scott and G. Saintsbury, eds., *John Dryden's Works* (Edinburgh: W. Paterson, 1892), XVII, "The Judgement of Charles Alphonse Du Fresnoy," pp. 503-504.

45. *Ibid.,* 318-319.

46. Compare also *Paradise Lost,* II.1, "High on a Throne of Royal State."

47. David Ogg, *England in the Reign of Charles II,* 2d ed. (Oxford: Oxford University Press, 1956), 2d ed. corrected, Oxford Paperbacks, 1963, "The Crown in Parliament," II, 450-454.

48. J. Rosenberg, "Rubens' Sketch," p. 9.

49. Alpers, *Decoration of the Torre de la Parada,* p. 173, notes that both Delacroix and Burckhardt "called Rubens the Homer of painters." See Burckhardt, *Recollections of Rubens,* p. 157.

50. *The Collected Poems of Wallace Stevens* (New York: Knopf, 1954), p. 222, quoted with permission of the publisher.

STEVEN MARCUS

Language into Structure: Pickwick Revisited

MYSTERIES IN real life exist in order to be solved, and literary mysteries exist in order to be consulted. As one who has already tried his hand in picking at the greatest of Dickens' mysteries—*Pickwick Papers*—I feel no need to apologize for frequenting these grounds again, nor for consulting the mystery in the hope that this time it will prove still more receptive and less resistant to critical interrogation. For the mystery has been and remains essentially a critical one: Where is the critical handle for such a work of genius to be found?

Let us begin then at the beginning. And, as it is only appropriate in such a perplexing context, we discover the beginning before the beginning and after the ending. I am referring to the advertisement that was published before the first number of *Pickwick Papers* appeared and to the prefaces that Dickens wrote after he had completed the novel. The advertisement begins as follows: "On the 31st of March will be published, to be continued Monthly, price One Shilling, the First Number of *The Posthumous Papers of the Pickwick Club;* containing a faithful record of the perambulations, perils, travels, adventures, and sporting transactions of the corresponding members. Edited by 'Boz.' And each Monthly Part embellished with Four Illustrations by Seymour." It is all thoroughly inauspicious and conventional. Amid these conventionalities, however, and indeed as part of them, three things persist in attracting the attention of the modern reader. First the papers are "posthumous"—but to what? To the club itself, presumably. But what does this mean, and why? It is not alive, it is not there, it is dead or has disappeared. It exists in a negative state or as a negation, in a condition of almost pure otherness. But the papers themselves may be posthumous as well in the sense that they are dead before they have ever come alive; they are being produced as a piece of hack work and will be or are dead as literature before they are even written.

Second, these papers are not "written" but "edited." This too was a convention of popular fiction and other writing, although Carlyle had recently made considerable creative play with it in *Sartor Resartus*. But it implies a statement similar to that contained in "posthumous." The agent

183

behind this publication is as it were not yet the novelist; he exists again in a kind of negative or not-yet-appeared or absent state. He is not writing the work; he does not create it or own or possess it. Somehow it is written through him. But at the same time once more there is a sense of some slight distance and disavowal present and being communicated. And third, the editor is Boz, not Dickens. Boz who did "sketches," not Dickens who wrote novels. Moreover, we are to learn in the future that Boz was not even in the first place Dickens' pseudonym for himself. It was a nickname that he had given to a younger brother, so that his using it for himself is on one of its sides another form of a complex, inexplicit disavowal, though on another side it is a characteristic gesture of aggrandizement. Boz contains the suggestion—retrospectively to be sure—that Dickens so to speak is not yet here, that he has not yet been created as he will eventually be. And thus the novel announces itself beforehand in a cluster of negations, of othernesses and circumstances which are not there, or are not yet there.

If we turn next to the preface to the first edition, we come across a number of equally arresting phrases and formulations. This was written some year and a half later, at the conclusion of the work, and with that work figuratively present in its entirety before the writer. We all know what had happened to *Pickwick Papers* in that interval; and we know in addition that an occurrence of similar magnitude had taken place in the young writer, that he had undergone a transformation and become Charles Dickens. It is to be supposed, therefore, that he would undertake to communicate some part of this momentousness in his prefatory leavetaking. But he does nothing of the kind. The first sentence of that preface begins as follows: "The author's object in this work was to place before the reader a constant succession of characters and incidents." We should note in passing that although he has become "the author," he has continued speaking in the distant and distancing convention of the authorial or editorial third person rather than the first person which he subsequently adopted on such occasions. What stops us, however, is his formulation of his "object"—"a constant succession." There is some notion here of endless movement, of incessant motion, an idea that is elaborated along one line later on when he tells us that the only sport at which he was really good (the word he uses is "great") was "all kinds of locomotion." But that is only one line of development, and we shall return to this conception in due course.

He then goes on to describe the conditions of the imaginative inception of the work. "Deferring to the judgement of others in the outset of the undertaking," he writes, "he [Dickens] adopted the machinery of the club, which was suggested as that best adapted to his purpose." It is always interesting to find an occasion on which Dickens refers in public to some act of deference on his part; and it is not surprising that he should do so with a touch of ill-nature—the supererogatory double emphasis and quasi-circularity of phrasing make his annoyance sufficiently clear. He did not, he is saying, want this "machinery" there at the beginning; and, he continues, finding as he wrote "that it tended rather to his embarrassment than otherwise, he gradually abandoned it, considering it a matter of very little importance to the work." The implication seems virtually to be that he wanted no machinery at all; that had he had his own way he would have begun without any machinery—that is to say, he would have begun in some other and almost entirely unimaginable way. He cannot of course tell us what that way would have been, but he does remark that the form or "general design" of the work, owing to its mode of publication, had to be as "simple" as possible. And the linking between the separate events and numbers, if they were to "form one tolerably harmonious whole," had to follow "a gentle and not-unnatural progress of adventure." After having misspent a certain number of years contemplating this utterance, I find that my response to it is to say—"meaning what?" A progress in what "not-unnatural" sense? A progress that is pure succession? The one thing that is indisputably clear about this assertion is that Dickens was in no position to understand discursively what it was that he had done—which may in point of creative fact have been exactly the most advantageous position for him to have occupied.

These observations are supported by what follows shortly, a description in one sentence by Dickens of his manner of writing *Pickwick Papers.* "The following pages," he states, "have been written from time to time, almost as the periodical occasion arose." Again, it is the subdued uncertainty and unintended ambiguity that draw the attention of the reader. On the one hand Dickens seems to be describing an activity that occurred spontaneously, and almost at random; on the other he tends to represent himself as writing by order for the occasion, or as the occasion "arose," which introduces an uncertainty of another kind. The point about this ambiguity is that it happens to correspond to an actuality. The parts were written by the yard, to prearranged mechanical specifications; at the same time they were composed spontaneously. It was not only Dickens who stood in puzzlement over this circumstance.

Ten years later the occasion arose again, and Dickens took the opportunity of the publication of the First Cheap Edition of his works to write a new preface in which he described more fully the circumstances of the inception of the now legendary novel. He recalls how William Hall came to his rooms in Furnivall's Inn to propose "a something that should be published in shilling numbers." This something soon becomes a "monthly something," both of the ironic phrases suggesting Dickens' growing awareness of the extraordinarily unformed and unconscious character of what it was that—ten years before—was then about to happen to him and unfold out of him. He next describes how it was proposed to him that his writing should be the "vehicle" for Seymour's plates, how he objected to this view of the project and proposed successfully to reverse it. "My views being deferred to," he states, "I thought of Mr. Pickwick and wrote the first number."

The deference of the preface to the first edition is now on the other foot. As for the famous statement about Mr. Pickwick, I have discussed its deceptive complexities elsewhere and there is no need to rehearse them here. But the second half of this sentence introduces still further difficulties, for after remarking that he "wrote the first number," Dickens goes on to add "from the proof-sheets of which, Mr. Seymour made his drawing of the club and that happy portrait of its founder, by which he is always recognized and which may be said to have made him a reality." Which may be said by whom? and in what sense? and for Dickens as well as for others? The confusion, however, was to be still worse confounded, for twenty years later Dickens revised the preface once again, took out the second half of that sentence, and substituted this: "from the proof sheets of which, Mr. Seymour made his drawing of the Club, and his happy portrait of its founder:—the latter on Mr. Edward Chapman's description of the dress and bearing of a real personage whom he had often seen." This revision had its origin in assertions that were made on Seymour's behalf, that had to do with the part he played in the primary imagination of the novel, and that cannot be discussed here. Dickens' "clarification," however, serves primarily to divert and distract one's attention. The sentence is still running in two directions—Seymour making his drawing now from both the proof sheets and Chapman's description of "a real personage" no less. Once more Dickens cannot withstand the impulse to introduce some such word as "real" or "reality." And each time that he does make such an introduction our sense of his permanent uncertainty about what it was that had happened to him is augmented. This observation holds for the well-known following paragraph about Mr. Pickwick's changing character as the novel develops, in which Dickens speaks about him as if he were a real and independent being from the very beginning and a complete invention at the same time.

What we are left with, then, after these extended prefatory marchings and countermarchings is a distinct conviction of how mysterious almost everything about *Pickwick Papers* remained to Dickens himself. We are therefore rather better off than we were when we began; we are still in darkness, but at least we have been joined there by the man who "may be said to have made [it] a reality." And if we can rely no further upon the teller, we have to turn to the tale, which begins thus:

The Pickwickians

The first ray of light which illumines the gloom, and converts into a dazzling brilliancy that obscurity in which the earlier history of the public career of the immortal Pickwick would appear to be involved, is derived from the perusal of the following entry in the Transactions of the Pickwick Club, which the editor of these papers feels the highest pleasure in laying before his readers, as a proof of the careful attention, indefatigable assiduity, and nice discrimination, with which his search among the multifarious documents confided to him has been conducted.

It opens with a title followed by a single epic sentence, a paragraph long, that closes in a dying fall. It is a parody, which later on and at length we learn is in part not a parody. It begins at the beginning, with the "creation" itself, with the Logos appearing out of "obscurity"—that is, the "earlier history . . . of the immortal Pickwick"—and into the light of creation. But it also dramatizes the fundamental activity of the Logos; it dramatizes the notion of cosmic creation as a word—which is how God, as the Logos, created the world: *fiat lux*, said God, when he was speaking Latin, and so it was. And here too, in this novel, we begin the creation with a word, with language; with Dickens' language on the one hand and the word "Pickwickians" on the other. Mr. Pickwick and Dickens are each of them the Logos as well, emerging brightly out of their immanence and creating. And each of them is in his separate, distinctive way the Word made flesh—as are those documents and papers mentioned by the "editor," which do not exist, or do not exist just yet, but will become another incarnation of language, a novel, a printed book. Thus we begin with a comic, cosmic creation in the form of the Logos, the word.[1]

There follows the second sentence of the novel, which is the first sentence of the mythical papers, enclosed in quotation marks. "May 12, 1827. Joseph Smiggers, Esq., P.V.P.M.P.C.,* presiding." The work is set in the past. And although the date is not 4004 B.C., there appears to be something equally accidental and gratuitous about May 12, 1827; in addition readers of *Pickwick Papers*, like readers of the Bible, have encountered certain difficulties in keeping its chronology straight or consistent. But that date is not in actuality gratuitous, although we have to go outside of the book to find its significance: May 1827 was the date at which the fifteen-year-old Charles Dickens first went to work as a clerk in the law firm of Ellis and Blackmore. In the popular idiom of the time, it was the moment at which he "began the world." Then there are those funny letters that follow Smiggers' name. At the risk of appearing absurd, we may ask why they are there; and if we put to one side the simple comic intention and effect of the long set of initials (and the extravagant title to which they refer), we may observe that letters arranged in such a novel and quasi-arbitrary way sometimes form words, or suggest a code that is different from though related to the codes by which we ordinarily communicate. They are almost a kind of doodling, which may be a first clue for us to hold onto. (What I am suggesting is that in this instance the letters P.V.P.M.P.C. are more important than the words to which they refer. It is the letters themselves that make one laugh at first; the humor in the footnoted explanation of their reference and of the inflation in the title is certainly there, but it is secondary.)

There follows an account of the meeting of the club, which first records that Mr. Pickwick had read his celebrated paper entitled "Speculations on the Source of the Hampstead Ponds, with some Observations on the Theory of Tittlebats." Whatever the theory of tittlebats may be, the term itself is of interest. It is, the *Oxford English Dictionary* records, a variant form of stickleback; it comes into use in about 1820, and has its origin in "childish" pronunciation of the fish's name.[2] Once again, as the novel feels about for its beginning, it presses itself and the reader back into words themselves, into matters connected with learning words and with some kind of fundamental or primitive relation to the language.

As for the meeting as a whole, it is conceived of at the outset as the mildest of burlesques upon the transactions of some scientific or scholarly association. It is that, but it is also a parody of a scene in heaven, a fanciful rendering of an unwritten episode of *Paradise Lost*. These comic-epic, immortally foolish creatures are going to visit the earth and report in their correspondence on what they see. And if Mr. Pickwick is the blandest of parodic imaginations of a traveler, explorer, observer, scientist, and scholar, he is just as much a parodic refraction of a god visiting his creation. There follows immediately upon the reading of the resolutions that assign their work of traveling and reporting to Mr. Pickwick and his companions a first description of this deity. "A casual observer, adds the secretary, . . . might possibly have remarked nothing extraordinary in the bald head, and circular spectacles, which were intently turned towards his (the secretary's) face, during the reading of the above resolutions: to those who knew that the gigantic brain of Pickwick was working beneath that forehead, and that the beaming eyes of Pickwick were twinkling behind those glasses, the sight was indeed an interesting one." The image of Pickwick's face is itself almost like a doodle: a number of blank circles to be filled in later—even the solid dots and lines of his "beaming eyes" are not there yet and have to be imagined.

Mr. Pickwick stands on a Windsor chair. His coat tails, tights, and gaiters are mentioned; Tupman, Snodgrass, and Winkle are cursorily sketched, while Dickens readies himself to do what comes next. What comes next is that Mr. Pickwick begins to speak; or more precisely the secretary begins to transcribe in the third person the speech of Mr. Pickwick. At once we see that a travesty parliamentary speech is in the course of being composed, and the best parliamentary reporter of his time is spitballing away in a Homeric doodle, letting the language improvisationally, incontinently, and inconsequentially run on. For example: "The praise of mankind was his [Mr. Pickwick's] Swing; philanthropy was his insurance office. (Vehement cheering) . . . Still he could not but feel that they had selected him for a service of great honour, and of some danger. Travelling was in a troubled state, and the minds of coachmen were unsettled. Let them look abroad and contemplate the scenes which were enacting around them. Stage coaches were upsetting in all directions, horses were bolting, boats were overturning, and boilers were bursting. (Cheers—a voice 'No.') No! (Cheers.)" It runs on until Blotton makes his objection, the altercation between him and Mr. Pickwick breaks out, he calls Pickwick a "humbug"[3]—

"Immense confusion, and loud cries of 'Chair,' and 'Order,'" and a compromise settlement is reached when Blotton asserts that he had used that word or expression "in its Pickwickian sense." At this point, of course, Dickens—and his readers—have hit upon something.

What is the Pickwickian sense? If we recall that the chapter begins with the Logos and with the word Pickwickians, we can begin by suggesting that it is a sense in which the word is seized creatively in the first instance almost as a kind of doodle, as a play of the pen, as a kind of verbal scribble or game. It is the word—or verbal expression—actively regarded not primarily as conscious imitation of either nature or preexistent models, but rather as largely unconscious invention, whose meaning is created essentially as it is spontaneously uttered or written down. It is the world, language, writing, as these exist in each other, as a complex process that is self-generating—so that beginning, so to say, either with the name Pickwick, or the word or title Pickwickian, the world, the language, and the writing implicit in or unfolded by such words appears to generate itself. It is language with the shackles removed from certain of its deeper creative powers, which henceforth becomes capable of a constant, rapid, and virtually limitless multiplication of its own effects and forms in new inventions and combinations and configurations. *Mutatis mutandis* it is the timely equivalent in written novelistic prose of the take-off into self-sustained growth. In *Pickwick Papers* the English novel becomes, as it were, airborne.[4]

What we have, in short, is something rather new and spectacular. Such a breakthrough in literature would in the nature of the case have to be largely unconsicous; it could not at first have been understood by the person who was the bearer of such a force. For Dickens has committed himself at the outset of *Pickwick Papers* to something like pure writing, to language itself. No novelist had, I believe, ever quite done this in such a measure before—certainly not Sterne. In addition, the commitment was paradoxically ensured and enforced by the circumstance of compelled spontaneity in which Dickens wrote, by the necessity he accepted of turning it out every month, of being regularly spontaneous and self-generatingly creative on demand. Dickens was, if it may be said, undertaking to let the writing write the book. There are several other ways of stating this notion and several explanatory means that may be applied to its elaboration—out of which I shall choose one. Dickens was able to abandon himself or give expression to what Freud called the primary process in a degree that was unprecedented in English fictional prose; he was able to let the fundamental and primitive mental processes of condensation, displacement, and equivalence or substitution find their way into consciousness with a minimum of inhibition, impedence, or resistance. These processes correspond to and are constituents of the deep nonlogical, the metaphoric and metonymic, processes of language—and it was these processes that Dickens allowed to have their run. It may be asked why such a development, in anything like a similar degree, had not occurred before in the English novel. Poets have, after all, often written in just such a way. Was it too frightening a prospect for novelists? Such a question inevitably involves historical circumstances of enormous complexity, and only a partial and provisional answer is possible here. In a sense the possibilities opened up by such an experience were too unnerving for most novelists. The novel had been built primarily on the secondary, logical processes, processes that develop ontogenetically at a later state of mental existence and form the essential structures of consciousness. The regression implied by this manner of composition, the threat of an ego overwhelmed by such regression and loss or abdication of control, must have appeared too alarming to English novelists hitherto. Or we can put it another way and state that before Dickens no English novelist had appeared with an ego of such imperial powers and with a sense of reality so secure that he could temporarily abandon those powers without fear of being overwhelmed or of their permanent loss. At the same time, such an abandonment, successfully carried through, marks the opening up of a new dimension of freedom for the English novel, if not for the human mind in general. Thus at the outset of *Pickwick Papers* Dickens has allowed the language to go into motion within him, and it is to the motion of that language, to its movement in writing, that we must first attend.

Chapter 2 opens with Mr. Pickwick about to begin experiencing the world, which is as yet unformed, undifferentiated, and uncreated, as he is himself. He has had almost no experience, but as we quickly learn the experience that he has not had is essentially linguistic experience. As his encounter with the cab man demonstrates at once:

"How old is that horse, my friend?" inquired Mr. Pickwick, rubbing his nose with the shilling he had reserved for the fare.

"Forty-two," replied the driver, eyeing him askant.

"What!" ejaculated Mr. Pickwick, laying his hand upon his notebook. The driver reiterated his former statement . . .

"And how long do you keep him out at a time?" inquired Mr. Pickwick, searching for further information.

"Two or three weeks," replied the man.

"Weeks!" said Mr. Pickwick in astonishment—and out came the notebook again.

"He lives at Pentonwil when he's at home," observed the driver, coolly, "but we seldom takes him home, on account of his veakness."

"On account of his weakness!" reiterated the perplexed Mr. Pickwick.

"He always falls down when he's took out o' the cab," continued the driver, "but when he's in it, we bears him up werry tight, and takes him in werry short, so as he can't werry well fall down; and we've got a pair o' precious large wheels on, so ven he *does* move, they run after him, and he must go on—he can't help it."

What we learn from this meeting of minds is that the cab man is using language in the Pickwickian sense, but Mr. Pickwick is not. Mr. Pickwick's use of the language is literal, abstractly symbolic, and almost entirely denotative and normative, and as the novel continues this characteristic of his becomes increasingly pronounced. He does not yet understand language, and his innocence is primarily a linguistic innocence. And yet we recall that he is supposed to be the Logos as well, whose principal creation is language, the means of which comprise all other creation, including those utterances that are his self-creation. In this reversal and paradox, Dickens has erected for himself a problem whose multiple workings-out will occupy considerable space throughout the novel.

But Dickens is not yet ready for that, and the affray between the Pickwickians and the cab man is brought to an end by the entrance of Jingle who delivers them from the embraces of the crowd that surrounds them and into the equally vigorous embrace of volubility and verbiage with which he succeeds to envelop them.

"Heads, heads—take care of your heads!" cried the loquacious stranger, as they came out under the low archway, which in those days formed the entrance to the coach-yard. "Terrible place—dangerous work—other day—five children—mother—tall lady, eating sandwiches—forgot the arch—crash—knock—children look round—mother's head off—sandwich in her hand—no mouth to put it in—head of a family off—shocking, shocking! Looking at Whitehall, sir?—fine place—little window—somebody else's head off there, eh, sir?—he didn't keep a sharp look-out enough either—eh, sir, eh?"

At this point, it may be said, *Pickwick Papers* is off and running, it has really begun to find itself. Jingle is an approximation of uninflected linguistic energy. He seems incoherent but he is not; his speech proceeds rapidly and by associations; his syntactical mode is abbreviatory and contracted; his logic is elliptical, abstractly minimal, and apropositional. He brings us into closer touch with the primary process. He is, moreover, the first expression of the "constant succession" that Dickens mentions in his preface to the first edition; but the constant succession, as it first appears here and will persist throughout the novel, is the constant succession of writing, of characters rising up to speak in print in unending torrents of words, of language in incessant motion, of writing apparently and extraordinarily writing itself —through the no less extraordinary means of Dickens. It is almost as if in Jingle Dickens had hit upon or invented a way of dramatizing or embodying this unconscious apprehension or conception, that somehow language itself is spontaneously creating this novel—and it is that conception that provides the dramatic substructure of rather more than half the novel.

But Jingle's speech is something more than this. At a slightly later point Dickens refers to it as a "system of stenography," and here we arrive on closer grounds. For Dickens had of course been a stenographer, a writer of shorthand, the very best shorthand writer of his time. He started to learn it soon after he went to work as a clerk at Ellis and Blackmore's, before he was sixteen years old; he had written in it for years in his work in Doctor's Commons and other courts and as a parliamentary reporter; and he was never to forget it, as he reminded his audience in a memorable speech made in his later life.[5] For a number of important formative years he had worked as a kind of written recording device for the human voice, for speech, for the English language. He had been a writing instrument for others, their language flowing through his writing. In one sense those written voices were all inside of him, wonderfully and instantaneously recorded on the most remarkable of all electronic tapes, and now were about to be played back and expressed—although the mechanical and electronic analogy is, I should forcibly state, far from being an adequate approximation to what it was that went on inside him. In another sense Dickens was acting as the stenographer of his characters and of the language itself as well as of its written form; he was transcribing writing, writing down what that particular mode of the language said to him and through him. And yet these notions of stenographic memory and transcription, however useful and suggestive they may be, are surely insufficient, for nothing is less mistakable about the writing of *Pickwick Papers* than its qualities of free inventiveness, of active, spontaneous creativity, of its movement in a higher imaginative order than that which is circumscribed by storage, memory, or recoverable transcriptions alone.

There is, however, another side to this experience that is relevant to our argument. Dickens describes what it was like to learn shorthand in a famous passage in *David Copperfield* (chap. 38). He had laid out the sum of half a guinea on "an approved scheme of the noble art and mystery of stenography"—it was Gurney's textbook, *Brachygraphy, or an Easy and Compendious System of Shorthand*—

and plunged into a sea of perplexity that brought me, in a few weeks, to the confines of distraction. The changes that were rung upon dots, which in such a position meant such a thing, and in another position something else, entirely different; the wonderful vagaries that were played by circles; the unaccountable consequences that resulted from marks like flies' legs; the tremendous effects of a curve in a wrong place; not only troubled my waking hours, but reappeared before me in my sleep. When I had groped my way, blindly, through these difficulties, and had mastered the alphabet, which was an Egyptian Temple in itself, there then appeared a procession of new horrors, called arbitrary characters; the most despotic characters I have ever known; who insisted, for instance, that a thing like the beginning of a cobweb, meant expectation, and that a pen-and-ink sky-rocket stood for disadvantageous. When I had fixed these wretches in my mind, I found that they had driven everything else out of it; then, beginning again, I forgot them; while I was picking them up, I dropped the other fragments of the system.

He goes on to describe how after three or four months, when he first made an attempt to take down a speech at Doctor's Commons, the "speaker walked off from me before I began, and left my imbecile pencil staggering about the paper as if it were in a fit!" He turns to practicing at night with Traddles, who reads out speeches to him from "Enfield's Speaker or a volume of parliamentary orations," which the aspiring young writer faithfully takes down. "But, as to reading them after I had got them, I might as well have copied the Chinese inscriptions on an immense collection of tea-chests, or the golden characters on all the great red and green bottles in the chemists' shops!" In short, he concludes, he spent this period "making the most desperate efforts to know these elusive characters by sight whenever I met them." I should like to suggest that Dickens' prolonged experience as a shorthand writer had a significant effect on what for a writer must be the most important of relations, the relation between speech and writing. The brachygraphic characters, as he describes them in recollection, were themselves doodles—apparently random plays of the pen, out of which figures or partial figures would emerge and to which meaning could be ascribed. It was almost as if the nascent novelist had providentially been given or discovered another way of structurally relating himself to the language. Speech could now be rendered not only in the abstract forms of cursive or printed letters and units; it could be represented *graphically* as well—the two other forms of written transcription that he refers to are Egyptian hieroglyphics and Chinese ideograms (along with the written code of science, chemistry). What I am suggesting is that this experience of an alternative, quasi-graphic way of representing speech had among other things the effect upon Dickens of loosening up the rigid relations between speech and writing that prevail in our linguistic and cultural system. By providing him with an experience of something that closely resembled a hieroglyphic means of preserving speech, it allowed the spoken language to enter into his writing with a parity it had never enjoyed before in English fictional prose. Speech here was not the traditional subordinate of its written representation; it could appear now in writing with a freedom and spontaneity that made it virtually, if momentarily, writing's equal. And yet whenever a development of this magnitude takes place in writing, in literature, the capacities and possibilities of that written art are themselves suddenly multiplied and enhanced.[6]

This kind of free, wild, inventive doodling language tends to break out in character after character in *Pickwick Papers*, even the most minor ones. The instances are almost limitless, and one more will have to stand for all the rest. After the Dingley Dell–Muggleton cricket match (at which, by the way, Jingle makes another sensational appearance with an account of his own epic match with Sir Thomas Blazo in the West Indies), little Mr. Staple arises to address the assembled company.

But, sir, while we remember that Muggleton has given birth to a Dumkins and a Podder, let us never forget that Dingley Dell can boast a Luffey and a Struggles . . . Every gentleman who hears me, is probably acquainted with the reply made by an individual, who—to use an ordinary figure of speech—"hung out" in a tub, to the emperor Alexander:—"If I were not Diogenes," said he, "I would be Alexander." I can well imagine these gentlemen to say, "If I were not Dumkins I would be Luffey; if I were not Podder I would be Struggles." (Enthusiasm.) But . . . is it in cricket alone that your fellow-townsmen stand preeminent? Have you never heard of Dumkins and determination? Have you never been taught to associate Podder with prosperity? (Great applause.)

But this kind of language in which the primary process is having a field day (which does not mean that it is pure fantasy without reference to realities of every description, external as well as internal and linguistic) gets into Dickens' authorial prose as well. It is to be found particularly in his metaphoric figures. Here are two examples: "The evening grew more dull every moment, and a melancholy wind sounded through the deserted fields, like a distant giant whistling for his house-dog" (chap. 2). Or there is this from Dingley Dell and the courtship of Tupman and Miss Wardle. "It was evening . . . the buxom servants were lounging at the side-door, enjoying the pleasantness of the hour, and the delights of a flirtation, on first principles, with certain unwieldy animals attached to the farm; and there sat the interesting pair, uncared for by all, caring for none, and dreaming only of themselves; there they sat, in short, like a pair of carefully-folded kid gloves—bound up in each other" (chap. 8).

As the novel advances Dickens becomes increasingly preoccupied with what it is he is doing in this connection, and at a crucial juncture in its early development this preoccupation surfaces and begins consciously to inform the entire substance of an episode. I am referring to the stone and "Bill Stumps, his mark." Mr. Pickwick discovers the stone and its "fragment of an inscription," but although he can make out the markings and letters, he cannot decipher their meaning. Writing and language remain a secret, a puzzle, an arcanum to him. What he finds is a species of writing, a hieroglyphic, that for him does not reduce to ordinary sense. He thereupon writes a pamphlet ninety-six pages long that contains "twenty-seven different readings of the inscription," and achieves great renown among the learned societies of the civilized world. At this point the vicious Blotton turns up again with another of his poisonous accusations. He denies "the antiquity of the inscription," accuses Pickwick of being a mystifier or a fool, and produces the evidence of the man who sold the stone to Mr. Pickwick. Yet if Blotton is correct what has he found except writing that is precisely a kind of doodling. It was written or inscribed "in an idle mood," that is to say at random; it is writing apparently for the sake of writing alone. Moreover, it contains still another paradox within itself, since what is supposed to have been written down is the traditional formula that is used when an illiterate man makes his mark. Hence this is the utterly confounding riddle of writing by a man who appears to be *illiterate,* and so perhaps Mr. Pickwick is right after all. In any case, right or wrong, Pickwick or Blotton, what we are confronted with here is writing in the Pickwickian sense once more. And so at this juncture too the book reveals itself as being at some deep structural level about the act of its own coming into existence. It is writing about writing, and writing itself—as is "BILL STUMPS, HIS MARK." As a result, Dickens remarks, the stone is "an illegible monument" to Mr. Pickwick, something written but mysteriously unreadable, as in a sense is Dickens in *Pickwick Papers.*

The importance I attribute to this episode is supported by what comes immediately after it. In the very next chapter the novel takes its first really large swerve of development, which is in fact a double swerve. Mr. Pickwick does two things. He sends for Sam Weller, the great master of language and invention, who by virtue of that mastery is going to protect Mr. Pickwick from the world. But while he is doing so he gets into trouble with Mrs. Bardell precisely by being betrayed by the language, which, Mr. Pickwick will never be quite able to learn, has an ambiguous social life all its own. The sexual and linguistic plays and implications of the scene need only be touched upon. While Mr. Pickwick is begetting his only begotten son—it is one of the few truly immaculate conceptions in world history—he is having a conversation with Mrs. Bardell that is full of sexual double entendres, none of which are apparent or intelligible to him. Although he has not committed criminal conversation with Mrs. Bardell, he is going to be found guilty of a linguistic offense at law, for which he will be punished, namely breach of promise. His bafflement by language, by the inescapable form in which the experience of this novel (and he himself) is created, is going to lead to his suffering. This eventuality is, however, postponed to a later part of the book, for at this moment with the active entry of Sam Weller, the novel's proportions are altered again, and it has at last settled into its full course. From now on Mr. Pickwick will be explicitly represented as employing the language in an essentially innocent or single-minded sense, and out of this his moral innocence and goodness will inexorably grow. At the same time, in Sam, Dickens has invented a virtuoso of language, of both the primary and secondary processes; he is a master hand at managing means and ends, of actively engaging reality through rational, symbolic language as well as appreciating it and playing with it through the other kind. He is unmistakeably Dickens' principal surrogate in the novel itself, the novelist-poet within the novel, and becomes from the moment of his effective entry its dominant creative center.

Hereafter the novel becomes even more clearly a "continuous succession" of language or writing in constant motion, moving itself. We pass directly on to Eatanswill where we have the language or diction of politics, generating its own obfuscation. Along with this there is Mr. Pott and his journalistic writings and style—in relation to which Mr. Pickwick remains the linguistic innocent. Pott asks Mr. Pickwick to read with him some of his leaders, upon which Dickens comments: "We have every reason to believe that he was perfectly enraptured with the vigour and freshness of the style; indeed . . . his eyes were closed, as if with excess of pleasure, during the whole time of their perusal" (chap. 13). And indeed one of the most charming moments in the entire novel is when Mr. Pickwick forgets how to speak altogether. Soon, however, everything is breaking into speech, including the furniture, as the chair does in "The Bagman's Tale" of Tom

Smart. There naturally follows Mrs. Leo Hunter and her literary breakfasts—the subject of which is literature and writing, and we find again
that the writing, the novel, takes itself for its subject in the very act of its
creation. Pope gets into it under false pretenses—"feasts of reason, sir, and
flows of soul," quotes Mr. Leo Hunter, who then adds "as somebody who
wrote a sonnet to Mrs. Leo Hunter on her breakfasts, feelingly and originally observed"—as do language and writing in almost innumerable forms,
some of them indescribable. Even foreigners are dragged into the act, as
in the passages about Count Smorltork and his pursuit of English under
difficulties, passages which Dickens was going to use again but to other
effects almost thirty years later in *Our Mutual Friend*.

By this time it seems evident that Dickens was intermittently and fleet-
ingly close to being aware of the extraordinary thing that was happening
to him or that he was doing—it is never quite clear which. There are any
number of instances that indicate such an oblique and partial awareness,
out of which mass I shall choose but one. It occurs at the beginning of
chapter 17, with Mr. Pickwick in bed with an attack of rheumatism brought
on by his night spent outdoors in the damp. The bulk of the chapter consists of the tale of "The Parish Clerk," which Mr. Pickwick produces, "with
sundry blushes . . . as having been 'edited' by himself, during his recent
indisposition, from his notes of Mr. Weller's unsophisticated recital." This
is a wonderful bit of play, and what we have is as follows: at this moment
Pickwick is to Sam as Dickens is to Mr. Pickwick. Yet we know as well
that Sam is in some closely intimate sense also Dickens. So Pickwick is to
Dickens as Dickens is to Pickwick—that is, for an instant Pickwick is
editing Dickens, or in other words writing his own book. Once again
writing seems to be reflexively writing itself. Another embodiment of this
circumstance begins to take shape with the increasing presence in the novel
of the law, which is another kind of language and another kind of writing.
Mr. Pickwick first becomes aware of its ominous presence when he receives
a letter from Dodson and Fogg informing him "that a writ has been issued
against you in this suit in the Court of Common Pleas" (chap. 18). The
novel thus proceeds to make itself by this continuous succession of kinds
of writing spontaneously introduced—and that for the most part is what
constitutes its structure. It is a structure that is, like the events themselves,
"a gross violation of all established rules and precedents," which may,
for all I know, be what Dickens meant when he referred to "a gentle and
not-unnatural progress of adventure."[7] For it constitutes itself in the main
by Dickens' repeatedly rising up in the form of one character after another
and bursting irrepressibly "into an animated torrent of words" (chap. 20).

But that is by no means all *Pickwick Papers* is. There are, for example,
those notorious interpolated tales. On this reading—as on others—they
dramatically represent the obverse principle to that which informs the body
of the novel. In them motion and movement of both language and event

come to a dead halt. In almost every one of them, even the funny ones, someone is paralyzed, immobilized, or locked up and imprisoned in something. Their language is not the free, wild, astonishingly creative language of the balance of the novel. It tends almost uniformly to be obsessed, imprisoned, anal, caught in various immobile, repetitive modes—to be for the largest part unmastered. One passage will remind us adequately of the effect of the whole. It comes from the most important of those tales, "The Old Man's Tale about the Queer Client."

> That night, in the silence and desolation of his miserable room, the wretched man knelt down by the dead body of his wife, and called on God to witness a terrible oath, that from that hour, he devoted himself to revenge her death and that of his child; that thenceforth to the last moment of his life, his whole energies should be directed to this *one object;* that his revenge should be protracted and terrible; that his hatred should be undying and inextinguishable; and should hunt its *object* through the world [my italics] (chap. 21).

The object in question is the antithesis of that "constant succession" which Dickens asserted to be his overarching creative intention. The language in which that object is represented is itself as yet utterly unfree; and the tales of that language are accordingly encapsulated, stuck, encysted, and imbedded in the movement of the novel which moves about and around them.

As that movement proceeds it takes a still wilder turn with the introduction of Tony Weller. Tony is in some measure a representation in language of the energies and workings of the primary process itself; he is Sam without the rationality, the logic, the instrumental relation to the world. Much of him may be caught from this one interchange with Mr. Pickwick, on the nature of the "Wery queer life" led by turnpike keepers.

> "They's all on 'em men as has met with some disappointment in life," said Mr. Weller senior.
> "Ay, ay?" said Mr. Pickwick.
> "Yes. Consequence of vich, they retires from the world, and shuts themselves up in pikes; partly vith the view of being solitary, and partly to rewenge themselves on mankind, by takin' tolls."
> "Dear me," said Mr. Pickwick, "I never knew that before."
> "Fact, sir," said Mr. Weller; "if they was gen'l'm'n you'd call them misanthropes, but as it is, they only takes to pike-keepin' " (chap. 22).

And Dickens proceeds to remark that Tony's conversation had "the inestimable charm" and virtue of "blending amusement with instruction," thus implying that he is in short literature itself. With Sam and Tony entering upon dialogue the novel finds its most creative moments, many of which are about its own mysterious nature, about the activity whereby it continues to bring itself into being. The *locus classicus,* of course, is chapter 33, which is about Sam's writing a valentine, and Mr. Weller "the elder" delivering "some Critical Sentiments respecting Literary Composition." Detail after detail is brought lightly to bear upon this fundamental preoccupation. There is, for example, the boy, who comes looking for Sam with a message from Tony—"young brockiley sprout" Sam calls him—who having delivered his message "walked away, awakening all the echoes in George Yard as he did so, with several chaste and extremely correct imitations of a drover's whistle, delivered in a tone of peculiar richness and volume." Then there is Sam, looking in a stationer's window and seeing a valentine, which Dickens thereupon describes:

The particular picture on which Sam Weller's eyes were fixed . . . was a highly coloured representation of a couple of human hearts skewered together with an arrow cooking before a cheerful fire, while a male and female cannibal in modern attire: the gentleman being clad in a blue coat and white trousers, and the lady in a deep red pelisse with a parasol of the same: were approaching the meal with hungry eyes, up a serpentine gravel path leading thereunto. A decidedly indelicate young gentleman, in a pair of wings and nothing else, was depicted as superintending the cooking; a representation of the spire of the church in Langham Place, London, appeared in the distance; and the whole formed a "valentine," of which, as a written inscription in the window testified, there was a large assortment within, which the shopkeeper pledged himself to dispose of, to his countrymen generally, at the reduced rate of one and sixpence each.

Sam then walks on toward Leadenhall Market in search of the Blue Boar, whence his father's summons had emanated. "Looking round him, he there beheld a sign-board on which the painter's art had delineated something remotely resembling a cerulean elephant with an aquiline nose in lieu of a trunk. Rightly conjecturing that this was the Blue Boar himself," he steps inside and begins to compose his valentine while waiting for his father. In due time Tony arrives and the immortal conversation about "literary composition" takes place. "Lovely creetur," begins Sam's valentine.

"'Tain't in poetry, is it?" interposed his father.
"No, no," replied Sam.
"Werry glad to hear it," said Mr. Weller. "Poetry's unnat'ral; no man ever talked poetry 'cept a beadle on boxin' day, or Warren's blackin', or Rowland's oil, or some o' them low fellows; never you let yourself down to talk poetry, my boy. Begin agin, Sammy."

And he goes on in the course of this conversation to make similar magisterial observations about words, style, metaphor, and writing in general.

In this chapter the young Dickens is writing at the very top of his inventive bent, and what he is implicitly and covertly asserting is that there is nothing he cannot capture and represent in his writing. He can gratuitously bring to life the sound of a drover's whistle, or even an extremely correct imitation of that sound, if that is what is wanted. He can turn pictures into writing which is more vivid, more graphic, more representational than the pictures themselves—as he does with the valentine. He can represent things more accurately and graphically than graphic art, as he does with the sign of the Blue Boar. His writing is superior even to poetry, both because it is more "natural" and because it can include all poetry, its agents and its objects, within its limitless range. It can even include Warren's blacking, and when we take note of this inclusion we understand that what Dickens is unconsciously asserting is that there is at this moment nothing he cannot overcome, there is nothing he cannot transcend, by writing about it, or through *writing it*. He genuinely feels free, for he is writing in freedom. He is perhaps the first novelist ever to have done so in such a degree.

It is very much to the point that it is at just this moment that Dickens chooses to emphasize that Sam, great poet and impresario of the language that he is, can hardly write. Dickens is the writer and Sam is what he is writing—that is, one brilliantly split off, deflected, and reorganized segment of himself. It was part of Dickens' genius as a writer to write Sam, or to tap that untapped resource of language in the near illiterate, and to get that speech and *its* genius into writing, into his writing. It was his genius, in other words, to be able *to write that as yet unwritten language*. It is at such a juncture that society and social change on the one hand and language and writing on the other all come richly together.

Correlative with this development, Dickens and Sam both become increasingly conscious of the meaning and value of Pickwick. At one point, it is asserted that Pickwick is a "magic word," and in a subsequent episode the cat is let entirely out of the bag. They are waiting in the travelers' room of the White Horse Cellar, when Sam emphatically draws his master's attention to a coach that is standing outside, and to what is written on its door: "and there, sure enough, in gilt letters of a goodly size, was the magic name of PICKWICK!" (chap. 35). At this moment both the magic and the reality that in collaboration go into the formation of creative originality are brought into active conjunction. For the name of Pickwick was clearly taken by Dickens from the actual man who ran the Bath coach. Moreover, as Sam does not fail indignantly to inform us, his first name was Moses. And at this point it becomes our turn to recall that "Boz" is a shortened version of Moses—and to realize again and in another way what we already know differently, that Boz and Pickwick are of course one. Even more, however, the real Pickwick was a coachman—and thus we realize once again that Mr. Pickwick and Tony are also in reality one, as in point of fact they were, both of them imaginative refractions and idealizations of John Dickens. It is Sam who voices Dickens' final comment on this nexus, saying something for once that is beyond his own enlarged understanding. To put the name Moses before Pickwick, he says, is what "I call addin' insult to injury, as the parrot said ven they not only took him from his native land, but made him talk the English langwidge arterwards" (chap. 35). The whole secret is in learning the English language; the secret lies in that primordial mystery that seems spontaneously to be creating out of itself, out of its own inherent resources, this marvelous work.

Finally there is the trial, which is a veritable mania of language in almost all the forms that have appeared before. There is the language, or languages, of the law itself; there is more court reporting on Dickens' part and more shorthand writing in an ideally transcribed form. There is the rhetoric of Buzfuz, and his masterful dealing with writing, with Mrs. Bardell's "written placard"—"I intreat the attention of the jury to the wording of this document. 'Apartments furnished for a single gentleman' !"—as well as with Mr. Pickwick's fatally compromising letters. There is the presiding judge, Mr. Justice Stareleigh, who wakening from the slumber in which he conducts almost all of the trial "immediately wrote down something with a pen without any ink in it," and whose questioning of Winkle follows a similar intelligible line.

"What's your Christian name, sir?" angrily inquired the little judge.
"Nathaniel, sir."
"Daniel,—any other name?"
"Nathaniel, sir—my Lord, I mean."
"Nathaniel Daniel, or Daniel Nathaniel?"
"No, my Lord, only Nathaniel; not Daniel at all."
"What did you tell me it was Daniel for, then, sir?" inquired the judge.
"I didn't, my Lord," replied Mr. Winkle.
"You did, sir," replied the judge, with a severe frown. "How could I have got Daniel on my notes, unless you told me so, sir?"
This argument was, of course, unanswerable.

Exactly. As are those arguments and circumstances through which Mr. Pickwick at length finds himself in prison, at which point, as everyone knows, the novel makes its final, momentous turn of development. Mr. Pickwick has in effect let himself be put in prison by the law, by its licentious abuse and misuse of language. And as he is thus confined within the world or precincts of the law, Dickens' writing too becomes imprisoned and immobile, preoccupied again as it was in the tales with intensities and obsessions and closeness and deprivation and filth, bound in by the law, by cases, by the past, by the accumulated weight of mold and dirt and misery that the prison and the law represent. But the writing in these crucial passages is not exactly the same as the writing in the interpolated tales; it is harder and has a greater bite to it. That writing, which before was free, has become like Mr. Pickwick himself engaged and involved, and engaged and involved with society. For in the person of the law Pickwick and Dickens have run into something which though it may seem at first to be an unalloyed linguistic universe is in fact much more than a world of words. It is and it represents society and its structures, in particular those structures known as property and money, both of them extralinguistic phenomena. Property and money are more than words, and words cannot make you free of them. It is a matter of the very largest moment for Dickens' development as a writer—and a testimony to his exceptional inner integrity—that he should in the midst of his greatest celebration of his freedom and transcendence as a genius of language, engage himself imaginatively in those very conditions which were calculated most powerfully to nullify that freedom. His entire future development is contained by anticipation in that nullification.

In one of his later utterances, Hegel undertook to settle a long-outstanding score between himself and Rousseau. As for the Rousseauian idea of some original state of freedom, he declared bluntly, it simply makes no sense. Hegel was a great genius, but he was an old man when he made this remark and had long since forgotten his childhood and youth, let alone his youthful writings. Dickens was also a great genius, who wrote *Pickwick Papers* in the flush of his young manhood, as a celebration of the positive sides of the childhood and youth that he yet remembered and as an exercise of what may be the highest kind of freedom that an individual person can enjoy, the freedom that consists in the exercise of one's native powers and that has as its consequence the creation out of one's self of an object that is of lasting value and that is at the same time an activity of self-creation. What Hegel goes on next to say, however, is of larger pertinence. It is true, he declares, that we are all unfree, that we all suffer from a pervasive sense of limitation, confinement, and constraint; yet that very constraint, he states, "is part of the process through which is first produced the consciousness of and the desire for freedom in its true, that is, its rational and ideal form." Indeed, he continues, every terrible limitation upon impulse, desire, and passion that we feel is itself "the very condition leading to liberation; and society and the state are the very conditions in which freedom is realized." What Hegel in his prodigious austerity is saying is that freedom can only come about, can only be realized, in and through its negation. A truly human freedom, that freedom which is the one goal worthy of being the "destination" of men as the human species, can only be achieved through the most profound historical experience of negativity. It is, it seems to me, no accident that Dickens installed that negativity at the dramatic center of his first and freest novel, at the very moment when he was sustaining himself with a freedom that was virtually unexampled in the history of the novel. The consequences that such a creative act of courage had are known to us all—they are nothing less than Dickens' long and arduous subsequent development, a development that as the later novels make increasingly clear is in fact a search for a wider, a more general, and a truly human freedom.

REFERENCES

1. It was Freud, of course, who preeminently taught us to distinguish between thoughts and behavior, disclosing how in the unconscious, intentions or verbal expressions are taken as the equivalent of deliberate actions. Yet it was also Freud who wrote to Thomas Mann that "an author's words are deeds," transfusing that commonplace with new kinds of meaning.

2. The *Oxford English Dictionary* misses out on an earlier appearance of the word in a variant form. In *An Island in the Moon* (1784), there occurs the following: "Here ladies and gentlemen said he I'll show you a louse [climing] or a flea or a butterfly or a cock chafer the blade bone of a tittle back no no heres a bottle of wind that I took up in the bog house." David V. Erdman, ed., *The Poetry and Prose of William Blake* (Garden City, N.Y.: Doubleday, 1965), p. 452.

3. Humbug, an expression to which Dickens would give memorable life on a later occasion, is another word whose etymological origin is cloaked in obscurity.

4. The analogy being drawn with terms taken from the language of economic historians is only partly fanciful, although this is not the place to work out the mediations that would provide it with substance. I annex the figure of being airborne from E. J. Hobsbawm.

5. "I have never forgotten the fascination of that old pursuit. The pleasure that I used to feel in the rapidity and dexterity of its exercise has never faded out of my breast. Whatever little cunning of hand or head I took to it, or acquired in it, I have so retained as that I fully believe I could resume it tomorrow, very little the worse from long disuse. To this present year of my life, when I sit in this hall, or where not, hearing a dull speech—the phenomenon does occur—I sometimes beguile the tedium of the moment by mentally following the speaker in the old way; and sometimes, if you can believe me, I even find my hand going on the table cloth, taking an imaginary note of it all." Speech to the Newspaper Press Fund, May 20, 1865, in K. J. Fielding, ed., *The Speeches of Charles Dickens* (Oxford: Oxford University Press, 1960), pp. 347-348.

6. In this section I have been adapting a number of analytical and speculative theses put forward separately and in concert by the psychoanalyst Ernst Kris and the art historian E. H. Gombrich. See *Psychoanalytic Explorations of Art* (New York, 1952), pp. 173-216; *Art and Illusion* (Princeton: Princeton University Press, 1961), pp. 330-358.

7. The characterizing "gross violation" and so forth is made by the gamekeeper as a heartfelt protest "against the introduction into a shooting party, of a gentleman in a barrow" (chap. 19).

ROBERT M. ADAMS

The Sense of Verification:
Pragmatic Commonplaces about Literary Criticism

IT IS with some hesitation and a sense that I may be taking an awful lot for granted that I lay down my premise: it is the aim of a literary critic to persuade his readers. The original work that he is writing about contains his primary problematic: something about it is unknown or uncertain—the exact nature of the basic work is somewhere in doubt. If nobody had any uncertainties about any aspect of an original text (either because it was completely unknown or completely known), there would be no occasion for critics to discuss it; one can at least hope that they would not. But ordinarily there is a blank or a blur in a context (something has not been seen, or being seen has not been understood, or being understood has been understood in several different, conflicting ways), and the critic writes in the hope of elucidating it. He is thus a persuader, an intermediary between the object and an eye which divides its focus between the object and his critique. In one direction, he must convince his reader that by seeing the object as his critique presents it, he will be seeing accurately, seeing what is "really there." I do not suppose any critic pretends he has access to the *Ding an sich,* or that he need necessarily be criticizing anything beyond the process of cognition itself. But the typical situation is that an original text exists, if only *in potentia,* in which the reader is at least as interested as he is in the critic, and to which the critic provides presumably superior access. In the other direction, the eye with which the object is seen is far from a uniform and predictable instrument. A reader or viewer (as E. H. Gombrich's *Art and Illusion* massively reminds us) sees with much more than his eyes; he sees with his mind, his memory, his emotions, his linguistic and visual habits, his culture patterns, his value systems, his expectations. His seeing thus changes in a social as well as a personal dimension, style giving way perpetually to style, generally under the slogan of doing away with style and getting back to the object "as it really is." In no way does the critic stand, by virtue of his office, above or outside this flux; he is himself of it, whether he openly recognizes the fact or not. At the same time he has an obligation to the ostensible object of his criticism. And thus he is involved in

203

a complex task of persuasion, comprising two separate tests which are ideally related to one another in one way, and practically related in another.

To look a little more closely at the object "itself": the critic must persuade the reader that together they have seen the object truly, in all its facets and emphases. This amounts to saying that what the reader sees with the critic's help must answer in some degree to the reader's direct perception of the object or some analogous object; the reader's final vision must appeal to him as an extension of what he has already seen on his own, and could have seen for himself, if he had pushed his processes a little further. (Criticism does not generally make us see something different; it helps us to see something more.) I thus deny by implication that simple coherence or consistency on the part of the critic is in itself sufficient ground of assurance on the part of the reader, since it is as good a mark of obsession as of insight, and since contradictories can claim it.* Directly or indirectly, then, new patterns are judged (in the typical situation of literary criticism) on their conformity with experience—either immediate experience or experience crystallized in accepted patterns and codes of belief. If the new pattern proposed by the critic seems to be, as we say, "completely out of touch with reality," and obstinately remains so after as much study as it seems to be worth, the reader's only recourse is to set it on the shelf.

On the other hand, that phrase "accepted patterns and codes of belief" contains a joker. The critic must persuade the reader that their two minds are in some sympathy, quite apart from the specific text. He is also limited, by these conditions, in what he can persuade the reader to accept. This test of direct persuasion is generally avowed less explicitly than the test-from-the-object, but it is no less pressing for the critic, especially if he pretends to offer some "meaning" to his reader. That quality of "meaning" can only be conferred by the assent of the reader himself, in terms of his own complex of expectations, understandings, desires. A reader who wants "meaning" wants it in terms of his own indefeasible economy, his own more or less precisely defined sense of what is believable. I can see, with brilliant clarity, the patterns of nineteenth-century melodramas (as outlined, for in-

* Not the fact or scope of consistency, but the quality of consistency in a pattern, may indeed and properly have a good deal to do with the judgment we make of it—subtlety of nuance and delicacy in perceiving relations being qualities of value in themselves, and imaginatively quickening in areas far removed from the specific subject they are exercised on. But there is a difference between being impressed by an intellectual performance and being instructed about a subject.

As for contradictory critical theories, it is no easy matter to say categorically under what circumstances we are bound to reject one or modify both into agreement. In matters of physical fact, it seems a good working rule that a thing cannot both be and not be at the same time. But an action of Milton's Satan can be seen at one and the same time as heroic and absurd and even contemptible. Though it is a more elastic concept in criticism than elsewhere, contradiction is an operative one. Within the limits of sanity, I cannot accept C. S. Lewis' view of Milton's god, and William Empson's.

stance, in M. Willson Disher's wonderful *Blood and Thunder*); I cannot believe them as proferred representations (literal, allegorical, anagogical, or tropological) of any human beings who ever lived on land or sea. Conceivably a brilliant critic could persuade me that these distortions and stylizings of representation had a consistent veracity on some significant level or other. The significance of that "some level or other" would have to be defined between me and the critic; and one major element in the definition would be his persuasion of me that the concept "significance" has a content for him, and his view of Victorian melodrama, that it also has for me.

Thus the task of the critic is to persuade. There is the work of literature as it was written and as it has become, with certain fixed limits and certain areas open to interpretation; and there is the contemporary reader, with *his* fixed limits and his areas of interpretive flexibility. To the best of his ability, the critic tries to mediate between these polarities, and his perception of patterns is a major resource in doing this.

The crucial problem in the perception of patterns can be stated in a sentence. One can not see them at all unless one presumes they exist; if one presumes they exist, one tends to see only the evidence that supports their existence.

This of course is a problem involved in all dialectical thinking: unless one has a hypothesis, one sees nothing but blur and confusion; if one has a hypothesis, one tends to become an advocate of it, at the expense of one's role as a judge. It is in this area of testing and verification that the rules of literary evidence would apply, if they could be properly formulated and agreed upon, and in which, for lack of them, we are driven back on rules of thumb, approximations, analogies, metaphors buried and ambulant—as well as some ambiguous imperatives, a couple of which can perhaps lead us on into the topic.

A frequent ambiguous imperative of critical persuasion is to show that the explanation one offers for some observed fact "works" in terms of the next larger unit. Interpreted as the critic would have it, the word "works" in terms of the line, stanza, sentence, or paragraph; the line, stanza, and so forth works in terms of the poem or novel; the poem or novel is understandable in terms of the biography (artistic or personal); the biography is comprehensible in terms of a tradition, a movement, a historical trend, a group of some sort. A unit "works" in terms of that larger unit of which it forms a part; one proves out a local hypothesis by momentarily widening the context to see how the solution "fits."

The principle behind this concept of "working" is obviously harmony. One assumes that the close integration of literary energies, as in an organism or a machine, is desirable to reader as well as to writer—that in seeking such a harmony, reader and writer share a common purpose. There are areas where this is true: for example, gross nonsense in the middle of an otherwise coherent poem calls for correction by interpretation or by textual emendation, if necessary. But there is a hidden analogy alongside the concept of "working" that gives the phrase an authority to which it is often not entitled; that is the parallel with logical method. An isolated and unrelated literary energy (outside a presumed pattern or in some measure disruptive of it) is thought to be like an unexplained observation within a scientific hypothesis, requiring any amount of necessary explanation to integrate it with the over-all theory. But, however true in the world of natural law, the supposition is wrong in the world of critical interpretation applied to works of imaginative art. The laws of an artistic structure (if laws they can be called) are far less strict than those of the natural world. A structural anomaly is a less serious thing, and a cumbersome, distracting, ambitious pattern may be aesthetically worse—if only because doomed to incoherence —than one which is unobtrusive, moderate, and approximate. (Approximate esthetic solutions, in which a plus value here is achieved at the cost of a minus value somewhere else, have a standing that in science does not generally attach to compromise solutions.) Thus the impulse to seek unified symbolic or allegorical patterns in authors like Spenser and Joyce has met, in recent criticism of these authors, with a certain check. The schema proposed, at least in the dimensions presumed necessary, has not been thought worth the effort it costs. In the nature of things, it is never possible to demonstrate that pushing the patterns a step or two further would not create a triumphant unity; but this is the old "light at the end of the tunnel" argument, and a lot of informed people seem to be saying that they do not see a glimmer. They may well be wrong; but, in the absence of revealed final truth, one has to make tentative and provisional judgments. Inherently, it is no more probable that an elaborate over-all pattern exists (especially when one already has a number of other, perhaps lesser, patterns) than that it does not. Even the most elaborately minded author may be unwilling or unable to maintain consistently all the levels of structure for which he has occasional uses. He may even find it aesthetically advantageous, now and then, to do what is (in isolation) structurally anomalous.

These thoughts may lead us to ask what is the proper boundary of the work of art within which the critic seeks to validate his patterns. Easy enough to say it is the printed words on the page and the concepts they were or are understood to symbolize. But with certain of the more public art forms, it is necessary to add that the years of their public history contribute to a definition of the work "itself." *Measure for Measure* may, indeed, be a merry, absurd comedy, as Miss J. W. Bennett proposed for the first time in 1966, but in that case it is not only a play of another coloration, it is a wholly different play from what audiences for three hundred years and more have supposed it to be. We thus explain the "facts" of the text, but at the expense of creating a massive kink in literary history. It is not only the total blindness, over all these years, of audiences and critics alike; it is their

acceptance of anguished discontent when they could readily have had com-
placent laughter that needs to be explained. Obviously, the play contains an
incongruity, and no way of seeing it can be correct that ignores (instead of
explaining or perhaps transcending) the history of that divided response.
The argument is not that one generation is bound to respect the limitations
of perception established as "standard" by another, but that new interpretive
patterns are bound to assert themselves, not only against the bare text,
but also against the circumstances of literary history. None of his contemporaries read Blake as Northrop Frye does, but that was because they
did not exercise the same care, sympathy, and intelligence. Their actual re-
actions are perfectly intelligible if the meaning of the text was as Mr. Frye
describes it. On the other hand, a reading of Wycherley or Etherege that
attributes to Restoration playgoers the ethical premises of a nineteenth-
century evangelical preacher, even supposing (for the sake of argument)
that it accounts splendidly for the details of the text, will not carry much
conviction: it leaves literary history in too much of a shambles.

A related ambiguous imperative draws on the supposition that we can
read a work of literary art "in the same spirit that it was read by its contemporaries." That of course is supposed to be a particularly authentic reading; the presumption is that the author wrote to be understood by his contemporaries, and if we find the two in agreement (or can interpret the
author to bring him into agreement with his contemporaries), nothing can
be pretended against them. But the whole assumption is questionable. A
Puritan contemporary of Bunyan or Milton might have been acclaimed in
so many words by both those authors as an ideal reader of their work (if
put to it, they might have settled on Thomas Ellwood); yet he would be so
narrow a reader, so fully persuaded in advance on the doctrinal level, that
the finest effects of literary artistry would be lost on him. In practice, the
argument suffers from an even grosser and more customary flaw; it is equat-
ing one articulate group in a society (the preachers, for example) with another less articulate (playgoers or poetry readers), or with the age as a
whole. These fallacies need no refuting. But on principle, the response of a
work's immediate audience is no more prescriptive than that of any other,
including the most recent. There are even reasons for thinking it less so.
The *idées reçues* of a contemporary audience may be precisely what an
artist wants to correct, outrage, or parody; they are hardly ever what he
wants to mirror mechanically. The first responses of a work's first readers
are often to its most superficial aspects; only over a period of time do its
deeper and more subtle aspects reveal themselves. (One can also phrase it
that only after the author is dead do the exegetes feel free to foist on him
pseudo-profundities and hairline distinctions of which he never thought
himself.)

In the other direction, one is bound to have a general impression of an
author's relation to the conventional opinions of his age; and the way in

which one interprets a particular work will be in some degree controlled by that perception. Blake is a man more radically alienated (by several light-years) from the public values of his day than, say, Horace Walpole. We know this from the constant tenor of the two men's lives and thoughts, not just from the interpretation of a single text. And it is a legitimate argument against the interpretation of a single text that it brings us into radical, un-explained conflict with the constant tenor of a man's life and thought. John Freccero's interpretation of Donne's "Valediction Forbidding Mourning" is magnificently coherent in itself (*English Literary History*, 30 [1963], 335-376), but it involves Donne in the intimate knowledge of books with which he shows no other signs of being acquainted, it implies a degree of intel-lectual complexity and allusive compression such as he never exemplified elsewhere, and it could hardly have failed to evoke a sort of comment from his contemporaries of which there is no sign. These are not conclusive argu-ments against Freccero's interpretation (probably there are no conclusive arguments one way or the other). They simply set before us some anomalies that result from acceptance of it, and these incongruities, unless explained or discounted, may justify a reserve or two against the internal virtues of the interpretation.

Historical hindsight is another potent and related source of anachronistic anomaly. Seeing where certain ideas "lead" by their own logic or the logic of history (and these two very different logics are fatally easy to identify), one assumes that what they become is a valid index to what they essentially were. Not so, or at least not necessarily so. The seed of a plant, if it develops at all, is bound to develop into that plant; if ideas follow any such strict inner logic, it has yet to be demonstrated. They pick up associated ideas and drop them; they are warped, dwarfed, contaminated, inverted, and perverted by circumstance. To read back from what they have become toward an image of what they originally were must be a vastly precarious enterprise—like trying to get an insight into the character of George Wash-ington by starting with the United States in 1971 and subtracting. The in-stance is deliberately grotesque. Yet I think I see in recent writing about the English romantics of the early nineteenth century an assumption that what points ahead to the symbolist movement of seventy to a hundred years later is the central element of romantic thought—even though the poets them-selves expressed it only obliquely or not at all—while the ideas they voiced explicitly and forthrightly are just epiphenomena, secondary and ephemeral.

Indeed, we can hardly fail to be contaminated by our own method-ologies, especially when they encourage independence of mere surface facts. Having supposed that the structure of language is a more crucial index to meaning than the external referents, we are in imminent danger of reading our original authors as if they thought so too, or were subject, in their ignorance, to a law with which we are happily acquainted. In other words, whatever they thought they meant, it was always (and very conveniently) just what our peculiar technique of analysis was designed to discover. I am not sure that this is wrong, only that, like all problems where the verification is inseparable from the premises, it suffers more from success than failure. "Deep" interpreters of literature can always find what they want by going a little deeper; and they tend to assume, by an ambiguous imperative derived from the psychiatrist, that what is "deep" in the sense of "buried, hard to uncover" is also "deep" in the sense of structural importance. But literature as a pattern of expression is almost always contaminated by literature as a pattern of formally manipulated effects. Discriminating overt from latent content in a work of literature is as hard as telling concealment from display. There may be more complex grounds for skepticism, but any level of critical interpretation that discards as secondary the arranged shapes, energies, profiles, and assertions of a literary work (such as earned it a standing in literary history in the first place) is of all theories least entitled to claim credit on the grounds of unity and coherence.

Structuralist criticism in some of its many variants seems to draw on still another ambiguous imperative: the parallel between the language structures of a primitive community and those of a literary artist. The crucial difference here lies not in the primitive/literary contrast but in that of community/artist. A symbol in a linguistic community is validated by the consensus of the members of that community: its relation to "experience" is less important in the degree that the symbol-users and symbol-acceptors employ a system of common counters. But the literary critic deals primarily with symbols about which there is less than perfect agreement. The artist in whom he is interested is often a maker of language, a giver to language of new and previously undefined meanings. Precisely at the moment when he departs from a norm (his own, or society's, or the language's) he becomes of special concern to the critic. There are of course basic ways in which every user of a language is controlled by its character, and by his own patterns of usage within it. Symbolist and post-symbolist writers particularly do often establish consciously a structure of varying but coordinate uses of a particular symbol, so that its "meaning" in one context can be illuminated (more properly, created) out of the range of its use in other contexts. The artist thus creates his own community, his own texture of consensus. But the application of this "anthology" or "concordance" method of interpretation varies widely in value from author to author; and, like all arguments by analogy, it serves better to suggest than to verify patterns.

Powerfully though obscurely operative throughout our judgment of interpretive patterns is a very hazy and only half-conscious horizon of interpretive norms that is controlled primarily (I suspect) by the specific examples with which one customarily works. Students of Dante or Mallarmé are tuned to a more elaborate level of exegetical possibility than students of Theodore Dreiser. So phrased, the idea is a commonplace. But one sees its operation more distinctly in students who, knowing Homer through a little paperback translation, then encounter a Renaissance allegorist or interpreter like Natale Conti. He is ready to see dozens of meanings—moral, psychological, political, religious, astronomical, botanical, chemical, historical, you name it—in what the modern reader, whose standards of narrative interpretation have been set, consciously or not, by novels of the "nineteenth century and after," can only consider fantastic excess. It is only when one goes back to the early commentators, to the glosses of Porphyry and those assembled by Eustathius, that one starts to become aware of a new norm for interpreting Homer—that one becomes seriously concerned about what the passage describing the cave of the nymphs or the shield of Achilles does actually mean, and conscious of a range and tradition of interpretive possibilities.

The problem is completely open. It is perfectly conceivable that the later allegorists of Homer burdened him with hundreds of meanings that never crossed his mind; on this latter point there is no external evidence at all. Nobody can claim much on the score of intimacy with Homer. The oldest allegorists are at least as remote from the poet as we are from them. Still, it is apparent that no poet writes intricate passages (like those about the cave of the nymphs and the shield of Achilles) without something being on his mind; if our choice is between a passage devoid of meaning altogether and an intricate interpretation, we can hardly fail to take the latter, if the alternative anomaly is gross enough. Whether it "crossed Homer's mind" is in any case only one element in the problem of whether an interpretation satisfies our minds. We cannot draw any positive inferences from the rest of the text and the way it seems to demand to be read, since it is absurd to suppose that all the passages in a long poem demand to be read alike. We may ultimately decide that there is no basis at all for a single "correct" reading of the questioned passage—that, faute de mieux, we have to make an individual decision based on nothing but individual taste and habit of mind. On a communicative level, the most we can then hope for is to encourage a range of alternatives to choose among and (by implication) the possibility of frankness in choosing.

Recapitulating, one test of a critical pattern (theory) is its capacity to order in a decisively better way the facts it pretends to control, that is, the text. The love of economy is the root of all intellectual virtue. If the test of the text is not conclusive, we may test in various ways the pattern's relation to the milieu, the tradition, the ambience. Freudian and Marxist theories, and those varieties of analysis that concentrate on the substructure of the author's linguistic "world" face up to these essentially pragmatic tests in reverse order; the critic offers insight into elements of which the author in his text may have been unconscious, which he revealed only in part, or which he deliberately distorted/suppressed. Thus the first factual test is biography for the Freudians, social situation for the Marxists, and mind, idiom, or total *oeuvre* for the analyst of substructures. Understanding of the specific text is derived from establishment of the larger schema or subordinated to it. (I do not deny the possibility of further relations between specifics and generals—I am only describing an order of approach.) But all theories, all patterns, are tested against an area of fact, variously defined, to which they propose to bring maximum order at minimum expense. Inseparable from this test against fact, but only darkly related to it, is a less distinct but radically operative criterion: the whole picture cannot be harshly incompatible with our sense of who we are, what is the texture of the world we inhabit—a definition of "meaning" that we create in the very process of living, and of which, the more powerfully operative it is, the less conscious we tend to be.

In one sense, all patterns are or can be meaningful, without exception: the pattern on my carpet, the scalene triangle formed by three dead flies in a dish, Sibelius' *Fifth Symphony*, any given minute's worth of noise or silence. The distinctions we make among them are quantitative, not qualitative; they include, inevitably, a sizable subjective as well as an objective element. What is meaningful to you is blank to me because of congruences or correlations within you of which I know nothing. On a street corner where I see "nothing in particular," you will see an aching absence that breaks your heart. An active eye or agitated sensibility hardly ever sees a random, meaningless pattern. In commanding our process of assent, the meaningful pattern relates to something—a set of particulars, a past experience, the concept of an intent, another pattern (perhaps only a potential one). Among the best tests of a theory is another theory—that is, the proof that your first theory has some validity is that it enables you to produce a second theory about some related matter. Naturally, no process of speculation is indefinitely self-validating; in a critical context (where consensus does not exist, where prophesy and vision are inappropriate, where the troubling crosscurrents of public performance are operative, where a history of literary response is part of the problem), the ultimate validation is bound to be, on one level or another, empirical. But "ultimately" may be quite a while coming.

Some patterns are more meaningful than others, absolutely or relatively, because they are specially related to facts, to other patterns, or to ourselves, generally to all three. Who we are is of course a matter that literature very often calls into question; how can we judge its relevance to our "selves" when its aim is precisely to enlarge our definition of what is possible within the world as we have hitherto conceived it? But the crucial word here is "within." A wholly different definition of reality can commend itself only on the basis of some known experience. This is the same paradox noted before, but inside out. We cannot see a new pattern unless we suppose it in advance, and then the supposition imposes on our sight; we cannot conceive a new reality except through past experience, and then it is not really new.

We are in a way of reducing ourselves to Zeno's despairing paradox, which would deprive our minds of the power to move at all.

In some small degree, however, the problem can be seen as its own solution. No individual is called by ineluctable destiny to serve as advocate and judge of his own thesis. The preconception that enables him to propose a pattern will not ordinarily be shared by those who judge it (or if it is, he will be acclaimed as the "spokesman for his generation");* though he is the victim of his own experience, that experience can be widened imaginatively, vicariously, by the pressure known as education. The whole process thus centers on persuasion. It is the honing of a thesis on the resistances of the unprepossessed and its adjustment to unquestioned (not necessarily un-questionable) patterns of assurance and expectation that produce an at least momentary and provisional conviction of meaning, an act of assent founded on a sense of verification. As it proves itself against resistance, every newly proposed critical pattern thus takes its place in the sluggish, unceasing stream of accepted opinion—is adopted into a structure, drained of its vitality, fossilized into a formula, repeated by rote for a while, re-newed perhaps for a fresh function, and finally cast aside to become a specimen in the "history of criticism" courses. Criticism is as profligate of patterns as nature is of seed; most perish at once (contributing, perhaps, to the humus), a few take root, a very few get adopted into the ecology, none are immortal. Hence criticism is always changing yet never "gets any-where," never "settles anything." Hence critical systems inevitably become obsolete without formal refutation. Hence the continual regurgitation of apparently exhaustively meditated books for one more go through the process of critical cud-chewing. The book has not changed, but the critic has, and so therefore has the potential meaning of the book.

From one point of view, this pragmatism can be parodied as a mere assertion that "whatever is, in criticism, is right." If one takes the primary function of the critic to be persuasion, then if (and so long as) he succeeds in persuading his contemporaries, he is right; and all critical ideas which fail to win large followings are wrong. But one need not be ignobly me-chanical in one's ideas of persuasion; it is not a matter of majority vote. The most recent opinion on a subject does have a certain practical claim on our attention, since if it is in every way satisfactory, there is no reason to say anything else. And if it persuades qualified, disinterested judges, so long as it persuades them, it is entitled to our provisional assent as probably the best thing on the subject so far. That does not preclude its being wholly inept; it just implies that it is probably less inept than what preceded it. If it is a radical departure from accepted thinking, or impinges sharply on vested

---

* This is not just a levity; a whole generation can be deluded in its perceptions, as no doubt the whole human race can; but who then is going to correct it? And what stand-ing does the next generation have vis-à-vis the previous one? A widespread delusion is generally a symptomatic, if not an instructive delusion.

interests, it can be expected to take time to establish itself, and in order to do so will be bound to display special depth and acuity of analysis. But, with one eye at least, I take a rather hopeful view of my colleagues. They have, within my lifetime, embraced a good deal of sophistry, and endured as well as inflicted an awful lot of pretentious confusion; in my memory, they have not refused a hearing to any major conceptions that had an evidential word to say for themselves.

But I am far from wanting to end on a note of complacency. It seems to me that current arrangements in the trade of literary criticism place a premium on the advancement of "new" patterns, while giving little opportunity for formalizing the act of assent or rejection which is so important. The new pattern customarily takes the form of a book or article: it is called a "contribution." The assessment of it is relegated to a review, exceptional when it is not perfunctory. How can it be otherwise, with the mass of literary commentary that pours forth these days, the drabness of much of it, and the difficulty of assessing critical points of view that have multiplied beyond calculation or encompassment? We are all prosecuting attorneys nowadays, and few of us judges: the first job is easier and pays better than the second. Yet what is the point of all these briefs, if there is no one to pass on their validity?

The inconvenience of letting an unlimited number of overlaid interpretive patterns build up around every work of literary art is not as great as rhetoric can make it seem. Every reader is free to choose among them, and does, according to the principles of his own assured taste, or his whim of the moment. If one does not like a pattern that has been proposed, there is nothing simpler than to put it aside. On the other hand, the beginning student (of Milton, say) can hardly fail to be depressed and intimidated by the sheer volume and variety of interpretive patterns through which he must struggle toward something "of his own." Even the practiced student, looking backward, must feel too much of his past to be a squalid litter of books, half-digested, too easily accepted or rejected, and never (for sheer lack of time and energy) properly organized in relation to one another. For this situation it is hard to think of any effectual remedy. Laissez faire in criticism is no more likely than laissez faire elsewhere to produce order, coherence, proportion. What it can produce, what one must not undervalue, is acuteness, ingenuity. Where every man builds his own house from his own plans, with the materials he has found lying to hand, we may expect interesting and ingenious structures in profusion; that they will have "meaning" in terms of one another, or in terms of any structure larger than the egocentric, must be essentially a matter of accident. To change that situation is probably not desirable and surely not feasible. Given the way things are, it is only the pattern that one personally makes out of the patterns that yields any effectual command of a subject. Criticism, like history, is thus a private art one of whose conventions is that the critic shall seem to use evidence in accordance with a public code. We feel that a critical pattern has "meaning" when it satisfies, confirms, and proves useful to our pre-existing habits of mind, that is, prejudices; we keep the shreds of our pro-fessional self-respect when the conventions of demonstration are observed. It ought to be the other way around, but it is not. About all we can do is mistrust our own culprit minds.

Notes on Contributors

ROBERT M. ADAMS, born in 1915, is professor of English at the University of California, Los Angeles. Mr. Adams is the author of *Ikon: John Milton and the Modern Critics* (Ithaca, 1955), *Surface and Symbol* (New York, 1962), and *Nil* (New York, 1966).

REUBEN A. BOWER, born in 1908, is Henry B. and Anne M. Cabot Professor of English Literature at Harvard University. His works include *The Fields of Light* (New York, 1951), *On Translation* (Cambridge, Mass., 1959), *Alexander Pope: The Poetry of Allusion* (Oxford and New York, 1959), *The Poetry of Robert Frost* (New York, 1963), *Hero and Saint: Shakespeare and the Graeco-Roman Heroic Tradition* (Oxford and New York, 1971). Mr. Brower is Phi Beta Kappa Visiting Scholar for 1971-1972.

MARY DOUGLAS, born in 1921, is professor of social anthropology at University College, London. She is the author of *The Lele of the Kasai* (London, 1963), *Purity and Danger: An Analysis of Concepts of Pollution and Taboo* (London, 1966), *Natural Symbols: Explorations in Cosmology* (London, 1970).

JAMES W. FERNANDEZ, born in 1930, is professor of anthropology at Dartmouth College. Mr. Fernandez has done field work in Natal, Ghana, Togo, Danomey, and Asturias on representations in culture. He is working on a forthcoming book, *Bwiti: An Equatorial Microcosm*.

CLIFFORD GEERTZ, born in 1926, is professor of social sciences at the Institute for Advanced Study, Princeton, New Jersey. He is the author of *Religion of Java* (Glencoe, Ill., 1960), *Agricultural Involution* (Berkeley, 1963), *Peddlers and and Princes* (Chicago, 1963), *The Social History of an Indonesian Town* (Cambridge, Mass., 1965), and *Islam Observed* (New Haven, 1968). Mr. Geertz has done three and a half years field work in Indonesia, including a year in Bali, and two and a half years field work in Morocco.

FRANK E. MANUEL, born in 1910, is Kenan Professor of History at New York University. He is the author of *The New World of Henri Saint-Simon* (Cambridge, Mass., 1956), *The Eighteenth Century Confronts the Gods* (Cambridge, Mass., 1959), *The Prophets of Paris* (Cambridge, Mass., 1962), *Isaac Newton, Historian* (Cambridge, Mass., 1963), *Shapes of Philosophical History* (Stanford, 1965), *A Portrait of Isaac Newton* (Cambridge, Mass., 1968), *Freedom from History and Other Untimely Essays* (New York, 1971).

FRITZIE P. MANUEL, born in 1914, has collaborated with her husband on a number of books and was coeditor of *French Utopias: An Anthology of Ideal Societies* (New York, 1966).

215

STEVEN MARCUS, born in 1928, is professor of English at Columbia University. Mr. Marcus is the author of *Dickens: From Pickwick to Dombey* (London, 1965), *The Other Victorians* (London, 1966), and *The World of Modern Fiction*, 2 vols. (New York, 1967); he is editor, with Lionel Trilling, of Ernest Jones, *The Life and Work of Sigmund Freud* (London, 1961).

JUDITH N. SHKLAR, born in 1928, is lecturer on government at Harvard University. She is the author of *After Utopia* (Princeton, 1957), *Legalism* (Cambridge, Mass., 1964), and *Men and Citizens* (Cambridge, Eng., 1969).

INDEX

Aaron (apocalyptic Messiah), 102
Abba, Ḥiyya ben, 95
Abraham, 75, 77, 95, 136
Achilles, 132, 158, 159, 210
Activity, as dimension in semantic space, 48
Adam, 99, 139, 142
Adam and Eve, in the *Zohar*, 107
Adams, Robert M., 203–16
Adapa myth, 91
Adeimantus, 88
Adonis, 99
Aeneas, 155, 167, 169, 175
Aeneid (Dryden), 155, 175–76, 178
Aeneid (Virgil), 155, 163, 171, 172
　moral values in, 164, 165
Aeolus, 155, 169, 173
Against the Heresies (Irenaeus), 103
Ailly, Pierre d', 118, 119
Ajax, 158
Akikos Zambi Avanga (god who creates), 51, 52
Albigensians, 104
Alexander the Great, 92
Alpers, Svetlana, 172
Ambrose, Saint, 119
Amphictyons, The, 89
Amphimachus, 158
Amphitrite Painter, the, 160
Anabaptists, 113, 115
Analogies
　assessment by, 42
　meals as systems of repeated, 69–70
Ancestor worship, 129
Andreae, Jakob, 120
Angelology, in Christian millenarianism, 102
Animal classification
　Hebrew dietary rules and, 70–75
　Thai, 71, 78–79
Animals
　Asturian preoccupation with, 39–41
　categories and values conferred on, 71
　self-identity found in, 5–7, 22, 46

see also Bali, cockfights; Hebrew dietary rules
Antilochus, 158
Aphrodite (Venus), 85, 99, 173
Apocalypse of John, 102
Apokalyptikforschung (Lücke), 100
Apostle's Revelation Society (Ghana), 54
Aquinas, Saint Thomas, 96, 106, 107
Aristotle, 27, 45, 85, 118
Armstrong, Robert P., 43
Art
　assimilation process in, 157
　Balinese cockfights as, 23–26
　Greek sculpture, 159–62
　Greek vases, 157–58
　history and criticism as private, 213
　Minoan vases, 158
　Neptune in visual, 155–82
　practice of imitation in, 154, 157
　see also Literary criticism; Poetry
Art and Illusion (Gombrich), 203
Asceticism, creativity versus, 146
Asch, S. E., 41
Assyrians, beast sacrifices by, 73
Asturias, 39–41
Astvatrta, 92
Athena, 158, 162
Athenaeus, 88
Auden, W. H., 23
Augustine, Saint, 97, 104–6

Baba Bathra Tractate, 95
Bacon, Sir Francis, 120, 121
"Bagman's Tale, The" (Dickens), 195
Bali
　child rearing in, 7
　cockfights in (*tetadjen; sabungan*), 1–37
　　anthropological significance of, 5
　　as art form, 23–26
　　betting on, 11–21
　　civil function of, 10
　　"Cockfighter, The," 22–23
　　as deep play, 15, 17, 22
　　described, 8–11

217

Near Eastern, 90
Norse, 120
old Canaanite, 100
visual and verbal translations of, 155–82
see also Creation myths; Eden, Garden
of; Messiah, Days of the; Paradise
Mythologiques (Lévi-Strauss), 62

Naḥmani, Samuel ben, 94
Napoleon I, 68, 142
Nationalism, radical, as source of puritanism, 2
Nature
. order of, in Virgil's works, 164
Rousseau's view of man and, 139–40
Near Eastern myths, 90
Nebuchadnezzar, 100
Neptune (Poseidon), 132, 155–82
Nero, 102
New Guinea, 71
New Testament, 76
Nietzsche, Friedrich, 105, 119, 130, 149
creation myth of, 141–46
Freud and, 147
Nihilism, 142, 145
Nile (river), 117
Njepi (The Day of Silence), 7
Noah, 77
Norse myths, 120
Nudity, Taborite view of, 114
Numerological symbolism, Joachite, 112

Odysseus, 143, 161, 162
Odyssey (Homer), 157, 158
Ogilby, John, 172–74
Oïleus, 158
Old Canaanite myths, 100
"Old Man's Tale about the Queer Client,
The" (Dickens), 197
Old Testament, 78
Adamic myth in, 136–38, 146
see also Torah
On Escalation: Metaphors and Scenarios
(Kahn), 42
Origen (church father), 98, 102
Original man, Rousseau's view of, 138–40,
143
Original sin, 99, 136, 138; *see also* Guilt
Orinoco River, Garden of Eden located
around, 118
Orphic doctrine, 87–89
Osgood, Charles E., 48
Otis, Brooks, 164
Our Mutual Friend (Dickens), 196
Ovid, 84, 86, 101, 172, 173

Oxford English Dictionary, 188

Pain, guilt and, 145
Pairidaëza (paradise), 92
Palabra house (*aba*)
activities in, 48–51
slicing (*akid adzô*) of, 49
Pallas Athene, 132
Pandora, 85, 134
Papias, 103
Paradeisos (paradise), 93
Paradise, 83–93, 99–107, 113–19
of church fathers, 104–7
on earth, common man's view of, 113–17
explorations as quest for, 92, 113, 117–19
female symbols in myths of, 87, 98–99,
119
giving birth to political movement, 84
as Greek Golden Age, 84–90, 120
human fetus in myths of, 87
innermost desires disclosed in visions of,
83
Jewish apocalyptic and Christian millenarian, 99–104
Joachite view of, 110–13
Kabbala doctrines of, *see* Kabbala doctrines
Midrashic, influenced by Islam, 96
primitivism in myths of, 91–92
Roman, 86, 91
sexual pleasures in myths of, 84–85, 89,
90, 114
as theological doctrine, 84
word not used in Talmud, 92, 93
see also Eden, Garden of; Elysium myth;
Judgment Day; Messiah, Days of
the; Utopias; World to Come
Paradise Lost (Milton), 188
Paradiso (Dante), 83
Parallel Alignment, Law of, 47
"Parallel Betwixt Poetry and Painting"
(Brower), 155
Parallel of Poetry and Painting (Dryden),
175
"Parish Clerk, The" (Dickens), 196
Patarians, 104
Patterns
ordered, of meals, 62, 66, 67
perception of, 205–6, 211–13
Paulicians, 104
Peccatum Originale (Beverland), 99
Persephone, 89
Persian civilization
influence of, on Jewish apocalyptic, 100
paradise in, 92–93